FINGERPRINTING POPULAR CULTURE

Popular cinema is a particularly potent political and cultural presence in highly diverse societies, where the audiovisual can cut across barriers of language and region, culture and class. The six essays in the volume span topics such as showmanship and stylization of images; the human characterization of abstract concepts such as good and evil; the open-ended, episodic, and fragmented nature of the narrative cemented together through devices such as family 'history' and 'filial love'; and the re-emergence of 'Hindustani' as a secular language of film. The essays also cover popular cinema's fear of using comedy when dealing with the legitimacy and authority of the state; the 'ideal' femininity conjured by Lata Mangeshkar's voice; and the debts to Hollywood and the carnivalesque that shape Guru Dutt's comedies.

Fingerprinting Popular Culture
The Mythic and the Iconic in Indian Cinema

Edited by
VINAY LAL
and
ASHIS NANDY

OXFORD
UNIVERSITY PRESS

YMCA Library Building, Jai Singh Road, New Delhi 110 001

Oxford University Press is a department of the University of Oxford. It furthers the University's objective of excellence in research, scholarship, and education by publishing worldwide in

Oxford New York

Auckland Cape Town Dar es Salaam Hong Kong Karachi Kuala Lumpur
Madrid Melbourne Mexico City Nairobi New Delhi Shanghai Taipei Toronto

With offices in

Argentina Austria Brazil Chile Czech Republic France Greece Guatemala
Hungary Italy Japan Poland Portugal Singapore South Korea Switzerland
Thailand Turkey Ukraine Vietnam

Oxford is a registered trademark of Oxford University Press
in the UK and in certain other countries

Published in India
by Oxford University Press, New Delhi

© Oxford University Press 2006

The moral rights of the author have been asserted
Database right Oxford University Press (maker)

First published 2006
Oxford India Paperbacks 2007
Fourth impression 2011

All rights reserved. No part of this publication may be reproduced, or transmitted in any form or by any means, electronic or mechanical, including photocopying, recording or by any information storage and retrieval system, without permission in writing from Oxford University Press. Enquiries concerning reproduction outside the scope of the above should be sent to the Rights Department, Oxford University Press, at the address above

You must not circulate this book in any other binding or cover
and you must impose this same condition on any acquirer

ISBN-13: 978-0-19-569267-9
ISBN-10: 0-19-569267-5

Typeset in Bembo 10.5/12.5
by Sai Grapgic Design, New Delhi 110 055
Printed in India by De Unique, New Delhi 110 018
Published by Oxford University Press
YMCA Library Building, Jai Singh Road, New Delhi 110 001

Contents

Contributors   vii

Introduction: Popular Cinema and the Culture of Indian Politics
Vinay Lal and *Ashis Nandy*   xi

1 Popular Cinema, India, and Fantasy
Probal Dasgupta   1

2 Structure and Form in Indian Popular Film Narrative
M.K. Raghavendra   24

3 All Kinds of Hindi: The Evolving Language of Hindi Cinema   51
Harish Trivedi

4 The Comic Collapse of Authority: An Essay on the Fears of the Public Spectator
D.R. Nagaraj   87

5 The Voice of the Nation and the Five-Year Plan Hero: Speculations on Gender, Space, and Popular Culture
Sanjay Srivastava   122

6 The Mapping of Guru Dutt's Comedic Vision
Darius Cooper   156

Index   186

Contributors

DARIUS COOPER is professor of literature and film in the department of English at San Diego Mesa College. He has a Ph.D. from the University of Southern California and he has published *Between Tradition and Modernity: The Cinema of Satyajit Ray* (1999). His new book on *Guru Dutt: Hollywood and Hindi Film Melodrama* is forthcoming. His stories and poems appear regularly in India and the US, and his creative work has been featured widely in Asian-American anthologies.

PROBAL DASGUPTA teaches applied linguistics at the University of Hyderabad, has written about ten books and over two hundred articles in Bangla, English, and Esperanto (in linguistics, sociolinguistics, literature, literary translation, and philosophy), is an honorary member of the Linguistics Society of America, is vice-president of the Akademio de Esperanto, and has co-edited *Language Problems and Language Planning*, and the Yearbook of *South Asian Languages and Linguistics*. His best-known writings include *The Otherness of English: India's Auntie Tongue Syndrome* (1993) and *Primico* (1977), his translation of some of Tagore's poems into Esperanto.

VINAY LAL teaches history and South Asian studies at the University of California, Los Angeles (UCLA). His most recent books include *Empire of Knowledge: Culture and Plurality in the Global Economy* (2002); *Of Cricket, Guinness and Gandhi: Essays on Indian History and Culture* (2003); *The History of History: Politics and Scholarship in Modern India* (OUP, 2003); *Introducing Hinduism* (with Borin van Loon, 2005); and (co-edited with Ashis Nandy), *The Future of Knowledge and Culture: A Dictionary for the Twenty-first Century* (2005).

D.R. NAGARAJ was a senior fellow at the Centre for the Study of Developing Societies and visiting professor at the Department of South

Asian Languages and Civilizations at the University of Chicago before he expired in 1998 in his 40s. He was a major figure in Kannada intellectual and literary circles, and among English readers is best known for his book *The Flaming Feet: A Study of the Dalit Movement* (1993).

ASHIS NANDY was senior fellow at the Centre for the Study of Developing Societies, New Delhi, for over three decades. His books include *The Intimate Enemy: Loss and Recovery of Self under Colonialism* (OUP, 1983); *Traditions, Tyranny, and Utopias* (OUP, 1987); *The Savage Freud* (OUP, 1995); *Time Warps: The Insistent Politics of Silent and Evasive Pasts* (2001); *An Ambiguous Journey to the City* (OUP, 2001); and *The Romance of the State and the Fate of Dissent in the Tropics* (OUP, 2003). His most recent work is *The Future of Knowledge and Culture: A Dictionary for the Twenty-first Century* (2005), co-edited with Vinay Lal.

M.K. RAGHAVENDRA is a film and literary critic, and has received the National Award (the *Swarna Kamal*) for best film critic for the year 1996. He was awarded a two-year Homi Bhabha Fellowship (2000–1) to research Indian popular film narrative and its transformation under the impetus of globalization. He has completed a book on Indian popular cinema, which attempts, among other things, to interpret it in the context of Indian social history. He has also just written a crime novel set in small-town India.

SANJAY SRIVASTAVA is an anthropologist and currently teaches in the School of Literary and Communication Studies, Deakin University, Melbourne, Australia. He is the author of *Constructing Postcolonial India. National Character and the Doon School* (1998), and co-author (with David Birch and Tony Schirato) of *Asia: Cultural Politics in the Global Age* (2001). His current research interests include masculinity, the role of 'sex-clinics', and Hindi pornography as sites of modernity and the media. He is also interested in the work of Rahul Sankrityayan. He recently completed a collection of essays around the themes of home, space, voice, sexuality and, 'post-coloniality'.

HARISH TRIVEDI is professor of English at the University of Delhi and has been visiting professor at the University of Chicago and the University of London. He is the author of *Colonial Transactions: English*

Literature and India (1993; 1995), and has co-edited *Literature and Nation: Britain and India 1800–1990* (2000), *Post-colonial Translation: Theory and Practice* (1999), and *Interrogating Post-colonialism: Theory, Text and Context* (1996; rpt., 2000). He has translated *Premchand: His Life and Times* by Amrit Rai (1982) from Hindi into English, and in addition, poems and short fiction by several modern writers.

Introduction:
Popular Cinema and the Culture of Indian Politics

VINAY LAL and ASHIS NANDY

Judging from the unusual number of scholarly and semi-academic books published over the past few years, it is no longer necessary to make a case for the study of popular Indian cinema. Such studies are now a respectable part of the research agenda of a number of established scholars and institutions, and dissertations on patriarchy, family values, and nationalism in mainstream Hindi cinema are proliferating. The gendering of the popular Hindi film is almost as likely to be studied nowadays, if one may be permitted a touch of exaggeration, as communalism. Much is beginning to be written in the Anglo-Saxon world on Indian 'musicals', and there is speculation that the 'Bollywood musical', as nearly every Hindi film is viewed from the perspective of those who associate musicals with song-and-dance routines, might even revive and energize a form that became largely moribund in Hollywood a few decades ago. All those Indians who view the approbation of the West as the ultimate litmus test of the success of Bollywood are awaiting precisely such an outcome, and many are hopeful that Bollywood stars will soon make their way into Hollywood. There are already signs of such a development, viewed as auspicious by Bollywood's financiers and stars, the Indian middle classes in India and abroad, and the firm proponents of the view that the world is becoming one large multicultural melting pot.

There was a time when festivals of Indian films furnished one of the few opportunities to view 'art', 'middle', or 'regional' cinema, and it was understood that popular Hindi films were much too lowbrow to warrant the attention of the likes of those who frequent film festivals. However, popular Hindi cinema has now made inroads into film festival circuits, and connoisseurs of the art of 'high cinema' need no longer feign disinterest or embarrassment. Indeed, we will soon have named chairs, annual lectures, and even perhaps museums on Indian popular culture, particularly popular cinema. Seminars and professional journals have already begun to resonate to the changing status of the subject. The film magazine of New York's Lincoln Center, which showcases world cinema and is a barometer of prevailing and emerging interests among America's cultural elite, devoted one of its recent issues to Bollywood.[1] Indian popular cinema has even attracted the attention of post-modernists and post-structuralists—a certain sign these days that a research area or discipline has got identified with political correctness and academic fashion. It is perhaps apposite that *Film Comment*'s special issue on Bollywood should feature Sushmita Sen flying, *apsara*-like, in the air: now that the Indian economy, having shed its notorious 'Hindu' rate of growth, is apparently burgeoning ahead in all departments—beauty, brains, and Bollywood—the country seems to be soaring to new heights.

If popular cinema has become an important subject of research in sectors that set the pace of the global academe, it is only natural for young researchers in the social sciences and the humanities in South Asia to find it attractive. This attraction has helped crystallize a new disciplinary area in the region. Often identified with post-modernist or post-structuralist schools of thought and theories of post-coloniality, the new discipline is also powered by the changing cultural politics in South Asia. Politically, English-speaking India has consistently lost ground in the culture of Indian politics during the last fifty years, though many observers in and outside India have, in this respect, been misled by apparently contrary trends.

Yet at no point has English occupied a more important place in the socio-economic and cultural life of the country as it does today. The demand for schooling in English-medium schools is relentless,[2] and the English-educated middle classes, particularly at the lower end of the spectrum, are creating a niche for themselves in the rapidly mushrooming call centres and outsourcing businesses. Though there is much discussion of the furious acceleration and even over-heating of the Chinese economy, which outpaced even the rapidly growing Indian economy in 2003, every commentator on the subject has gestured at some of the long-term advantages that the presence of a large pool of people educated in English confers upon India in relation to China. India is even exporting its English-medium schoolteachers to schools strapped for teachers in the United States, and Indian nurses, fluent in English, are slowly making inroads into the nearly worldwide monopoly hitherto exercised by Filipino nurses. The Indian novel in English has, for its part, become so much a part of global culture that people might be forgiven for thinking that English-speaking Indians set the cultural and political agendas of the nation. The renowned British linguist, David Crystal, who is an authority on the English language, has even predicted that Indian English, 'Hinglish', will soon circulate globally and become the most common form of spoken English.[3]

Notwithstanding all this, the status of English as a marker of the old, colonial concept of cosmopolitanism has declined, and to a new generation of South Asians the language is now, as the developments of recent years clearly indicate, more a vocational tool than a cultural index. Their attitude, one might say, resembles the outlook of Malaysia's long-serving (and recently retired) Prime Minister, Mahathir Mohammed, who was adamant that Malaysians should know English not as the language of Shakespeare and Jane Austen but rather as the vehicle of global commerce. Nor can these developments disguise the fact that the new vernacular forces thrown up by the democratic order are trying to push Anglophone India to the periphery. The result is the diminishing access of English-speaking, middle-class India to the new forces and forms of consciousness emerging in India's political horizon. For that class, studying popular cinema is the farthest one can go to access the popular mind; it is the outer rim of the accessible social universe for English India.

Yet, while commercial cinema remains a window to popular India's English-speaking, globalized intelligentsia, a certain ambivalence persists. It is a cinema that appears terribly flawed by the canons of global film theory and almost entirely disjunctive with the globally dominant aesthetics and concept of good cinema. Its principal attractions—the carnivalesque atmosphere, the centrifugal story-line, the larger-than-life characters, and stilted dialogue—also mark it out as flawed art and a curious intrusion into the world of modern art forms. How can one, if brought up on a steady diet of Frederico Fellini, Akira Kurosawa, Satyajit Ray, or Jean-Luc Godard, gulp such meaningless digressions from the core narrative, maudlin melodrama, an embarrassingly juvenile conception of the comic as well as the romantic, and ahistoric, inconsistent sequencing? The new cultural studies of cinema allow anyone facing such questions to set up criteria by which to judge the popular; they allow one to find respectable, intellectually sustainable reasons why one can see and even secretly enjoy popular films and, at the same time, publicly ridicule this cinema. Indeed, even as the reasons for condemning popular cinema have become more forceful—in terms of the conversations generally encountered in respectable middle-class homes, women are portrayed in increasingly scantier clothing, rape scenes have become nearly mandatory, and violence is both rampant as well as senselessly brutal—sociologists and advocates of cultural studies have become more emboldened in laying claim to it as a fruitful subject of inquiry. The very films that steer clear of violence and villainy, apparently setting up an alternative universe of family values and 'good, clean fun', have likewise come under the predictable scrutiny of film scholars who construe their mandate as one of puncturing the sanctimonious pieties of those who would champion the nation and the hearth.

There is a peculiar anomaly here. Nobody has any problem with lowbrow literature, such as penny romances, how-to-do books, comics, or the various series of books for 'dummies' or those which prescribe chicken soup for the soul. Their status is known and the producers and writers of such books also know their place. Serious journals do not review them; university libraries do not catalogue them—unless some enterprising academic decides to study them as instances of popular culture; and few people any longer care to attack them as representing cultural decadence, though everyone also knows that they are immensely influential and sell in millions. There is little confusion about their genre. Entirely different is the reaction to lowbrow cinema. In India, as in the US, popular cinema has increasingly tended to become a battleground of cultures, tastes, aesthetics, and political ideologies. Yet, at least in India, more than one reasonably clear genre of films has evolved during the past five decades. The critic's expectations from these genres should, one would imagine, be different, particularly when there seems to be a tacit admission that Satyajit Ray and Raj Kapoor do not belong to the same class. This does not mean that serious studies of the works of Raj Kapoor have not been attempted, but even these studies acknowledge that Raj Kapoor has a different audience and that he survives in the history of Indian public consciousness and art forms in a different way.

Nonetheless, it is usually by implicitly blurring genres that studies in the political ideology of films are made in India. This is partly because, among film theorists and social scientists, there is no intrinsic generic legitimacy for lowbrow cinema as mass entertainment, not even as a window to the social universe of South Asia. There is even less legitimacy for the cinematic language and narrative style developed by such cinema. Style, some of these highbrow theorists will contend, is almost too lofty a word to be used apropos films that, like emerging small towns in north India, give every impression of having been hastily put together without much thought to planning and order. What legitimacy, they may well ask, can there be for films that often lack a script, where the script is altered by actors on demand, and even bystanders chip in with observations and suggestions? As a result, film theorists and social scientists usually act as a second line of censors when seeing these films. In many writings on such films, the author usually is at once an advocate, witness, and judge: 'If you have [a] few rupees to spare in your pocket, you can always become a film critic', Ray used to grumble, waiting to pass a judgement that the readers know beforehand. Such judgements adduce sophisticated reasons for disliking the films and the author strikes the pose that s/he has not yielded to the seductive charms of these films and has viewed them only for scholarly purposes.

Correctives to such studies can come in only two ways. First, one could self-consciously shift the emphasis from the thematic concerns, cinematic language, and style—as they are understood or interpreted by conventional film theory—to the varied reactions and exegetic manoeuvres of the audience. These reactions and manoeuvres cannot be presumed on the basis of existing film studies in the West or in India, but have to be sought out painfully and laboriously. Our attention to the empirical part of the story was first drawn by documentary film-maker and sociologist Anjali Monteiro's work on television audiences in a Goan slum.[4] In her painstaking fieldwork, she reaffirmed what such studies have always shown in other countries, namely, that what were construed as messages by the audience were often dramatically different from what sophisticated media analysts and urban, middle-class viewers presumed. Only given India's mind-boggling cultural and linguistic diversity, these differences were often more dramatic. For instance, many viewers in the slum saw TV serials that we would classify as thrillers or tales of detection as documentaries produced by the police. Also, at least one viewer found a spot on national unity, in which famous sportspersons of India participated, to be obscene—because the breasts of a woman athlete bobbled while she ran. What different sections of the people see and what we think they see are entirely different things, and no serious student of culture and society would claim that the second set of meanings should have priority over the first.

The second way, to us a slightly less satisfactory strategy, could be to opt for frames of analysis and models of interpretation closer to the viewers. This is not easy and we are doubtful that even the likes of the formidable Abhinavagupta and his *rasa* theory can be, by itself, a good guide to the diverse aesthetic traditions in South Asia. The traditional is rarely the classical. Perhaps the frameworks that combine the classical with the local and the contemporary would go farther and a new generation of researchers will produce more appropriate blends of the two that will establish a new kind of bonding between film critics and film viewers. However, if your interests are culture and politics, even unalloyed Abhinavagupta is better than Marie Seton. After all, his framework has, over the centuries, been in dialogue with the tacit aesthetic frames that inform the various modes of popular self-expression, ranging from kathakali to Ramleela to jatra.

The disjunction between what we are proposing and what actually obtains in the world of film writing in India is neatly illustrated by the controversy not so very long ago about the film *Border*. It is an instance of how sensitivity or insensitivity to the language and style of the commercial Bombay film shape critical reactions to films. Most urban, sophisticated film viewers and reviewers found *Border* a one-dimensional, overly nationalistic, war film which dispensed with even some of the 'good' conventions of popular Hindi films. *Border* is supposed to be based on the 'history' of a specific battle during the 1971 India–Pakistan war; in such films, it is important to have one or two loveable Muslim characters among the heroes to draw a line between Pakistan and Muslims. The phenomenon of the 'good Muslim' is widely

INTRODUCTION   xvii

encountered in popular Hindi films, and *Border*'s storyline appears to be extraordinarily apposite for such representations. *Border* dispensed with this convention.

A specific exchange that took place on *Border* furnishes a good example.[5] Let us recall that *Border* is supposedly based on the real-life history of a night's battle in the India–Pakistan war of 1971, and the debate is over the values projected by the film. As it happens, in commercial Indian cinema genres like 'war films' mean little; all films have to have an element of an all-purpose carnival. When one talks of real-life history in the context of commercial Bombay cinema, one actually has in mind its mythic and partly trivialized versions. Nikhat Kazmi, the usually witty and occasionally brilliant film reviewer of the *Times of India*, misses this in her humourless column with the tell-all title: 'It is no celebration of patriotism, but jingoism all the way'. The veteran film reviewer, Firoze Rangoonwalla, objects to this kind of reading. His argument, at places unintentionally witty, reflects his life spent writing on Bombay cinema:

Commercial films, which are purely 'box-office oriented'...cannot really make a strong impact with their themes or work up a frenzy of feeling in the audience. More so in Asian countries, where viewers start with the basic premise that such films are pure fiction or 'fictionalized' from reality, and therefore do not take the subject too seriously, even if it is a depiction of a past war with a neighbouring country.

To that extent, J. P. Dutt's film *Border*...does not 'cross the line' in inciting passions, rekindling communal hatred or jeopardizing relations between the two countries. ...[T]he film's impact is neutralized by the fact that it uses popular devices like multi-star cast—with heroes acting like demi-gods—far-fetched lyrics, orchestrated songs, highly dramatic dialogues and the picture of war as a spectacle. ...

Border is more akin to films like *Roja* or *Bombay*, which diluted terrorism and communal riots with romance and fantasy. Viewers would find it difficult, I daresay, to go berserk when they see *Roja*—a film that talks of 24-hour curfews and hazards of free movement and then shows Kashmiri girls doing a group dance on a hill at night while the leading pair sings a song. Ditto in the case of *Bombay*. ...[I]f there was any prick of the collective conscious, it was soon removed by the main characters singing and dancing about in a dream sequence about having a third baby, while still being in the riot jungle. ...

...Satyajit Ray once told me in a taped interview: 'Films are not meant to bring about changes in society. ...See how the best anti-war films were made on the verge of World War II but did not prevent the holocaust.'[6]

Bombay films have a way of saying something entirely different to their audience even when they deal with contemporary issues of life and death. The challenge is to identify that message as it is beamed by the film-makers and read by a highly diverse audience, many of whom are not even acquainted with the culture the films depict and the language they use. By not recognizing this and ignoring the specific meanings different audiences impose on these films, most academic film studies, which assume some universal spectator, have loaded the dice against themselves. Ordinary viewers in South Asia, not surprisingly, know this. Expatriate Pakistanis tried to stop video stores in Britain from circulating copies of *Border* because it depicted the humiliation of Pakistan. Despite all Indian films being banned in Pakistan, Pakistanis in Pakistan knew better. The songs of *Border* were big hits there.

The profuse academic and quasi-academic exchanges over the film *Lagaan* (Land Tax, 2001) furnish another entry point into our observations about the various cultures of viewing and the frequent disjunctions between the reactions of allegedly sophisticated viewers, critics, and scholarly commentators, on the one hand, and ordinary audiences, on the other hand. Few recent films have excited as much attention as *Lagaan*, and not only because of its Oscar nomination in the best foreign film category—indeed, one can attribute the hullabaloo over that to the sentiment prevailing among middle-class audiences that such recognition validates Bollywood and is a sign of the maturity of commercial Indian cinema. An argument has been advanced that popular Hindi films are increasingly turning to the diaspora for their audience as well as for their themes, and films such as *Dilwale Dulhaniya Le Jayenge, Pardes, Jeans, Aa Ab Laut Chalen*, and *Kal Ho Na Ho* point convincingly towards this trend. Indians from the diaspora may have lobbied extensively on behalf of *Lagaan*, and the milk-drinking Ganesh was doubtless placated with immense, American-size offerings, but *Lagaan*'s success with Indian audiences requires different narratives. The Hindi film at its best has always been, it is suggested, a spectacle, and the makers of *Lagaan* had the good common sense, on this view, to marry the two great obsessions of modern India, cricket and popular Hindi films, to each other. However, the invocation of these twin passions has, everyone knows, furnished no magic formula which Bollywood could draw upon to ensure at least a few more box-office hits over the next few years.

Some of the elements that endeared *Lagaan* to highly diverse audiences are precisely those which the academic critics and political activists found objectionable. No brilliant feat of the imagination is required to understand that the most common criticism of *Lagaan* is that it allows Indians to take pride in an easy, shallow, and oppressive nationalism. The labour of an entire generation of scholars around the world has had no purpose other than to demonstrate that the task of forging a nation has always been a messy, even bloody, business. Where, earlier histories of nationalism were predominantly written in registers of inclusion, increasingly they are being written as histories of exclusion. Even as nationalism attracted entire communities that might otherwise have been at odds with one another, it privileged some communities over others and, much worse, had no space within its parameters for various others. *Lagaan*, its critics argue, is misleadingly 'written' in the inclusivist mode and has an absurdly optimistic view of Indian nationalism as a benevolent enterprise which, on account of a strident anti-colonialism, brought together subjects of the British Raj in India who were otherwise inclined to view themselves only as rajas, kisans, taluqdars, Brahmins, Kshatriyas, Dalits, Muslims, Hindus, Sikhs, and so on.

Writing from an explicitly Marxist standpoint, one commentator describes the Hindu raja of *Lagaan*, who is etched in a sympathetic light as himself a victim of the arrogance of British officials, as bearing no relationship to the 'protected princes' of the Raj who lived in opulent splendour, were indifferent to the sufferings of their subjects, tolerated no dissent, and actively collaborated in suppressing the Congress and other bodies of nationalist opinion. The native princes, as the historical record suggests, were no friends of their own subjects. As subalternity is a relational concept, we should remember that the native rulers, whatever the real or alleged humiliations to which they were subjected by the British, were not particularly restrained in their brutal exploitation of the peasantry. The '"tridentine oppression" perpetrated by the "sarkar", "zamindar", "sahukar" in coalition with other classes on the peasants' is, this writer argues, conveniently ignored 'in favour of a simple binary of all "Indian" groups versus the white colonizer'.[7] In a similar vein, the Dalit writer Siriyavan Anand, who is quite certain that cricket is a 'truly casteist game', best suited to an 'oppressive' religion such as Hinduism, argues that *Lagaan* obscures the historical links that in India have always bound cricket to Brahminical dominance. (Somewhere, in the immense variety of representations of the most malleable Ganesh, there is doubtless a bat-wielding image of the deity.) He finds it intolerable that *Lagaan* should have attempted to assimilate to the project of nationalism the figure of the dalit, Kachra. Not only do Brahmins and Dalits share nothing in common, but cricket, avers Anand, involves 'a colossal waste of time', and hard-working Dalits, whom everyone loves to exploit, never had the luxury of squandering days over a mere game.[8]

Admirers of *Lagaan*, by contrast, are struck by the film's boldness in suggesting that the nation excludes no one, and that Dalits, Muslims, women, Sikhs, and villagers will have as much a hand in forging the nation-state of India as they did in liberating the country from the yoke of foreign rule. Makarand Paranjape is ebullient in his praise of *Lagaan* as a 'classic instance of what postcolonials like to call the empire writing back'. Somewhere Marx had written that those who cannot represent themselves must be represented by others. The villagers of Champaner beat the British at their own game; they author their own representations.[9] Rejecting some kind of 'transnational globalism' as well as 'fragmentary post-modern subalternism', Paranjape is appreciative of the 'critical, self-reflexive, pluralistic and progressive nationalism' of *Lagaan* as both a 'safety valve' and as a 'sort of civic religion for the one billion different entities that inhabit India'.[10] Not only does Kachra, the Dalit, find a place on the team, but his heroic spell with the ball allows Champaner's villagers to enter something of a level playing field. However, representation is rarely innocuous, and Kachra also suffers from a disability which apparently enables him to produce brilliant spins. One might say that, from the standpoint of 'self-reflexive' and 'progressive' nationalism, the disabled yet victorious Kachra becomes emblematic of the possibilities of subaltern achievements in a nation aspiring to open itself to hitherto marginalized and oppressed peoples. Even so, the opposite conclusion will resonate among others with at least as much conviction: Kachra's achievement owes nothing to his intrinsic abilities, to his will to win and avenge the insults thrown at him by white men and upper-caste Hindus alike, but rather to a physical disability over which he has no control.

Whatever the differences in the most widely prevalent readings of *Lagaan*, it is also remarkable that all such readings are deeply grounded in historicist frameworks. This is self-evidently so in Marxist critique. Mannathukkaren, supposing (for no evident reason) *Lagaan* to be set in some village in Awadh, consciously contrasts 'the "history" that Lagaan portrays' with the 'actual conditions prevalent in Awadh at the end of the 19th century'. Thus, in this rendering, *Lagaan* is best treated as a historical novel, and the film-maker, having exercised the choice to remain partly within the framework of history, must be subjected to the same exacting standards customarily applied to works of history. Anand, likewise, adamantly argues that in actual fact the gentlemanly game of cricket was always the preserve of Brahmins, and that the comforting fictions of *Lagaan* cannot be reconciled with the unpleasantly casteist history of cricket in India. And yet, lurking behind these self-consciously realist readings are other, more complex, considerations. If we allow Gandhi to stand in for *Lagaan*, we might see how the various readings are expressive of the differences that emerged over Gandhi's leadership of the Congress and his views on social reform and political change. The Marxist and Ambedkarite critiques of Gandhi are well-known; and equally familiar is the defence of Gandhi as the political genius who somehow drew to himself and the greater cause of Indian nationalism people of vastly different sensibilities. *Lagaan* is proof enough that, notwithstanding the ascendancy of Hindutva and the glitter of globalization, the spectre of Gandhi still looms large. Notwithstanding also the attempts to bludgeon Indians into becoming historically-minded citizens, to render the language of history as familiar to them as the languages of puranas, kathas, bhajans, and *kavya*, the mythic has an annoying way of creeping back into Indian sensibilities. For instance, are Indian audiences likely to read the wager that sets into motion the plot of *Lagaan* as a kind of Faustian pact or, as is far more likely, a modern version of the improbable wager that brought Yudhishthira and the Pandavas into conflict with the Kauravas? *Lagaan*, for all its nationalism and anti-colonialism, is not at all far removed from the mythic materials that have occupied so substantive a place in shaping the culture of the popular Hindi film.

If it is not the mythic inheritance of Indian civilization upon which social and political activists and researchers draw, is there some other inheritance which might help to explain the interest that some of them have lately taken in popular Hindi cinema? Might any such inheritance have a qualitatively different bonding with democratic politics in India?

All inheritances have their own past and tell the story of that past differently. The present flurry of activities and research in popular culture, especially popular cinema, began in Indian intellectual and academic circles in a small way two decades ago, a little after, and in direct response to the Emergency imposed in India in 1975. During the two years when civil rights were suspended in the country, India had its brief, if distinctive, flirtation with a home-grown style of authoritarianism—actually, the petty tyranny of a small caucus of court politicians, bureaucrats, and hangers-on among the academics, artists, and scientists. The Emergency meant different things to different political analysts and scholars, but it did manage to subvert crucial aspects of conventional wisdom about Indian public life. True, many continued as if nothing had changed. For them it was business as usual. For others, the Emergency was only an attempt to institutionalize forms of dominance that already existed. At most, it was an hour of reckoning when the backlogs and liabilities of the Indian system had caught up with its pretences. However, for many others the period was one of intellectual confusion. The older forms of political analysis did not seem to work and many of the academically popular slogans—progress, development, secularism, and national security—were in any case taken over by the authorities.

The Emergency also had other less-known consequences in the culture of Indian politics. Many of them—such as the growing role of the media, the increased attractions of populism, and the decline of ideologies of all hues, including mainstream radicalism—are now a part of the folklore of Indian politics, though they may not yet have percolated into academic studies of Indian politics.[11] (It is a pity that almost thirty years after the event there is as yet scarcely a serious academic study of the Emergency.) These changes were to alter the contents of political respectability in India once and for all.

Not only did the existing ideologically tinged categories that dominated academic studies of Indian politics—derived mainly from various schools of constitutional studies, pre-war Marxism, and theories of modernization—not work, they were a distinct liability. For instance, contrary to the expectations of the mainstream intellectuals, the Akalis, the DMK, and the RSS opposed the Emergency. Few believed these 'ethnonationalists', 'fundamentalists' and 'fascists' would proffer such spirited resistance to the Emergency and fight for democratic rights. Likewise, important members of the Left either collaborated or offered mealy-mouthed opposition to the Emergency. The Left that resisted, largely the various schools of Maoists, had previously been looked upon by the rest of the parties as woolly-headed visionaries or as acknowledged agents of evil. Even the wishy-washy, sanctimonious Gandhians—by then looking like retired visionaries enjoying state-supported sinecures at institutions peripheral to Indian public life—fought the Emergency hard. Many of them defied Vinoba Bhave's legitimization of the Emergency as 'a time for discipline' and belied the widespread belief that they would cave in.

The rediscovery of M.K. Gandhi by a new generation of Indians was partly a product of the category-confusion the Emergency induced. This Gandhi did not look like the one that the noted Gandhians and the Indian establishment knew.[12] It was a new Gandhi who became the icon of militant environmentalists, critics of conventional science and development, anti-nuclear movements, and human rights activism. He now attracted the young political and intellectual activists, looking for post-Marxist models of dissent and frames of radical social criticism that would be simultaneously culturally rooted, less statist, and less dependent on the global institutions of capitalism as counterplayers.

The new interest in popular culture grew in this environment and got identified as an alternative entry into Indian public consciousness. With many old ideas collapsing and conventional social sciences failing to respond to the changing content of Indian politics, many began to explore the myths and fantasies that seemed to shape public expectations from politics, politicians, and the state. The search became more serious after the Indian electorate threw out in 1977 the rulers who had imposed the Emergency, including the charismatic but now tainted Indira Gandhi. Why did ordinary people, after apparently accepting passively the suspension of civil rights, show such political acumen? Why was their verdict more decisive than that of many intellectuals and other public figures, so many of whom supported the suspension of civil rights in India? Also, why did the same electorate, after dumping the Congress Party and the Nehru–Gandhis so unceremoniously, vote them back to power in less than three years? Why, on her part, did Indira Gandhi, if she was such a single-minded despot, call elections in 1977?

Many, including the editors of this volume, turned to Indian popular culture, particularly popular cinema, as a form of cultural and political self-expression that might throw up answers to these questions. They did not have any sustained professional interest in the evaluation and analysis of films or in an academic history of commercial Bombay cinema. However, it was also obvious to them that formal film studies could not really give a clue to the meanings of popular films without hard empirical work or direct contact with viewers from diverse segments of Indian society. It was also fairly obvious that the conventional social sciences could not supply adequate clues to the public sentiments that ringed Indian politics, especially those that could be neither traced to India's classical traditions nor to the stratificatory systems and local cultures in village India. Popular culture, especially popular cinema, now began to look like a crucial battleground where the battles between the old and the new, the traditional and the modern, the global and the local were being fought through the re-negotiation of myths and fantasy life.

This re-negotiation has begun to look even more important because of the re-emergence of urban, modernizing, media-exposed, middle-class India as an important player in Indian politics. This India sees commercial cinema as the form that has become particularly expressive of middle-class sensibilities and aspirations. Such cinema supplies, as one of us has argued elsewhere, a slum's-eye view of Indian public life.[13] There is in it an attempt to capture and keep the past alive, tame the new, and make a virtue out of the transient bonds the uprooted forge between experience and hope, the past and the future. Technically, the middle-class is still a relatively small 'minority' in electoral politics, but it is no longer that marginal to mainstream India, presumably dominated by the consociational politics of caste and communities in rural India, that even a few years ago would have been considered the heart of 'normal' politics in South Asia. Indira Gandhi's populism systematically built upon, some may say cynically exploited, the sentiments of the middle class, especially its fear of the growing political power of the peripheries of the society, its old, unself-critical enthusiasm for every variety of social engineering (especially when directed against non-modern India), and its easy, paternalistic radicalism. In the process, she made the media and the literati allies and accomplices in her political battles, and others aware that middle-class India's fantasies of power, nationhood, and political transformation mattered.[14]

In the late 1980s, the awareness of this part of the story was further sharpened by the electoral campaigns and victories, and the rapid rise and steep decline in the popularity of Prime Ministers Rajiv Gandhi and Vishwanath Pratap Singh, in each instance crucially shaped and led by changes in middle-class consciousness. For the first time, many discovered that a new, media-exposed India was not merely a political reality but also accessible and sometimes manipulable through the symbols and the mythic structures encoded in popular non-traditional modes of self-expression. Even the more 'incorruptible' film analysts and historians of Indian cinema, who would not have deigned to touch popular cinema as a subject of serious scholarly attention, began to reluctantly admit that the genre had something to say to us, even if it chose to do so unwittingly, incompetently, and inartistically.

The language that this newly powerful sector uses in its political self-expression has close links with popular cinema. True, this cinema is also simultaneously a form of kitsch—albeit a powerful, pan-Indian, politically meaningful kitsch—of ideas derived from the dominant ideology of the state, categories thrown up by the clash between the memories of the encounters between India and the West during the past two hundred years, and the various surviving vernacular constructions of desirable life and society. There *are* in this middle-class culture many of the standard ingredients of the global mass culture but, notwithstanding its dedicated critics, there are also in it elements derived from everyday life that are self-subversive. They subvert the grandiloquence of the idioms of the state, the nation, the dominant ideology of rationality and, ultimately, even sanity. The kitsch is after all meant to entertain and be consumed by people who carry within themselves the contradictory pulls of, on the one hand, the experience of living with a functioning nation-state desperately trying to modernize itself and join the big league of global political economy and mass culture, and, on the other, the experience of living with the myriad vernacular cultures and traditional lifestyles associated with the civilizational entity called India.

This book is, like its companion, *The Secret Politics of Our Desires* (1998), a product of that awareness. All except one of its contributors are from outside the world of formal film studies and film criticism. They may not agree with our reading of the origins of the new interest in popular cinema in India, but they are likely to acknowledge that this volume is a response to the new political presence and culture of the urban middle classes of South Asia as a whole.[15]

It is this peculiar mix that has made popular cinema an important political document in some parts of the southern world. This book's political project is to work unabashedly with this stretched meaning of the 'political' that popular cinema has produced, for such cinema has brought within critical focus modern India as well as its distinctive style of social criticism. In the process, the volume also explores the nature and role of fantasy in Indian public life and the way a new, exogenous medium has entered it to become a major vehicle of Indian imagination.

That brings us to our final word of caution. We reaffirm that this collection of essays, like its predecessor, *The Secret Politics of Our Desires*, inverts the usual approach to popular cinema. It presumes that the case for more serious attention to Indian popular cinema has been made and, indeed, the time has now arrived for us to explore how a transdisciplinary yet less formal approach to such a cinema can open up new possibilities in other disciplines and, more importantly, in our understanding of society, politics, and culture. That is what this volume seeks to do, sometimes successfully, sometimes not. Yes, we have taken that risk, defying what some social psychologists call the fear of failure, for we believe that a road map of dead-ends is also important in this instance. Like all other means of human self-expression, India's commercial cinema too has its major deficiencies and limitations. One must know not only what it can do, but also what it cannot. Thus, we are well aware that the studies assembled here neither reflect the state of scholarship on popular cinema nor constitute in every case a serious contribution to the sociology, cultural history, and psychology of popular cinema in India. Our aim has been to include essays that seriously seek to extend the boundaries of existing disciplines of social knowledge grappling with India—from literary theory to social history to philosophy—and indeed expand the very range of social and political analyses of public awareness. Risk is inherent in such an enterprise.

NOTES AND REFERENCES

1. David Chute et al., 'Bollywood 101', *Film Comment* 38, no. 3 (May–June 2002), pp. 35–57.
2. The subject of English-medium schools in India has even made it to the *New York Times*: Amy Waldman, 'India's Poor Bet Precious Sums on Private Schools' (15 Nov. 2003), pp. A1, 5.

3. 'Indian English will become most spoken form of English', (10 Oct. 2004), online at: *http://in.news.yahoo.com/041010/43/2h7wq.html*.
4. Anjali Monteiro, 'Official Television and Unofficial Fabrications of the Self: The Spectator as Subject', in Ashis Nandy (ed.), *The Secret Politics of Our Desires: Innocence, Culpability and Popular Cinema* (New Delhi and London: Oxford University Press, and London: Zed Press, 1998), pp. 157-207.
5. Nikhat Kazmi, 'It is not a Celebration of Patriotism, But Jingoism all the Way'; and Firoze Rangoonwalla, 'The Song and Dance Format will Ensure It's Never Taken Seriously', 'Does *Border* Cross the Line?', *Times of India*, (29 June 1997).
6. Ibid.
7. Nissim Mannathukkaren, 'Subaltern, Cricket and the "Nation": The Silences of "Lagaan"', *Economic and Political Weekly* (8 Dec. 2001).
8. Siriyavan Anand, 'Eating with Our Fingers, Watching Hindi Cinema and Consuming Cricket', *Himal* (March 2002), online at: *http://www.himalmag.com/2002/march/essay.htm*.
9. Makarand Paranjape, 'Postcolonial Bollywood', *Evam* 1, nos. 1–2 (2002), pp. 268–76.
10. Ibid., p. 276.
11. The singular exception, and also quite recent, is Emma Tarlo, *Unsettling Memories: Narratives of the 'Emergency' in Delhi* (London: C. Hurst, 2001; and Delhi: Permanent Black, 2003).
12. For a more detailed reading, see Ashis Nandy, 'Gandhi after Gandhi', *The Little Magazine* 1, no. 1 (May 2000), pp. 38–41.
13. Ashis Nandy, 'Introduction', *The Secret Politics of Our Desires*, pp. 1–18.
14. There is an implicit definition of middle class used here. It includes any family that owns a private TV and is thus wired to a centralized command structure of messages. A slightly stricter definition along the same lines is that of M.N. Srinivas: a class that includes any family which has one working member abroad, either in the first world or in West Asia. M.N. Srinivas, presentation on 'Grambharat', at Samskritishivira (workshop on cultural studies) organized by Ninasam, Heggodu, Karnataka, 10–20 Oct. 1994.
15. One of the contributors, D.R. Nagaraj, died shortly after drafting his contribution to this volume.

Popular Cinema, India, and Fantasy[1]

PROBAL DASGUPTA

I begin with a theme that conjoins the topics of fantasy, India, and the popular cinema: nudity.[2] A theme like nudity-on-the-screen leads one to something like the seminal essay by Laura Mulvey and psychoanalytic works on the construction of gender and the role of explicit sexuality in films.[3] However, this essay is not an enterprise of that kind; it assumes that nudity-on-the-screen as a topic of research can lead one also to the culture of critical discourse. In that, this essay sets the stage to say something else.

Nudity has something to do with the crisis of our denuded world and the growing feeling that the crisis can be overcome only by re-clothing the world. Overtly, denudation is the destruction of the planet's forest cover; to re-clothe is to restore the earth's green finery. There are however other levels of denudation and re-clothing.[4] Those who believe that the denudation that implies a broad, non-technical understanding of re-clothing—to stop or reverse the denudation—may not, despite sharing the global concern with environment and women, accept technical ecology and rigorous, scholarly feminism as privileged bodies of wisdom. They may feel that the degradation of the portrayal (and consequently the existence) of women and the degradation of the earth are largely due to an overvaluation of experts who claim to have technical knowledge and whose claims are not critically inspected by the public through open discourse. They may resist the proliferation of experts, including those who claim to speak for us, for it is expertise as a category that they see as denuding our world. Re-clothing the world for them also means the public learning how to tame its sub-communities of experts.

To put it differently, the ecologists may have taught us about the reversal of the devastation of the environment, but such a reversal involves going beyond the economism, technologism, and cost–benefit analyses in ecology itself, viewed as a theoretical and applied natural-science enterprise. One way of going beyond these symptoms of the denudation of our life-world is to try to deepen our understanding of the general categories of nudity, clothing, cover, privacy, violation: themes that link feminist concerns to environmental ones but go unexamined in the aggressive, rigorous codifications of feminist and ecological theory. Such rigour becomes an obstacle when we try to see feminism and environmentalism as twin concerns in an emerging post-Enlightenment consensus. It subverts an integrated articulation of the revolt of the life-world against the Enlightenment-sponsored 'conquest of nature'—read conquest of the natural—by the technical.

Let us, then, make a special effort to be non-rigorous and non-technical, and engage with the popular. One place to begin is the popular science version of the Enlightenment's culture-free, disenchanted view of human reality, as is obvious in the bestseller *The Naked Ape* by Desmond Morris. When bad guys tell you that you are really naked apes, we can retort that we are non-naked non-apes. The retort hides two insights. First, that the human race is not just a species of organism, for unlike other species it is non-naked. We clothe ourselves in the clothing we make. Clothing in the sense of apparel is a case of what one may call privacy or cover in human life. Our animal bodies and organic existences are covered by many layers of humanness. (We entertain ourselves by singing, using modes of voice control that do not come naturally but are cultivated and shaped by cultural transmission. We conduct our lives in the framework of language, another cultural artifact that is not instinctual and independent of the community's educational system). In contrast to our closest biological kin, the ape, it is not 'aping' that keeps human cultural transmission going. People learn actively/creatively, not passively/imitatively. For learning to be more than being taught, for apprenticeship to be more than slavery, the human learner must have an inner basis for cultural innovation and creative representation. This basis is obviously the faculty of human imagination, which expresses itself most clearly in the representational arts, such as painting, fiction, drama, and (at a very late stage of technology) the cinema.

Let me now reformulate my point of departure. If clothing is important, we may want to interrogate India—the world's traditional merchant of clothing and purveyor of serpent-and-rope enchantment, idolatry, and other illusionary wares—because we want to ask India about clothing.[5] Such questioning should be fruitful, as this civilization has already given some thought to the theme of clothing and nakedness.

Likewise, if the imaginative inner basis of freedom is in such arts as the cinema, we should interrogate the cinema while being in dialogue with India as the world's illusion supplier. Such dual questioning makes sense not only because the cinema is based on illusion, and film theory has made a fuss about it, but also because India, in its own self-imaging, has given a prominent place to reflection about fantasy as the root of desire and as the agency which, in giving itself illusions and realities, establishes itself as an ego for which realities are inter-definable with correlated objective realities and irrealities.

The identifying features of India's popular cinema include the extensive use of music and dance, and the explicit stylization of roles and speech acts. A scrutiny of this 'anti-naturalism' forces us beyond the limits of ordinary thinking about the cinema, taking us into the regions normally occupied by Indian philosophy.

MASTER NARRATIVE MODELS

The well-known role of the novel in the formation of the modern period, and the novel's ultimate icon, the autonomous individual, can serve as our second point of departure. The novel became the model of a master narrative because its conventions governed the individual's narrative construction of his or her biographical self. Evidently, the individuals of late modernity—let us call them interdependent individuals—construct their biographical selves according to laws that find their clearest artistic correlate in the conventions of the feature film. The feature film is a second master narrative in ordinary life today. It upstages but does not entirely supersede the novel.

It is normal for a theoretical discussion of cinema to take its categories from the Enlightenment vision; the period when the novel takes over as the major artistic representation of the master narrative. For the Enlightenment project has been the theoretical base for the emergence of the independent individual and the utopian telos of modernity.

Modernity is a pursuit of universal freedom based on a growing body of open, general, and, therefore, universal knowledge.

Assumptions about inquiry and theory derived from the Enlightenment lead film theoreticians to regard the filmic representation of reality as 'assimilable' to the conventional pursuit of knowledge and freedom. Such a perspective raises questions about realism in representation and about the relations between struggles in society and such struggles in films, the problems of presenting conflict-portraying works through an ambiguous market mechanism to a problematic public, the effect of vivid or potent audio-visual imaging of struggles on the public arena, the social reinforcement of the fetishized vividness and potency of the film image, and the spillover from the iconicity of the film star into political representations. Such discussions of the problems of cinema are familiar.[6]

This framework deserves the influence it exercises over all debates in this domain, but it has become clear from these debates that the framework is in serious trouble. Here, as in many other spheres, the Enlightenment has reached a dead end. It may not soon be over; but it may continue to mark time in this terminal mode for an exasperatingly long period, during which the Enlightenment project bends back and caves in on itself even as it strives to follow its standard line of progress.

To make the point clear, let me overstate the case and propose that the emergence of film as a master narrative constitutes a termination of the Enlightenment insofar as its twilight form belies modernity's pursuit of eternal wakefulness, vigil, vigilance. If one accepts this, even if by suspending disbelief, cinema becomes a point of termination that needs other analytic approaches. These 'other approaches' neither preclude the mainstream treatment of cinema nor claim to be the only alternatives.

Can there be a common ground where these different approaches meet and interact? There can be no dogmatic answer to such a question. The rights of those who feel that cross-paradigm conversations are useless must be respected, but those who feel otherwise also have a right to inter-paradigmatic conversations. There is, however, an empirical point on which various approaches will have to converge: cinema does serve as the master narrative governing the conventions of the ordinary self-construction of individuals in our times, regardless of how one characterizes these times and the individual. This is a reasonably clear, theory-free fact on which there is some consensus. It can be used, then, as a point of entry into our inter-theoretical discussion.

NATURALISM, CONTROL, AND HISTORY

The hegemony of the cognitive and political discourse of mainstream film theory forces me to define my position in relation to the standard positions which many readers take for granted. We therefore begin with the idea of naturalism in films as a case of the more general Enlightenment idea of the natural.

Enlightenment builds its project around the enterprise of science and the pursuit of true knowledge of the nature of everything that enables the knower to achieve control. As its partisans would put it, human beings are endowed with individual skills of discovery and collective skills of cognitive accumulation and transmission. These skills underpin the hope that all people, together, will eventually know enough about the nature of a large enough tract of the universe to be able to control phenomena within it and sustain a satisfying and fulfilling life. Existence, seen as steps towards the deliberate realization of that universalist utopia, is History, which must itself be preserved in its cognitive continuity. Such preservation entails methodical archiving and rigorous periodic stocktaking of how the archive looks. It is this recounting that one calls 'history' in the narrower, disciplinary sense. Representation in the service of this history must serve the general goals of cognitive exactitude and archival continuity. Hence the naturalist imperative of accurate portrayal, hitched to the regulative principles of scientific description and explanation. Thus, we return to science, the centre of the Enlightenment.

This quick recapitulation of some standard explanations of how science, control, history, and naturalism are interrelated—and why they belong to the general conquest-of-nature narrative associated with progress—also shows why the standard forms of dissent or innovations, such as ecological critiques of industrialism, do not upset the overall cognitive or historical frame. Such critiques after all quarrel over details about who is going to control what for whose sake and at what cost, not about the point of it all, or about the style of cognition that prizes exactitude in recording natural facts over all other values.

If nature as a whole, including human reality, is the object of natural science, the subject of the project can only be an idealized natural human being: an unsleeping, self-examining, ever-enlightened being, discovering and illuminating things and fighting secrets, ambiguities, darknesses, twilights; a naked ape. Clothing symbolizes reticence, an unwillingness to reveal, a respect for the privacy of potential objects of one's curiosity. It is only fitting that India, committed more to covering or clothing than to discovery, should have prized the twilight regions of dreaming (*svapna*) and deep sleep (*susupti*), and the ultra-darkness of a symbolic fourth state of consciousness (*turiiya*) beyond waking, dreaming, and deep sleep in its philosophical systems.

Such a philosophy is of a piece with the features of the Indian popular film that we have called anti-naturalist. Indian society calls its principal cultural language Sanskrit, or *samskrta*. This name does not identify any region or tribe but, by its other meaning that connotes 'sophisticated' or 'refined' or 'stylized' seeks to dress up a speech that comes naturally in a systematically embellished disguise. The other part of the story emerges in Ashis Nandy's observation in *The Intimate Enemy* that Gandhi taps deep strands of Indian experience when he elaborates a non-aggressive, non-objectivist approach to the past that is mythical rather than historical in the Enlightenment's sense of history.[7] Myth is after all a form of clothing, while history seeks direct carnal possession of the past.

The oppositions between the Indian approaches to aesthetics and that of the Enlightenment are many. Even the erotic art of the Gupta empire underwrites a mythographic approach to the past, and could be viewed as resolutely anti-naturalistic.

Against this background, this chapter will attempt to link the ancient India of the philosophies to the modern India of the film industry.

INDIA'S LOGICAL FACE

There has been a shift from the idealist reading of the history of Indian thought to the paradigm that informs, say, one of Bimal Krishna Matilal's last books.[8] The new construal holds that the hallmark of Indian philosophizing has always been a total commitment to meticulously rational argumentation and polemic, involving the deployment of rigorous systems of conceptual representation based on sophisticated grammatical theories, so that the logical points being made have real teeth. Thanks to this atmosphere of careful debate, all Indian philosophers have to account for the pedestrian empirical points that the ever-present realists have kept on the agenda. Consequently, there is a solid core of realism shared by all the epistemologies in their account of empirical facts about perception and action.

Also in the air is a historical commentary that supports the cause of the new reading of Indian philosophy. The commentary explains the earlier idealistic tellings of the story in terms of a sociology of knowledge that stresses the dominance of Bradley-style idealism in Britain when our nationalist histories—including those of Indian philosophy—were being written. (For reasons I do not fully understand, the commentary does not go on to point out that the new historiographers of philosophy are also working under the supervision of a realist, logic-oriented Western master-narrative.)

The foregoing comments do not commit me to the old readings of the history of Indian thought. I focus only on a point that the older historians often emphasized. Namely, that the six systems of orthodox, *astika* Indian philosophy (those that accept the authority of the Vedas), while they vary from the emphatic realism of the Nyaya and Vaisesika schools to the combination of ontological idealism and empirical realism proposed by elements of Uttara-Mimamsa (better known as Vedanta), all explicitly recognize the separate role of cognitive activity in constructing the experiential world. Also, they all attribute this activity to desire, the root of the *samsara* process, whereby the human agent is situated in, and must perceptually construct, this world.

Thus, it is unnecessary to reject the new, 'logical' image of Indian thought in order to make our point; I can appeal for a consensus.

FANTASY AND DISCOURSE

I stretch this consensus to suggest that the emphatic stylization of Indian art, and of language at the Sanskrit or *samskrta* level, reflects the consensual recognition of the specificity of desire-as-the-source-of-worlding. I shall call this specific agency fantasy. On the whole, ancient Indian thought sees fantasy as the source of the personal ego and of the world-constructing cognitive activity in terms of which this ego situates itself. That fantasy is also discursive; it may be cogently represented by constitutive discursive acts which create and destroy substructures of the world (such acts as curses and boons); and these properties of fantasy in such a civilization make the invocation of the sacred and the magical in our classical narratives—from the epics, through the *kavya*s, right down to the re-telling by Gandhi of the story of the Bihar earthquake to insert it into our stylized narrative of the good and bad karmic record of Indian society—a normal and central constituent of the causal trajectory of the plot.

Are the magical and the sacred real dimensions of the discursive labour of fantasy; of the agency responsible for the cognitive situatedness of the self? Let me quote from a modern scriptural authority, Jean-Paul Sartre's *Being and Nothingness*. On page 457 of my 1966 Washington Square Press paperback edition, there is the following passage:

> ...this first aspect of language—in so far as it is I who employ it for the Other—is *sacred*. The sacred object is an object which is in the world and which points to a transcendence beyond the world. Language reveals to me the freedom (the transcendence) of the one who listens to me in silence.
>
> But at the same moment I remain for the Other a meaningful object—that which I have always been. There is no path which departing from my object-state can lead the Other to my transcendence... Thus language remains for him a simple property of a magical object—and this magical object itself. It is an action at a distance whose effect the Other exactly knows. Thus the word is *sacred* when I employ it and *magic* when the Other hears it. Thus I do not know my language any more than I know my body for the Other. I cannot hear myself speak nor see myself smile...

Language, when it is received, is understood and produces effects that are determinate in principle. Readers who feel uncomfortable with the designation 'magical' for this aspect of language may prefer the term 'technological'. Lewis Mumford has said that any sufficiently complex technology is indistinguishable from magic. Also, when a person speaks to an audience that listens in silence, the language is for the speaker an open, indeterminate beginning, which seeks association with the audience's power to interpret it; to give it a place in another existence. This aspect of language is sacred and theoretical.

My second step is to acknowledge that the equations can be turned around: not only is the sacred theoretical and magic technological, one may say that theory is intrinsically sacred and that technology is intrinsically magical. This, of course, challenges the idea that technology and theory, as we understand these terms, either belong to the Enlightenment or take on the shapes we recognize in the Enlightenment. How can one relate them to the magical and the sacred, except in jest or in a metaphor? The Enlightenment's standard portrayal of technology and theory as rational spaces of transparency, devoid of any mystery, is valid only within what may be called attention bubbles. During short stretches of activity involving a few participants, the participants can attain and hold on to a rational, controlled, teachable understanding of how some body of technology or theory works. However, this transparent controllability extends only up to the limits of the attention bubble they inhabit. This bubble can, at best, be as large as a discipline, though even this assumption seems too generous if one bears in mind the proliferating sub-disciplines and the growth of interdisciplinarity. The participants themselves regard all technology and theory outside their own bubble in the way the laity does, as magical and sacred.

In other words, technology is magical and theory sacred under normal conditions. The Enlightenment has 'cognitivized' magic into technology and the sacred into theory. It has, thus, disrupted the ancient traffic between the animistic production of the magical and the theistic production of the sacred and starts a new game with technology on the consumption side and theory on the production side. This recoding may be seen especially clearly in fiction. The consolidation of the natural sciences in the late nineteenth century coincided with the ascendancy of detective and science fiction. One global by-product of the process has been the focus on the investment of desire in knowledge, not merely in its contents, but in the game of knowing its players, hierarchies, and claims to objectivity.

As for self-reference and self-construction, the game of discursive knowing is played in two modes: the high or élite mode, as in the theory-oriented art films, dealing with critical constructions of the self, and the low or public mode of technology-oriented popular films, representing the world of desires with which fantasy clothes the self. The heart of my argument is that the popular film alone can directly represent both the inter-bubble category of technology as magic and the Enlightenment's partly successful recoding of the magical as the technological. Popular cinema holds the key to the self–world equation in our times. The art film's exploration of reality is a continuing one with the typically modern forms of cognitive inquiry such as in the sciences, humanities, and journalism. It formally inhabits the theoretical/ sacred space within the attention bubble of the Enlightenment and is bound by the rules of wakefulness. Those rules, that prevent it from thematizing the twilight, we have talked about.

If the Enlightened self can encounter the fantasy-rooted construction of the ego and the desires that its world-making and objectification embody in a discourse of twilight alone; if the popular cinema provides a unique artistic representation of the twilight today; and if Indian thought is where the rootedness of the ego and its objectification in fantasy and the twilight that fantasy inhabits have been classically thematized, we begin to see how questions of classical Indian philosophy and narratives can be brought to bear upon an analysis of popular cinema.

INDIA AND ILLUSION

In the stereotype of India, there is the element of enchantment. Indians are not seen as powerful sorcerers but as playful rope tricksters and snake charmers. The magic that India sells is the stuff of which illusion is made.

An element of showmanship and ornamental stylization has always been crucial to the theory and practice of image-making in India. One author, Mukund Lath, who makes this point in detail, with examples drawn from several popular films, notes that the constitutive (plot-affecting) role of song in the popular Hindi cinema and the juxtaposition of such numbers with mimetic episodes are among the many points at which modern practice corresponds to the traditional aesthetics codified in Bharata's *Natyashastra*.[9] Lath argues that stylization and heterogeneity of discourse have been consistent features of narrative representation in India. These features are non-linear (in terms of the heterogeneity of discourse) and frequently depart from the mimetic–naturalistic modes of representing action. Lath reinforces the view that non-linear conventions of representation embody an epistemology in which the spectacle is produced and construed as an illusion.

Also, there is the slippage between mimetic dialogue and stylized song. This slippage takes place in a liminal zone where the naturalistic ordering of languages and meta-languages becomes fuzzy and the attention bubble sometimes fuses with other spaces. Non-linearity enables the representation to cope with the problem of both having your self and also transcending it. *Dhyanabhanga*, enchantment's victory over meditative attention, may then be taken as iconic of the Indian aesthetics' solution to the level ordering problem of languages and meta-languages (a problem which makes self-reference logically paradoxical and which critical–cinematic representations cannot solve in relation to the self of the Enlightenment subjectivity).

I turn now to the enchantment of the twilight, under which one can speak in the same breath of the discoveries of the day and the mysterious concealments of night. Twilight is the discursive free play of fantasy that reveals the consubstantiality of wishful dreams with serious wakefulness (for seriousness is itself a wish or a desire). If serious and wishful thinking did not share the same perceptual matrix, the sage's meditation in *dhyana* would be completely focused and the very idea of a semi-divine temptress seducing him would be ungrammatical. Again, one must resist the desire to plunge into standard metaphysics (such as an appeal to the *Mandukya Upanisad*, which literally asks what the unity of breath must be, for it to be possible to speak of wakefulness, dream, repose, and the mysterious and numinous meta-repose in the same breath). It will not, after all, directly help us face the issues of representation, such as: how does the twilight represent pieces of day and pieces of night in such a way as to bring out their consubstantiality qua desire? Our suggested answer is: through overt productions of images. I can here attempt only a defence of the answer.

Some readers may find it easy to follow our story if I explain how it might have been told in the language made fashionable by some contemporary Western works reclaiming the sophists of pre-Socratic Greece. Consider my claim that the classical Indian deployment of discourse, particularly in the twilight mode, stages overt productions of images and sets up an amphibian traffic in which wakefulness and liquid dreams participate indiscriminately. Neo-pre-Socratics can read this as a rejection of a Platonic dichotomy between the day as the visible or sensible form/signifier and the night as the intelligible content/signified. Readers who know of Nietzsche's reversal of Plato on this issue may take it that we are rejecting the conventional placement of dreams and night in Plato's sky. Readers who are into Heidegger or Derrida will read our move as a rejection of the metaphysics of presence, for we deny that day and night can be distinguished because day is present to perception and night absent. Those acquainted with Derrida may note the relatedness between this project and Derrida's obsession with the sunlit day as the environment that Western metaphysics presupposes for perception. Readers intimate with Foucault may notice that the production of images, as I visualize it, is a discursive practice; it resists logical closure and subverts the will to truth, and the like. However, these contacts should not be confused with the central point I am making.

Some other readers may want this account to be offset against Ramana Maharshi's use of the metaphor of cinema to elucidate his advaitin view of the self and the world. For example, in *Talks with Sri Ramana Maharshi* one of his typical formulations leads up to this theme:

This 'I' is the one who experiences the waking, dream and sleep states. The three states are changes which do not affect the individual. The experiences are like pictures passing on a screen in the cinema. The appearance and disappearance of the pictures do not affect the screen. So also, the three states alternate with one another, leaving the self unaffected. The waking and dream states are creations of the mind. So the self covers them all.[10]

Both my account and this analysis face the question: How exactly 'the waking and the dream states are creations of the mind'? Perhaps the answer broadly is: Pure fantasy is on its own in the twilight of the dream state. It is fantasy's ability to imagine that it is not imagining (that the objects it presents to itself are 'really there') that produces wakefulness. To the extent that these vicissitudes of the mode of objectification do not affect the agential character of fantasy, my assumptions approach those of Sri Ramana. This hasty piece of bridge-building is obviously no substitute for a rigorous analysis of the issues involved. I offer here only a possible point of entry.

For some readers, it may be important to connect all this to a recognizably classical Indian theory of language. I refer such readers to Harold G. Coward's account of Bhartrihar's *sphota* theory,[11] and to my appropriation of *sphota* theory as a 'spark theory' in my work on Western theories of translation and the viability of a classically based Indian resistance to Western theories.[12] A spark, or an individual embodiment of charged or meaningful form, is always a production of an image, and that imagination is always a constructive activity. Thus every *vaikhari* unpacking of the level called *madhyama* (treated not transcendentally but as a stage) is always a performance and thus counts as a contingent production of substance. Given this formulation, where the postulation of forms and meanings becomes a merely technical grammatical exercise and does not affect the substantiality or the contingent character of discourse, the present theory of art becomes fully congruent with the classical Indian tradition in linguistic theory.

The theoretical unity (and technical distinction) of form and sense in the spark underwrites a discourse that can, in principle, switch between languages and meta-languages. The philosophical analysis of art shows the power of this principle by holding up for our attention not the routine sparks of ordinary language but the charged images of life. (Charge is my rethinking of *rasa*, just as sparks are my rewritten *sphota*s). The charge implies such questions as: Who must you, and the protagonists with whom you identify be, to perceive and respond to this charge as a charge? The attraction of the spectacle implicitly draws attention to your position as someone who receives and consumes it as spectacular. The anti-naturalism of the aesthetics of production expresses the forces that enable you to receive and consume—call them desires—in shapes that embody the spectator's position within the work of art itself.

Thus, the spectacle includes factors of self-construction that tell you who to be while watching and how to consume the spectacle. These factors do not necessarily narrow down the range of who and how, but the popular film is an art form that does present one type of consumer's position most invitingly, leaving other options in the background for those who read popular films as critical texts and write theoretical essays about them. This is the position of the formula consumer. The popular film constructs this position by making a variety of desire-marking strategies converge on the types of desire that the consumer is supposed to replicate. Conventional attractions, such as the faces of stars and postcard sceneries, for example, are invitations to take a position from which such charges look attractive. Stylized exaggerations of speech and plot, coupled with song and other such accessories, help specify what one is supposed to attend to and the conventions one must obey.

The high degree of stylization and illusion-making puts the spectator in a position of constant awareness of the constructed and performed nature of the spectacle; you know that you are not seeing reality, and the way your complicity is elicited ensures that you know that the spectacle appeals to you by bringing your fantasies and desires directly into play. As you are co-constructing the spectacle while watching it, you knowingly let the pieces of fantasy presented to you play on your own desires in a stylized fashion, and thus get an opportunity to re-explore them.

Thus, you come to know not quite yourself but a certain self that you consent to be vis-à-vis the film. You know a facet of your fantasy and you obtain or re-clarify this knowledge by watching the film. It is then fantasy, not reality, with which such a film puts you into contact. Note that 'fantasy' here strictly means the agency responsible for our perceiving the real world in terms of certain object-types rather than in terms of conceivable alternatives that could have encoded other intentions, interests, and decisions on inclusions and exclusions: the agency that constitutes you as the ego is compelled to populate your world with the objects that your desires encourage you to perceive.

The account thus far, we believe, offers one fruitful way of understanding India's popular cinema. We continue to assume that there is still a need for standard sociological, film-theoretic, aesthetic, and other Enlightenment-linked modes of inquiry in this domain, and that my work only seeks to supplement them. However, I do claim that though my formulation reflects specifically Indian theoretical and practical circumstances, it can be extended to other film industries, to turn the twilight into a crucial element in late-modern self-definitions everywhere. I explain this part of the story in the following section.

THE CRITIQUE OF REASON

I have said that the art film's exploration of reality is continuous with typically modern forms of cognitive inquiry; it is ultimately bound by the rules of wakefulness. These rules prevent it from thematizing the twilight and cause it to share the predicament of most critical and theoretical work in modern India. It is basically colonized, while leaving some gaps where resistance against this colonization is possible. The methods of analysis overwhelmingly reflect paradigms shaped and re-shaped by the Western master discourses which limit representation to a controlled set of options bound by the rules of the Enlightenment.

Popular cinema, in contrast, has tended to play an anti-theoretical role, occasionally offering an explicit critique of the application of Enlightenment assumptions to the Indian context. In playing up the element of public entertainment, popular cinema has implicitly claimed that, if a cinematic proposition (critical or otherwise) is indeed a valid representation, one should be able to turn it into a piece of normal and potentially entertaining public discourse, that is, into a stretch of popular cinema. The possibility of the public having fun at a spectacle becomes, on this assumption, a test of the validity, for that public, of such a discourse.

There is a whole spectrum of positions that go with this assumption, some of them exemplified by India's popular cinema. All these positions help us make sense of the contrast between the popular and the theoretical. The dialogical concept of the ludic as a mode of popular deflation of official visions (which must accompany a culture's heavy excesses and which embodies the authentic eudaemonism of the labouring classes) may appeal to some of us; others may prefer to undertake a close reading of, say, Raj Kapoor's film *Aawara* (1951) as a critique of the social embodiment of the Enlightenment (and thus of theory as such). Unfortunately, this essay cannot deal with any of these approaches in detail.

What I can do here is to explore whether the Indian popular cinema's critique (if such it is) of the Enlightenment agrees in mood, if not in detail, with the central idea of classical Indian philosophy vis-à-vis the attention bubble. The Enlightenment takes seriously, and incorporates in its conception of the theoretical, the account that an attention bubble gives of the phenomenon it studies (the high mode of this seriousness is science). The Indian philosophical tradition qualifies this seriousness by thematizing both the content of the attention, seriously, and by specifying its limits, not seriously, stressing that bubbles are performances and no bubble can underwrite any lasting theoretical stand, being at most a stance and thus contingent. It is in the category of the spectacle, of the notion that the existence of the world itself may be due to processes of the show biz variety, that our philosophical tradition seems to find itself in the improbable intellectual company of Indian popular cinema and pitted against the world projected by official modernity and critical cinema. To the extent that relatively uninterrupted commercial traffic of images has operated throughout India's idolatrous history, along with spectacular salesmanship, the analysis of classical India and that of popular cinema meet at the level of the spectacle.

IMAGES AND CODES

Let us place this convergence within more general concerns. The spectacle presents images to an audience that sees them in terms of codes embodying certain systematic investments of desire. These codes are simultaneously cognitive and aesthetic–fantastic arrangements. Only by understanding the codes can one hope to understand how images are set up and how they work. Also, such analysis, in a cognitivized cultural space, is inseparable from the specifically aesthetic perception of images by the typical or ordinary viewer at some point in time.

The problem transcends the limits of India as a place or the cinema as a domain. Nineteenth-century science, confidently implementing the Enlightenment project, had a theory of the concept called logic, rather than a question about the concept. Promethean poetry and fiction, usually called Romantic and nationalistic, built an aesthetic architecture for the categorial dualism of the concept and the percept. This century's crisis of the cognitive, epitomized in the transition from the fictional master-narrative to the cinematic, has unsettled the foundations of logic and of the belief that the operative tools of reasoning are concepts in the sense of a dualistic logic. It has been known, ever since the early twentieth century discovered the limits of the classical paradigm of logic, that conceptual systems can never be formally self-sponsoring or complete, for it always initiates an infinite regress of meta-concepts sponsoring concepts. More recent decades have made it clear that clarity is not a matter of sharp boundaries delimiting concepts, but of loose families of cases clustering around typical (familiar or strikingly unfamiliar) images that do not add up to a conceptual system but come together in plural, codified sets of networks that elude total systematization. Finally, a third way in which systems of concepts are of limited validity has been brought out by psychoanalysis and its surrealist appropriation. Consequently, the twentieth century has posed, in shifting forms, a question about the concept to which many diverse images offer some kind of answer.

The infinite regress, for instance, does not arise with the meta-image, for a highly charged image is capable of thematizing itself and subsuming the levels of meta-image, meta-meta-image, etc. A network of images, being a code and not a system, is free to overlap with other codes without self-contradiction, and thus becomes indefinitely extensible and contextualizable. As for the unconscious, images have been considered the most salient representation possible of that territory. It seems, speaking abstractly, that the image overcomes all the problems surrounding the concept.

In practice, many domains of inquiry have indeed made the image their central tool. Cognitive psychology assumes that the real 'concepts' people use while reasoning are largely 'prototype-based' or 'natural categories' clustering around 'typical' examples. Much of linguistics today rests on this base; so does the work of many philosophers, whose tradition includes the later Wittgenstein's theory of family resemblances, focus on images, and familiarity as meta-conceptual criteria. In Gramsci, and to some degree Althusser, theoretical Marxism has freed itself from a concept-based logicalistic reading of Hegel and has come up with an understanding of hegemony that sees images and their force as the mechanism sustaining the cognitive asymmetries constituting hegemony. Thus, the image not only looks abstractly like the answer to the question of the concept, but has even been accepted as such by many influential scholars. Even the post-structural-deconstructionism, the last bastion of the classical formality that insists on inhabiting the old structure only to seriously dismantle it and thus gets caught in the nitty-gritty of archaic seriousness, abandons the concept for the image in its gesture of using concepts 'under erasure' ('*sous rature*').

We appear to have an avant-garde consensus in favour of the image. An alliance between Indian philosophy and cinema should be able to coalesce with this global imagination and even celebrate it. However, some questions remain. All images may be on the same logical level and formally equal, in that they are already meta-images and so forth, but inequality persists in the practicalities of show biz: the question of who is in business, showing what to whom. If images are self-consciously constructed and are designed to make the audience aware of its own practices of self-construction, it becomes necessary to face questions about the construction of such images and about the political and economic arenas of those who do the constructing.

Such questions cannot simply be about Indian popular cinema, but must concern themselves with the broader traffic of images. We sell idols for worship; we sell religious systems and personalities. We build and market various types of charisma, including hybrids of artistic and political performance, with or without a religious dimension. If our inquiry is to be global, we must also look at what the missionaries of Buddhism, Christianity, and Islam did with their markets and their styles of charismatic performance, seeking to explain the success of the Indian spiritual industry in recent times vis-à-vis its global competitors.

Nevertheless, for the moment let us remain with the question of the forces governing the construction and dissemination of the images and codes that make modern India's popular cinema tick. For one thing, critical cinema and its spokespersons and allies—among, say, the feminists—have been dubious about the genuineness of the contact between the popular cinema and the actual, as opposed to the induced or manufactured, self-construction of the viewers. It is of course clear that their usual critique of the formula film fails to address the issue of fantasy and the attention bubble, and thus, fails to step out of the Enlightenment paradigm. That critique, therefore, is complicit with the normal colonial structure of India's official academic life. However, notwithstanding its inappropriate mode, there is in the critique a serious critical point: the danger of popular art being 'taken over' through market mechanisms. In particular, the imitative relationship between American and European popular films and their Bollywood remakes cannot easily be explained away in terms of a portrayal of the relation between the typical desire systems in the West and in India. It does not seem that the Indian re-interpreters of the material are taking any semiotic initiative or being ironic. The most plausible reading of such imitation is the standard one: that the Indian popular cinema is in part engaged in a retail trade for which it permits the metropolitan master industry to call the shots, though this is obviously only a small fraction of what keeps the Indian industry going.

To summarize, the transition from a cognitive world dominated by concepts to a meta-cognitive world of images brings to the fore some questions about the image and its presuppositions. These questions can be examined in the context of the Indian image industry in general (including its philosophical self-commentary usually called classical Indian philosophy) and the modern Indian popular cinema in particular. In the light of these questions, it can be seen that India's critical cinema, being continuous with the Enlightenment problematic and its contextualizing culture, is relatively dependent on the Western conceptual structure and is in that sense 'colonized'. On the other hand, the formally relaxed and entertaining nature of popular cinema invites and makes possible more obvious and traditional forms of subversion, enabling the first world film industries and the assumptions and constraints imposed by Indian cinema's business mafias to shape the limits within which cinematic images must be made and circulated. The image in and of itself is defenceless against such subversion. That is why the critical culture of the concept, and the Enlightenment project associated with it, retain their vitality and relevance even as we learn how to spell out the termination of the Enlightenment in terms of the image.

This obvious counter-critique from the Enlightenment point of view, which many readers must have been constructing in their minds while reading the earlier sections, certainly cannot be wished away, and it is an open question to what extent the magic of the popular, or the present theoretical celebration of that magic, can face and absorb this counter-critique. In the final section, I address that question.

LIGHTNESS AND THE ENLIGHTENMENT

The theory trip is heavy; the magic trip is light. A light element that needs to face and absorb a heavy counter-critique must learn how to take it lightly. Indian popular cinema has already risen to the challenge. Films like Shekhar Kapoor's *Mr India* (1987) and Sooraj Barjatya's *Maine Pyar Kiya* (1990) manifest the latent conceptuality and self-referentiality of the image and solve, in practice, the problem of going beyond the Enlightenment's obvious counter-critique. The analytic task today, far too large for a chapter like this to handle, is to pick up and theoretically re-state that practical solution by commenting on popular cinema's reflexive turn. I can here only point out some factors that will have to form a part of a fuller statement.

One 'answer' to the counter-critique could be that the Enlightenment is right about the need to question the making of the images, and it is possible to have a popular cinema that questions this making without ceasing to be a part of the fantasy industry. This answer eliminates the Enlightenment's monopoly over the critical function and sets up the concept and the image as competing models, not only of representation but even of analysis and critique.

To see more clearly how the concept and the image may serve as alternative models, we can think about the old problem of the Enlightenment, formulated by Rousseau. In his book *Emile* and in his political writings, he assumes that the archaic forces of tradition maintain the power of artificial and therefore complex thrones. He proposes to demystify the magic of this complexity by general enlightenment or education. This education would make it obvious to the public that such complexity could be analysed or broken up into this or that aggregation of simple primes. Rousseau's point is that you have to make education universal to make it clear to the public how the distinct perceptual elements of Cartesian common sense combine to form structures and complexes. Once this analysis is publicly available, Rousseau believes, it would show the public how to distinguish the good from the bad complexities. The public will then apply its 'general will' against the illicit complexities of the throne and in favour of the legitimate complexities of genuinely representative structures. In that classical Enlightenment argument, theory is a matter of critically deploying concepts in the service of analysis. This process empowers the clear and distinct simplicities of Light, which then triumph over the temporary power, and archaic complexities of obscurity. Magic could then only be seen as a reactionary means of concealment enabling the throne to hide its inequities and exercise illegitimate power over the people.

With hindsight, I can say that the simplicity of that classical argument depends on an empirical assumption: that you can posit, on the one hand, some readily available precepts or maximally transparent easy elements in terms of which children can be given an elementary education and, on the other, posit a set of elementary simple items for adult readers as the foundational concept. You also assume, and this is crucial, that these easy percepts are going to prove to be the same set on the basis of the systematic builders of disciplines of science and discursive systems of popular science. This proves to be false.

We can show that this equation of the easy percept with the simple concept is a product of the illusion of unrestricted interdisciplinary traffic from one attention bubble to another, for only within a given bubble does the equation hold. It breaks down the moment we cross the boundary between, say, the physics and the sociology and ask if the two disciplines use exactly the same notions of 'action' or 'force'. Ultimately, the images that shape the public's perception and the concepts deployed in the specialists' sophisticated re-interpretations do not meet. Correspondingly, the 'easy' image-element and the 'simple' concept-element cannot be brought together in any general notion of the elementary in a serious programme of education (making analysis available to the public and leading to political action). This was what split the Enlightenment itself, at the point of Rousseau, into the Enlightenment proper of a Voltaire and the Romanticism of a Blake, one cultivating the analytic culture of the concept and the other the integrative culture of the image. In this they located supreme cognitive authority in, respectively, the community of experts working with theory and in the general public working with technology. Today's polarization of the critical and the popular in cinema is one of the many continuations of that old duality within the Enlightenment. Romanticism has long been the Enlightenment's internal 'other', aligning itself in crucial ways with non-Enlightenment and pre-Enlightenment traditions in and outside the European crucible of modernity. Popular cinema shares with its Romantic heritage the capacity to directly appropriate magic from the image itself, bypassing both the power of the throne and the anti-royalist claims of the culture of the concept.

Readers who even partly accept this reading of the history of modernity may grant that the image today, in its popular cinematic deployment, has matured to a point where its lightness can afford to take conceptuality lightly. After all, it can replicate the work of the critical concept within the play of the post-critical (and no longer pre-critical) image as meta-image. When *Mr India* simultaneously entertains and serves as a cognitively self-conscious send-up of the formula film, it goes beyond both the heroic period of a national people's narrative presenting the *dil* as a Hindustani synthesis and the anti-heroic counterpoint offered by the conventional critical cinema. The meta-images in *Mr India* present a field of *dil* or desire which very much includes *dimaagh*, cognitive and critical consciousness, as a species of desire, and present a complexity of desire that subsumes the cognitive as a special case of the creative. This presentation is made possible by turning the formulaic code into a spectacular object with which to have fun.

One consequence of this complexity is that a new question becomes possible about the distribution of critical and discursive power. The monopoly of the critical Enlightenment culture has been broken and, with it, that of India's essentially colonized intellectual élite. Now that mass culture is becoming an alternative locus of critical discourse (as a reflexive function within entertainment itself), one must ask how this configuration differentiates between the kinds of questioning one would expect in the 'serious' critical cinema and in the realm of 'fun' popular cinema.

If we explore this question, accepting fantasy as an agency of self-construction, it becomes: To what extent are the image-based, perceptual self-interrogations available in the fantasy mode of popular cinema different, or could be so in the long run, from the concept-oriented, problem-featuring criticisms couched in the realistic idiom of art films?

This question does not have an answer that can survive repeated examination. However, one available answer is that the critical cinema, following the modernist paradigm that works through Verfremdung and other forms of defamiliarization, tends to present problems in terms of external social forces. Such forces obey historical laws. Artistic and other sectors of intellectual critique can mobilize systematic popular resistance against them, utilizing knowledge of these to overcome the negative forces artistically set up as the other. The critical depiction eventually shows up the narrative self as embroiled in a play of external forces and, therefore, as essentially reactive, caught in the enemy's game in the manner of the macho anti-British resistance in the Swadeshi period.[13] In contrast, the popular cinema's basic gesture is familiarization and narrative confidence, usually condemned by conceptualist critics as 'closure'. So, when the popular cinema thematizes basic contradictions, not only is it formally bound to show the evil Mogambo of *Mr India* as a familiar, selflike figure within the field of confident empathy, but its reliance on convention at the deepest level of representation, coupled with its anti-naturalism, commits popular cinema to a non-mimetic, representational view of problems. Thus its fundamental gesture, (i) frames the problems in the image, (ii) distances them from any notion of an all-powerful 'nature' or 'society', supposedly constituted by autonomous laws (unavailable for questioning within the representation-bound framework of the cinematic master narrative of our period; a framework that is narrative and visual-pleasure-oriented in Laura Mulvey's sense)[14] and, thus, (iii) by 'familiarizing' them into the representational framework of confident conventions, placing them in the self, conveys the message that the problems of life do not obey objective 'laws of life' outside us. Rather, life and its problems are made of the same shadows and tinsel with which the rest of show biz works and are as magical and as tame in principle as the screen itself.

NOTES AND REFERENCES

1. The production of these images was made possible by several friends who helped in various ways: R. Abel, T. Bhattacharya, S. Chakrabarti Dasgupta, G. Chatterjee, R. Gandhi, A. Nandy, R. Sankara Sastry, A. Sen, A. Shah, and R. Velicheti. The usual disclaimers apply.

2. I am invoking the *theme* of nudity, not the *topic*. A topic invites systematic study, preferably in the framework of one or more disciplines; a theme may or may not. Themes, however, do often preoccupy one and shape the way one approaches individual topics or connect one topic to another.
3. Laura Mulvey, 'Visual Pleasure and Narrative Cinema', *Screen* 3 (1975), pp. 6–18.
4. I speak here of the *world*, not the *planet*. The idiom that objectifies the earth as a planet is itself part of the denudation of our existence; the invasion of its privacy in the name of a knowedge that seeks to strip off all cultural artificialities and to uncover the nakedness of the natural body of life and its environment.
5. For instance, a worshipper of the naked goddess Kali, Ramprasad Sen, has sung 'Basan Paro, Ma' (Dress yourself, mother): Song 158 in 'Ramprasad's Padavali', in Bulbul Basu (ed.), *Ramprasad-Bharatchandra Rachanasamagra* (Calcutta: Reflect Publications, 1986), p. 147.
6. Readers not familiar with it should at least take a look at Colin McCabe's *Theoretical Essays: Film, Linguistics, Literature* (Manchester: Manchester University Press, 1985) and the references it cites.
7. Ashis Nandy, *The Intimate Enemy: Loss and Recovery of Self Under Colonialism* (New Delhi: Oxford University Press, 1983).
8. Bimal Krishna Matilal, *The Word and the World: India's Contribution to the Study of Language* (New Delhi: Oxford University Press, 1990).
9. 'Bharata and the Hindi film Revisited', in Sudhakar Marathe and Meenakshi Mukherjee (eds.), *Narrative: Forms and Transformations* (Delhi: Chanakya, 1986), pp. 139–49.
10. *Talks with Sri Ramana Maharshi* (Tiruvannamalai: Sri Ramanasraman, T.N. Venkatraman, 1978), 6th ed., 3 vols, p. 467.
11. Harold G. Coward, *Sphota Theory of Language* (Delhi: Motilal Banarsidass, 1980).
12. Probal Dasgupta, 'Outgrowing Quine: Towards Substantivism in the Theory of Translation', *International Journal of Translation* 1, no. 2 (1989), pp. 13–41.
13. On this, see Ashis Nandy, *The Intimate Enemy: Loss and Recovery of Self Under Colonialism* (New Delhi: Oxford University Press, 1983).
14. Laura Mulvey, 'Visual Pleasure and the Narrative Cinema', *Screen* 3 (1975), pp. 6–18.

Structure and Form in Indian Popular Film Narrative

M.K. RAGHAVENDRA

WHY TAKE POPULAR CINEMA SERIOUSLY?

The ideas contained in this essay emerged, largely, in 1991 after a viewing of the Hindi film *Saudagar* directed by Subhash Ghai, because at the time this film seemed, to me, to illustrate the liberties that Indian popular cinema takes in its story-telling methods. The narrative of *Saudagar* is, to someone brought up on a staple of Hollywood, quite bizarre but the film leaves us wondering if it employs another set of codes and if these codes are legitimate. If popular cinema is treated with derision,[1] it is the opinion of its detractors that is often cited outside India.[2] Let us, however, consider the aspects of *Saudagar* that, rather than meriting derision, might enable audiences to respond to it wholeheartedly.

Indians see more of their own cinema than the audiences of other film-producing nations and the inroads made by Hollywood into Indian film distribution have been relatively limited. A significant study of popular culture therefore seems unimaginable without popular cinema receiving its share of the attention. Sudhir Kakar[3] tentatively suggested that this cinema could be a collective daydream in which the audience partly becomes creator, and this view is echoed by many practitioners of media studies, who are now alive to the concept of 'co-authorship' by the spectator:

Co-authorship in media culture takes two forms: the 'creator co-author' and the 'consumer co-author'. One initiates the process of generating meaning and the other concludes it.

We are, each of us, a 'consumer co-author' of our media experience. We select what media we use, what products from those media we view, hear or read, how much attention we give each, and what kind of credibility we give to the experience.

As co-authors, we have genuine responsibility for the shape of the culture to which we expose ourselves. At the same time, we are only co-authors. The other author, the 'creator co-author,' in the form of media industries that provide us the menu from which we select, also has a direct influence on the culture we experience. Creator co-authors may not distribute cultural products of refreshing variety and high quality. Alternatively, more commonly, they may collectively submerge quality products within the huge and heavily promoted mainstream of mediocrity. Creative co-authors may be more interested in making income from me than enlightening or challenging me. However, whatever the shortcomings, I take from the creator co-authors and shape my own experience of media culture.[4]

If we propose a natural selection of stories[5] based on the success of films and individual 'formulae', the role of the consumer-co-author becomes even more significant.

FANTASY OR FAIRY TALE?

The terms employed most often to characterize Indian popular cinema are generic terms such as 'fantasy', 'fairy tale', and 'melodrama' but these terms have specific Western connotations that render their usage in the Indian context somewhat loose and imprecise. To Tzvetan Todorov, a work belongs to the realm of fantastic narrative only if the spectator/reader hesitates between a natural and a supernatural explanation for the events depicted.[6] Indian popular cinema evidently does not fulfil this criterion because its 'fantastic' side does not force the spectator to examine the issue of plausibility before s/he reaches for 'supernatural' explanations.

The designation 'fairy tale' is apparently less problematic. Like the fairy tale,[7] popular cinema resists categorization by themes; it is deliberate fiction and does not pass itself off as reality but it is also sententious in a way that the fairy tale is not.[8] The category commonly called 'melodrama' is different, and it cannot be denied that most Indian popular films belong to it, but what has also been demonstrated is that Western melodrama emerged through a specific historical impetus pertinent to Europe.[9] It is also true that Indian popular cinema is melodramatic in a different way from its Hollywood counterpart, such as the films of Douglas Sirk. Indian popular films place less emphasis upon individual motivation, subscribing to a more deterministic viewpoint. The more pejorative term 'escapism' has perhaps fewer culture-specific connotations and many popular films are perhaps vulnerable to the charge of being 'escapist'.[10] Still, the same accusation was once also made against Hollywood and the codes governing Indian popular cinema deserve the same understanding that has since been accorded to Hollywood.

The most productive approaches to Indian popular cinema have either attempted, following the trend initiated by cultural studies, to examine its texts as sites of ideological conflict,[11] or employed psycho-analytical methods (derived from Freud or Lacan) to read films.[12] The validity of the ideological or the psychoanalytical approach cannot be disputed, but a film like *Saudagar* has us wondering whether the 'content' of Indian cinema is as singular as its form and convention. Several key characteristics relating to narrative convention have been identified by academics and critics. For instance, it has been noticed by both its detractors and those sympathetic to it that popular cinema gives human representation to abstract notions like good and evil, often using character stereotypes embodying qualities.[13] The titles of Hindi films—*Sholay, Kismet, Sangam*, to mention only three—are also more metaphoric than metonymic.[14] Indian popular cinema is generally indifferent to the attractions of suspense and surprise.[15] What will happen next is usually known to the spectator, who waits to see how it will happen.[16] While some work has been done to identify narrative conventions, there have been fewer inquiries into popular cinema's form and structure. In most accounts of popular Hindi films, they are merely reckoned to be loosely structured and episodic.

This essay does not claim to be a comprehensive study of popular cinema because what began as a study of *Saudagar* has been extended to only two more Hindi films. The study has also been restricted to Hindi cinema because it reaches a 'pan-Indian' audience; regional films also perform a more complicated 'local' function within India and deserve a separate study. Here I restrict myself to films that are unabashedly 'mainstream' and not part of 'middle cinema' or 'art cinema' which apparently functions by different codes.[17]

SAUDAGAR

Returning to *Saudagar* (1991), the film is a saga spanning three generations and its story is narrated in flashback by a chorus-like figure, a wandering 'mendicant' named Mandhari who plays a small part in the narrative. We first encounter him as a bearded figure on horseback, meeting a group of schoolchildren whom he counsels through the following tale:

Raju (Rajeshwar Singh, a Thakur) and Biru (Bir Singh, a farmer) grow up together to adulthood and share a friendship that the years do nothing to diminish. Raju's sister Palikantha loses her heart to Biru and the two are to be married. Circumstances, however, intervene and force Biru to wed another woman. The heartbroken Palikantha sees no life without Biru and kills herself. Raju believes himself wronged by his best friend, and his scheming brother-in-law Chunya exploits the situation to drive Raju and Biru further apart. The two therefore become sworn enemies.

Twenty-five years go by. Rajeshwar is settled abroad, very much the non-resident Indian, and Bir Singh is headman of Sanathanpur, their native village. Rajeshwar's two sons are industrialists, having founded an industrial town named Palinagar (after their late aunt) across the river from Sanathanpur. Bir Singh also has two sons and the respective offspring of Rajeshwar and Bir Singh are perpetually at war with one another. When Vishal, the more reasonable of Bir Singh's sons, attempts to mend fences with the other side, Chunya has him murdered and this leads to some more bloodshed. Vishal's infant son Vasu is therefore sent away hastily to the Himalayas to be trained by an *acharya* in the arts of war. Rajeshwar returns home at this juncture and is on the point of learning the truth from 'the Collector' but Chunya contrives to have the official murdered and his brother-in-law blamed. Rajeshwar is duly arrested and he spends the next fourteen years in prison believing Bir Singh responsible for his predicament.

The fourteen years go by and Rajeshwar's grandchildren Kunal and Radha are back from schooling in Delhi. Vasu has also returned home equipped with the knowledge imparted to him by the acharya. Vasu and Radha meet one day and fall in love. Kunal loves a girl named Amla also from the hated village of Sanathanpur. Kunal and Amla marry secretly and Amla gives birth to a child. The liaison between Kunal and Amla comes to the attention of the alert Chunya, who is apprehensive of the good that the relationship might do. Amla obliges him by falling into his hands, and she is raped and murdered. Kunal is too weak to accept responsibility for Amla's child, and this leads to another conflagration. When the angry Bir Singh confronts Rajeshwar (who has completed his term in prison), the latter denies his grandson's connection with the child but Kunal says and does nothing. As hostilities between the two families intensify, Vasu and Radha also despair and contemplate suicide but Mandhari comes to their rescue.

Radha is planted in Bir Singh's house as a maid and Vasu finds employment with Raju through his martial prowess and native wisdom. In time, Vasu and Radha wear down the two old men who begin to show signs of mutual affection amidst their habitual obstinacy. When Chunya miscalculates and suggests the marriage of his own son Monty to Radha, Raju is annoyed and Chunya defaults on a mysterious deal with a shadowy 'Chinaman' named Michael Thapa. Now desperate, Chunya holds Vasu captive and attempts to force Radha into marriage with Monty. Raju now understands Chunya's true nature and he and Biru become friends again. To save Radha and Vasu, however, he agrees to help honour the agreement with Michael Thapa. There are a few more twists and turns but at the conclusion Rajeshwar, Bir Singh, Chunya, and Michael Thapa are all killed. Mandhari comes to the end of his tale but we are shown Vasu and Radha whose love survives the carnage. The schoolboys listening to Mandhari lower their gazes, as if acknowledging the tragic greatness of the protagonists and the moral significance of the story.

SAUDAGAR'S EXTRAVAGANT METHODS

The narrative of *Saudagar* has been briefly related and several details have been omitted. The film is more than three hours long, and as it conforms to no established aesthetic this makes the task of 'understanding' its narrative logic daunting. Several aspects of the film, nonetheless, deserve special examination, the first of these evidently the dependence of the film on mythological elements borrowed from the Mahabharata. Sanathanpur is intended to remind us of the Pandava capital Hastinapur, and Chunya is modelled on Shakuni, Gandhari's brother in the epic. Rajeshwar tests Vasu's wisdom through questions related to the abstract notions of friendship, enmity, courage, and death, just as the Yaksha tests Yudhishthira at the enchanted pool. Radha and Vasu are themselves intended to remind us of Radha and Krishna, and the name assumed by Vasu in Rajeshwar's employment is also Krishna. No Indian would need to be reminded that the fourteen years during which Rajeshwar is falsely confined to jail parallel the fourteen years during which the Pandavas were banished into exile.

The film, as is commonly the case, also takes several liberties with the epic: it does not respect the narrative's 'purity' and grafts elements from Western literature on to it. Radha and Vasu's love story is not like Radha's and Krishna's in the Mahabharata, inasmuch as motifs borrowed liberally from Shakespeare's *Romeo and Juliet* find a place in it. The figure of Mandhari combines aspects of Vidhura from the Mahabharata with Friar Lawrence from *Romeo and Juliet*; and he assists the lovers in the same way.[18] This medley of motifs perhaps finds a reflection in Rajeshwar's family mansion, which acknowledges equally the architectural styles of Victorian England and Central India of the medieval period.

Another aspect of *Saudagar* that attracts notice is the way it accommodates characteristics of the contemporary world within an archaic world-view. Rajeshwar is a Thakur who wears emerald earrings but lives abroad as a non-resident. A 'peace-keeping force' separates Sanathanpur from Palinagar. Vasu learns the art of using firearms from an acharya. Riders on horseback and motorcyclists mingle freely in the action sequences. Rajeshwar signs an agreement with Michael Thapa on a ping-pong table. There is enough in *Saudagar* to send hybridity theorists reeling. The film also extends these anachronisms to offer a discourse on traditional and 'Western' values. Bir Singh and Rajeshwar are differentiated from each other through their attitudes towards them. Biru is traditional to the core and does not leave his native village but Rajeshwar dresses in Western clothes and rides in a helicopter. His descendents cavort to Western music on a dance floor and Radha frequently breaks into English. Vasu is traditionally dressed and shuns English although he is not ignorant of its nuances (T means *chai* and C means *dekhna*, he says: another one for linguists and hybridists). Bir Singh also exhorts Rajeshwar to 'come down to earth', to abandon scotch whisky for the local *daru* and mimics his lofty ways with a few sentences of terse English punctuated by swear words. As Rajeshwar moves closer to Bir Singh, his attire changes noticeably, becoming entirely traditional by the end.

The two aspects of *Saudagar* gain importance only in the context of the third, most important one, which is the way it structures time. The film is formally conceived in two parts separated by the appearance of the titles, an event that takes place a full twenty-five minutes after the commencement of the film. Examining the film closely, the first part covers forty-five years of narrative time: twenty years for Raju and Biru to grow fully into adulthood and twenty-five years of enmity between them until Rajeshwar returns to India. The second part commences with Vasu's return home, shortly after which Rajeshwar is released from prison. As Rajeshwar is imprisoned immediately after the title sequence, the fourteen years of his sentence are not experienced on-screen, in the sense that no important event in the narrative occurs within this span. It is not far-fetched to argue that *narrative time is discontinuous*, and that the fourteen-year period separates the preamble or prologue from the central narrative of the film dealing with Vasu and Radha.

If the preamble accounts for forty-five years and the 'gap' accounts for fourteen more, the time spanned by the central story—dealing with Vasu and Radha—is uncertain and there are reasons for this. First, this part of the film is more episodic; secondly, the songs sung are all duets. It is difficult to remember the order in which the songs appear. The duets in *Saudagar* are sung under the same timeless circumstances, the first of these being rendered (from separate spaces) *even before Radha and Vasu have met each other!* It is likely that as in many songs today, this one was written without a narrative function in mind, but what is interesting is the ease with which the song fits into the narrative with no questions being asked about how a duet can precede the first meeting.

There are also sequences in the film in which spaces are miraculously bridged: Radha and Vasu visualizing each other within their respective homes and heading to a common place to find the other waiting. Rajeshwar and Bir Singh privately recall each other as children but, as they do this, their remarks about each other are inter-cut as if the two are facing each other. At a third moment, Vasu and Radha sing a duet, not together but in their respective villages, followed by choruses of their own. This miraculous bridging of spaces undermines the possibility of an 'elsewhere', a space outside our attention that is nevertheless the location for simultaneous action and everything is taking place here and now.

Structure and Form in Indian Popular Film Narrative

The non-causal or 'episodic' character of *Saudagar* is also different from that of an American or European film with a comparable structure. A 'road film', for example, is often episodic because its events are not held together by direct causal linking. There is, however, inevitability in the order of arrangement of the episodes, the arrangement reflecting in some way an emotional progression directed towards a climax. In *Saudagar*, this is not the case because each event in the central drama is virtually autonomous. The love between Radha and Vasu, for example, does not follow their initial meeting. The mythological references and the singing of the duet before their first encounter suggests that, in some ideal way, their love *always* existed, and Mandhari assures us at the conclusion that it is 'eternal'. Their love does not grow with each meeting because each meeting is complete in its own right.

The progress of the relationship between Rajeshwar and Bir Singh is more complicated. When Mandhari begins his tale we are shown garlanded oil portraits of the two and presume that they are dead. Apart from the obvious significance of the garlands, it is one of the conventions of the popular film that the subject of an oil portrait cannot be living. During the last moments of the film, for example, we are shown portraits of the two and of Vishal but not of any of the survivors. Another portrait of Rajeshwar and Bir Singh sitting shoulder-to-shoulder is shown to us during the period of their estrangement to signify their lost friendship. Somewhere during the course of the film, Rajeshwar cleaves the painting with a blow of a sword and the two pieces lie around for Vasu to discover and attempt to rejoin. At the end of Mandhari's tale we observe that the portrait has become whole again and shows no signs of the damage once caused to it. The recurring presence of the portrait in the central part of the film is therefore not only a perpetual reminder of the friendship they shared in the preamble but also a pointer to its eventual restoration and the tragic deaths of the two. Judging from these factors, we may conclude that the relationship between the two does not 'develop' in time but, rather, that its history is encoded in each of the narrative's individual moments, all of them existing side by side.

While the same observations can be made about the delineation of Chunya's character, the important aspect is that the episodes tend to work as tableaux that follow one another chronologically, but with no causal links between them.[19] The love story of Kunal and Amla, for example, performs no essential function and can be excised from the film without in any way affecting its narrative, and a few more episodes could have been squeezed into the film if it hadn't been long enough already. Each episode in the central narrative is only connected to a 'first cause' contained in the preamble. The preamble is like a previous existence; it is separated from the present by a schism in time, but influences its course to a degree that events in the present do not.

CLASSICAL HOLLYWOOD CINEMA AS THE 'NORM'

The narrative of *Saudagar* may strike someone unaccustomed to popular cinema as eccentric because it respects few 'rules' of filmic storytelling. These rules, however, cannot be regarded as 'universal' but are actually culture-specific. Film theorists nonetheless tend to regard 'classical' Hollywood cinema—or studio feature film-making from Hollywood after 1920—as the basic model from which all other narrative styles are derived:

> ...In constructing alternatives to Hollywood, we must recognize that the historical centrality of that mode creates a constant and complex interchange with other modes. No absolute, pure alternative to Hollywood exists. Godard's use of Hollywood conventions,...Fassbinder's borrowings from melodramas and gangster films, Rivette's revision of Lang and Jansco's of Ford—all attest to the filmmaker's impulse to use classicism as a reference point... Hollywood's mode of production continues to exert a power that can only be opposed by a knowledge of its past and its functions. The historical and aesthetic importance of the classical Hollywood cinema lies in the fact that to go beyond it we must go through it.[20]

It is difficult to accept the contention that all kinds of filmic storytelling proceed from classical cinema, although Hollywood does represent the dominant mode. Consequently, while the remark cited above applies to most of the cinemas from around the world, it is certainly not pertinent to Indian popular cinema and the extreme case of *Saudagar* quite plainly demonstrates this. While this essay does not pretend to instal Indian popular cinema's narrative methods as a counterpoint to those of classical Hollywood cinema, it does try to point in that direction, and its arguments can perhaps be further extended.

Classical Hollywood cinema has a set of broad rules, and those pertinent to my arguments can be enumerated briefly as follows:[21]

1. The narrative logic should be driven by psychological causation. The narrative must be character centred and the drive should be towards overcoming obstacles.
2. The narrative must take the shape of a causal chain. To maintain continuity in time, causes must be left dangling to be subsequently taken up by effects. This also ensures the creation of off-screen space, which becomes a 'screen', a blank space that invites the spectator to project hypothetical events on to it.
3. Unity of action must be maintained and all incidents must cluster around a single animating idea. One purpose must run through the series of incidents.
4. The representation of time is done to make the chronology and the duration clear to the spectator. Duration is usually indicated by introducing appointments and deadlines into the narrative. Cross-cutting usually denotes parallel action: two or three lines of action in different locales woven together.

Classical Hollywood cinema insists that causality is the backbone of narrative, and this viewpoint evidently has its basis in dialectics: the linkage of development to binary conflict. Indian cinema 'strays' from classical Hollywood cinema because it derives from a world-view that places its emphasis upon the immutable rather than upon change through conflict. One of the cornerstones of Indian dramaturgy, for example, is the notion of *rasa*. Rasa is held to be a generalized emotion out of which all elements of a particular consciousness have been expunged, and perhaps corresponds to an 'essence'. According to one view:

Art is a kind of mimesis according to the rasa theory, but it is an imitation of a very special kind, for rasa does not imitate things or actions in their particularity, in their actuality, but rather in their universality, in their potentiality—and this imitation is said to be more real than any particular real thing.[22]

The sense of the transcendental 'real' that does not reside in the particularity of any real thing can be read as an affirmation of the immutable, and this eventually sees *development* and *change* not receiving the same emphasis in Indian art and dramaturgy that they get in the West, and this evidently affects popular film narrative. Returning once again to Subhash Ghai's film, what we observe in *Saudagar* is the absence of *becoming* in its narrative: the disinclination of the narrative to deal with change as a continuous process. We have already received an indication of the fundamental difference between the Western and the Indian approach to art but this may need further exploration.

TIME IN INDIA ART

In writing about a well-known painting by Rembrandt Van Rijn, an Indian critic remarks:

...let us take...the well-known portrait 'Christ before The Pilate'. We find here the judge sitting upon his high seat of honour, and before him the Jewish priests are making angry...complaints about Jesus. In front of Jesus, on a high pillar, there is a large statue of Caesar; at some distance from it, in a dark corner, Jesus is standing...surrounded by Roman soldiers. Rembrandt...chose for his portrayal the moment when at the end of his strivings in the cause of the religion he regarded to be true, he was discarded by his own people and brought before a Roman judge. The choice of this particular moment, though revealing the great artistic insight of Rembrandt fails to put Jesus in proper perspective...Indian artists [on the other hand]...did not lay emphasis on any passing [moment]...but tried to discover [the essence of]...the object of creation. This was perceived by them as dominating over individual moments...and could be regarded as characterizing the soul or essence of the artist's object of creation.[23]

We see here how in a medium like painting, which is essentially spatial in character, the seizing of a transitory moment is crucial in Western art. The subject of Rembrandt's canvas is religious narrative, but even when the subject is more abstract, more concerned with form, the preoccupation is evident:

Two sculptors are carving a sphere out of stone. One of them wants to achieve the most perfect form of the sphere and sees the meaning of his work in turning a mass of stone into a perfect sphere. The other is also carving a sphere but only to convey the inner tension expressed in the form of a sphere filled to bursting point. The first will be the work of a craftsman and the second, that of an artist.[24]

The difference between the two spheres is that the latter, the 'work of the artist', captures a moment of equilibrium between two opposing forces; an instant in a continuum while the former ignores the notion of time altogether. Progress is dialectical and embodied in a series of conflicts. The natural consequence of conflict being change, each moment develops into the next through a series of binary oppositions.

Thus, 'change' becomes synonymous with continuing, irreversible time. To illustrate the difference between the Indian and Western approach further, the Western artist studied the human anatomy, the intricacies of skeletal and muscular structure, not for its own sake but because muscle and bone together produce movement. We do not, in Indian art, see an emphasis upon muscle and bone as the basis of movement. Movement itself is not a transition between two states involving a defined interval of time but, is more exactly, 'ceaseless flow'. The dancing figure in Indian sculpture, for example, has been so described:

> The Indian artist in portraying a figure did not take it in a merely static attitude, but from that static state abstracted it as a piece from a concrete flow of motion... It may be remembered in this connection that according to Indian mythology, the whole universe was regarded as having emanated from the rhythmic dance of Lord Narayana on the waves of the great ocean at the beginning of creation... The movement of dance thus represents in itself the rhythmic motion leading to creation and the opposite rhythm of dissolution. From this point of view, the whole universe may be regarded...as congealed or sliced off states of rhythmic motion of dance.[25]

Indian art is therefore not preoccupied with the seizing of a transitory moment in a temporal continuum but as an expression of what is eternal and unchanging. If even the pictorial and plastic arts of the West attempt to include change and continuing time as constituent elements, the traditional performing arts of India, which unfold in time, have disregarded time's 'reality'. Here is a description of Sanskrit drama, comparing it to the frescoes of Ajanta:

> as we have seen the 'continuous narrative' of the Ajanta frescos is cyclical and non-sequential. Similarly, the dramatized structure of a Sanskrit play is cyclical, based on the themes of separation and reunion; it ends as it begins; various devices are used such as the dream, the trance, the premonition, the flashback, to disrupt the linearity of time and make the action recoil upon itself. Both media rely on the theory of modal music...devise a sequence of movements, scenes or acts which is cyclical...[26]

TIME AND HISTORICITY

If the notion of linear, continuing time is traditionally alien to the Indian sensibility it cannot but have consequences for film narrative, and this is evidenced in the 'ahistoricity' of the Indian popular film. The drama in much of Western cinema is anchored in history and the advantage this confers upon film narrative needs some comment. If the opening frame of a film says '1945' and the film itself is set in the United States we recognize an allusion to the end of the war; we anticipate the tumult, the music, and the returning soldiers. We perhaps also expect to see a wife waiting for her husband or a girl for her sweetheart. In the same way, an American street in 1930 and a pedestrian in tattered clothes can indicate the great economic depression. The allusion is a sign that creates an instantaneous context. We become involved in the story on the basis of what we already know of the moment and we expect the drama in the film to be driven by its implications. The historical anchoring of the narrative is compulsive, and even a futuristic fantasy like *Star Wars* employs historical signifiers. It gives us intimation of its principal villain through his 'Nazi' headgear.

The meta-narrative of history presents each film with the opportunity of linking its own narrative to universal time, also providing a ready context with reference to which the drama in the film can be conceived. Popular Indian cinema never has a ready context to which it can relate its concerns, and therefore each film must create or define its own. Whole stories must be told where a single sign might have sufficed, and this makes the films inordinately long. When each narrative is not linked to the meta-narrative of universal time, each film exists only autonomously and in relation to its own context. Sequels are also impossible because this would mean situating one narrative in relation to another one within the meta-narrative.

If popular cinema has drawn sustenance from a body of myth, this does not, still, single it out. According to Roland Barthes, myth is essentially a kind of language and a set of conventions by which the exigencies of a historical moment are given eternal justification.[27] Hollywood genre films refer back to mythologies with their foundations in history. The Western, for example, draws upon the mythology associated with the origins of the American nation. The mythology of the cold war created its own genres—James Bond and Rambo, to name two—and some sub-categories under film noir can perhaps be traced to the depression of 1930. The curious fact about popular cinema in India is that history seems to have created no myths of its own, and one is hard-pressed to find more than a film or two that uses even 1947 for its narrative thrust notwithstanding the efforts of the state to build a durable mythology out of the Freedom Struggle. Popular cinema refers persistently to pre-history and myth—the Ramayana and the Mahabharata—perhaps because history has produced no enduring myths to be transformed into generic convention.

The reluctance of popular cinema to depend upon history for 'contexts' implies that each film must create its own contexts. The most enduring of these is the family. The only 'past' known to this cinema is family history, and hence the most permanent of the motifs exhibited by this cinema is that of family and the parental figure. Hollywood family dramas are about the family under threat. Indian 'family dramas' are not about families in danger of disintegration but, rather, romantic stories about love with the family merely as context or background.

We also recall no other cinema in the world that brings 'love' as compulsively into its narratives and most Indian popular films are about the triumph of love, and love can be regarded as 'triumphant' if it is reciprocated—even if tragedy prevents mutual love from being finally consummated. One way of interpreting the formal use of the family in Indian film narrative is that it is the largest social unit that can exist autonomously within the narrative without referential links to history and absolute time. The parental figure furnishes the required 'context' that the historical moment cannot provide in Indian cinema. Similarly, 'triumphant love' closes the narrative, keeping its mythical universe clearly apart from the historical one.

The term 'closure' has been used in a different sense in the Bazinian debate about realism in cinema and the present usage of the term may need further illustration. In the way that the terms have been generally used, a film has been described as 'open' when the world of the film is a momentary frame around an ongoing reality. The objects and characters existed before the camera focused upon them and they will exist after the film is over. As in the *Bicycle Thief*, they achieve their significance or interest within the story of the film but, unlike the objects and people in a closed film, the story of the open film does not exhaust the meaning of what it contains.[28] Genre films like the Western or the historical film are closed because the conventions impose a final meaning upon the moment in a way that history itself does not. Indian popular films are closed in a more fundamental way because their narratives are not located in the stream of history. The narrative definitely 'ceases' at the conclusion of the film, and this would not have been the case if it had links with the meta-narrative of universal time. As an illustration, Roland Emmerich's *The Patriot* (2000), an adventure set in the American Revolution, is a genre film with the Englishman Lord Cornwallis as one of its villains. This man surrenders to the Revolution at the conclusion, and this act brings the narrative to closure. Yet, our awareness that the same Lord Cornwallis went on to become governor-general of India works, in some sense, against our seeing the closure as final.

The structure and the conventions of Indian popular cinema make it impossible for it to accommodate continuing, universal time as one of its constituents, but the contemporary references in *Saudagar*—peacekeeping forces, ping pong diplomacy, non-residents—gain significance only in historical time. The incorporation of these elements into the narrative is an attempt to be 'topical' but the film evidently lacks the capability to assimilate their larger significance. What the film does is to simply take each of these elements, detach it from its own historical significance, and physically introduce it into the narrative.[29]

SHOLAY AND THE CONGLOMERATE NARRATIVE

Saudagar is a rather extreme example, but the scrutiny of other films shows us that its methods are not singular although each film may employ its own motifs and work differently within the same structural paradigms. Ramesh Sippy's *Sholay* (1975), for example, is more 'realistic' than *Saudagar* on many counts but works on the same narrative principles, and an examination of it is bound to be instructive. *Sholay* is one of the best known of Indian films and its story therefore does not bear retelling. The film is founded on the knowledge that the *daku* (dacoit) film has several characteristics in common with the Western. It takes many stylistic devices from Sergio Leone's spaghetti classic, *Once Upon a Time in the West* (1968), and also borrows liberally from other films. Indeed, *Sholay* can be said to use bits and pieces from American films or spaghetti Western—*Once Upon a Time in the West; The Good, the Bad, and the Ugly; The Magnificent Seven; The Secret of Santa Vittoria*—in much the same way that *Saudagar* inserts fragments of Shakespeare into a concoction made from scraps of Indian mythology. One finds a curious parallel between the way *Sholay* 'borrows' from the body of world cinema[30] and an observation made about Sanskrit theatre by one Western scholar:

The Sanskrit dramatists show considerable skill in weaving the incidents of the plot and in the portrayal of individual character, but do not show much fertility of invention, commonly borrowing the story of their plays from history or epic legend.[31]

Leone's film is constructed around the great railroad to the West but, in keeping with the requirements of Indian cinema, *Sholay* abandons all claims to historicity. The action in the film is located at a nondescript place named Ramgarh and its principal protagonists are two ex-criminals, Jai and Viru, who are engaged by a former police officer, Thakur Baldev Singh, to capture a notorious dacoit named Gabbar Singh.

The narrative of *Sholay* does not apparently take place over a period exceeding a decade, and this is largely responsible for making the film's methods seem less extreme than *Saudagar*, but it is constructed in the same episodic way and is indifferent to chronology. The film does not begin with a prologue but the 'prehistory' of the central narrative takes the shape of several flashbacks regarding the Thakur, his family, and his past dealings with Gabbar. Re-arranged chronologically, this part of the narrative ends with the killing of the Thakur's kin and the severing of his arms by Gabbar. By the time the adventures of Jai and Viru commence the Thakur is noticeably older and his hair has started to turn grey. If the greying of the Thakur's hair is understood to be an indication of the passage of time, it can be said that an interval of about ten years separates the Thakur's tragedy from his employment of Jai and Viru. This is so although it must be emphasized that apart from the changing hues of the Thakur's hair there is no other evidence of the passage of such an interval. If this interval is, however, conceded, we still don't know what befell him during this period or why the Thakur waited ten years before deciding to avenge himself upon Gabbar.

The 'prehistory' of the central narrative (represented by the flashbacks) also provides the film with its driving logic and, like the story of Raju and Biru in *Saudagar*, is tightly constructed. What is interesting is that this sub-narrative also provides the 'first cause' with regard to two of the remaining three sub-narratives identified. It sets the tone for the love story between Jai and Radha, and if Jai and Viru are the Thakur's surrogate children, it gives a new impetus to their relationship by making them 'brothers'. It is only the farcical love story of Viru and Basanti that resists being driven by its logic of vengeance, and this explains why it is the weakest part of the film. Still, this sub-narrative provides the film with its only opportunity for closure, and it is difficult to imagine an alternative strategy that would effect this closure more efficiently.

The episodic quality of the film also deserves some comment. When we say that a work is 'episodic' we mean that the work frustrates us in our efforts to make causal connections in its narrative, and this is exactly what much of *Sholay* does because of the discontinuities in its structure.[32] Just as the two parts of the Thakur's life are arranged as tableaux with an unexplained period in between, the younger daughter-in-law Radha is also shown before her marriage as playful and vivacious and, after her widowhood, as perpetually in mourning. We fail to see any continuity in her behaviour, and when she is attracted to Jai, her demeanour still doesn't change. *Sholay* 'arranges' Jai's death because he cannot be permitted to marry a widow, but this may not be due to any social stigma attached to the act. Radha is conceived 'in essence' as a widow and the conventions of popular cinema, not allowing for the notion of continuing change, cannot show Radha's conduct undergoing transformation. Gabbar himself is a curious creation because we don't know what motivates him or why the loyalty of his men is so unwavering. For all the rewards he carries on his head there is also no excitement in tracking Gabbar because his enemies always reach his hideout without trouble. As he is conceived, Gabbar does not develop but is meant to represent 'pure evil' in a singularly static or rigid way.

Another aspect of *Sholay* that needs examination is the characterization of Jai and Viru. The two protagonists of *Sholay* have been described as 'rootless and traditionless', and the conclusion has been that they are 'representatives of the mercantile capitalism emerging traditionally'.[33] Jai's and Viru's 'rootlessness' is presumably deduced from the absence of parental figures securing them firmly to a 'context', but this absence is disputable. In the first place, the childhood friendship (*Sangam*, 1964) or '*dosti*' has often provided the popular film with the same guiding ethical thrust as the parental figure and the relationship between Jai and Viru exhibits all the characteristics of companionship developed in childhood.[34] More importantly, parental links are made through allusion. Gabbar liquidated the Thakur's two sons along with the elder daughter-in-law and a grandchild. A strange attraction now develops between the widowed younger daughter-in-law Radha and Jai, the younger of the two protagonists. When the relationships within the Thakur's family are suggested in the longest of four flashbacks, care is taken to avoid showing the younger son and Radha together. The attraction between Jai and Radha thus becomes, technically, the first that either experiences on-screen. It is also revealed in an earlier flashback that the two saved the Thakur's life although this entailed surrendering to the law and being imprisoned. The subsequent period of imprisonment is also shown, but comically making the punishment seem nominal. The two also refuse money for capturing Gabbar when they learn the Thakur's true story. All these factors influence our reading of the relationship between Thakur Baldev Singh and the two ex-convicts and it appears, increasingly to resemble one between a stern but well-meaning father and his two prankish sons.

Sholay exhibits the characteristics of Hollywood genre cinema with much of the inspiration for it coming from the Western genre. At the same time, it shows generic inconsistencies that would be inadmissible in American cinema. Genres like the Western gangster film, and the horror film all have their own conventions that create mutually exclusive worlds and motifs from one genre do not easily find a place in the others. The episodic nature of Indian popular cinema, its song and dance sequences, dreams and premonitions disrupt the flow of continuous linear time and prepare the audience for events that defy prediction. They prepare them for sudden thematic or generic shifts, and the characteristics mentioned above perform the task of cementing the incompatible fragments together, facilitating a 'conglomeration' of individual narrative strands.³⁵

The conglomerate structure of *Sholay* makes it possible for at least four major sub-narratives to exist side by side with no authentic links connecting them. The tones or moods that dominate each of the sub-narratives vary and whenever the film moves from one to another the effect is abrupt. Thakur Baldev Singh's story takes up the issues of hatred and vengeance. The story of Jai and Radha concerns unfulfilled love and is a melancholy one. The story of the friendship between Jai and Viru is high adventure, and the romance between Viru and Basanti is conceived as low farce. Each sub-narrative has its own climax and resolution and the film makes no attempt to subordinate them to a single end. Thus, at the conclusion of *Sholay*, Thakur Baldev Singh sees Viru off at the railway station and the atmosphere is heavy with what the two have lost. However, a moment later, Viru finds Basanti 'accidentally' on the train and the mood lightens instantaneously. It is tempting to see the conclusion of *Sholay* as signifying an emotional 'renewal', but the relaxation in the mood results, evidently, from the sub-narrative being switched.

HUM AAPKE HAIN KOUN AND THE ABSENT 'FIRST CAUSE'

A more recent but apparently different kind of film that nevertheless follows the same principles of construction is Sooraj Barjatya's *Hum Aapke Hain Koun* (1994). This film can be regarded as a pioneer of sorts and has the capacity to repay detailed analysis generously but we are here concerned only with the aspects relevant to its structure.

Hum Aapke Hain Koun is a family drama that begins when a marriage proposal is brought for Kailas Nath's elder nephew Rajesh. The girl proposed is Professor Siddharth Chaudhury's elder daughter Pooja. Kailas Nath is an industrialist and a bachelor who lives in a palatial house with his two nephews, Rajesh and the younger Prem. Professor Chaudhury lives with his wife and two daughters Pooja and Nisha. The instant the proposal is made, Kailas Nath recognizes an old college friend in Professor Chaudhury, and it takes only one meeting for the alliance to be considered an eminently desirable one by all concerned, and the understanding is duly celebrated with songs and festivities.

Hum Aapke Hain Koun moves from one celebration to another, and the first is followed by an official engagement ceremony and, a little later, by the actual wedding. Prem and Nisha have begun to see more and more of each other and it is evident from the first moments that they find each other extremely attractive. Nisha plays a prank on Prem but the family dog, gifted with miraculous powers, saves him at the last moment. Prem, however, demonstrates his sporting qualities by admitting defeat and this endears him to Nisha even more. Professor Chaudhury and Kailas Nath themselves revere each other not only because the two men were friends earlier but also because the latter was an ardent admirer of Mrs Chaudhury and made way for the man who ultimately became her husband.

After the wedding Pooja moves to her husband's home and it is evident that more happiness cannot be expected from a union. The next celebration takes place when Pooja conceives, and the one after that when the child is born. The Chaudhurys and Nisha stay on in Kailas Nath's home long after the child is born, and the time is spent in community games like passing the pillow. Prem and Nisha have more or less agreed upon their own marriage and Prem promises Nisha that he will bring the matter up in the right place and at the right time. Kailas Nath's new business undertaking 'Prem Motors (P) Ltd' also has its opening and all continues to be well.

At this point, however, the loyal family servant Lallu receives bad news from his village and has to leave, but Pooja is financially generous and he leaves with much gratitude. Pooja and her child are now driven by Prem to her father's house and, during the conversation, Prem reveals to her that he and Nisha want to marry. Pooja is overjoyed and all three of them celebrate briefly but, in trying to get downstairs to answer the telephone, Pooja slips on the staircase, hurtles downward, and is fatally injured.

Once the mourning is over, the family comes to recognize the problem posed by the motherless baby and one well-wisher urges that Rajesh remarry. An unpleasant aunt promptly brings in a marriage proposal but a condition is made that the baby must not live with the couple after the wedding. After some discussion Professor Chaudhury suggests that as a complete stranger cannot be expected to care about the child, it would make sense for Nisha to marry Rajesh. The others approve of the idea but the rider is that Nisha herself must give her consent. Professor Chaudhury approaches his daughter, but before the proposal is made clear, Nisha assumes it is Prem she is being asked to marry and agrees. The film now skips one or two celebrations and goes straight to the wedding arrangements. Nisha is blissful until someone reads out the wedding invitation and the horror of the situation dawns on her. Both she and Prem decide that duty must have priority and she decides to go ahead, but the loyal family servant is in tears and makes a desperate application to divinity. As happened in an earlier scene, the family dog is miraculously empowered with the knowledge of the situation and he deliberately carries a farewell message from Nisha to Rajesh instead of to Prem. Rajesh now understands and makes way for his younger brother. Prem and Nisha are finally united.

Compared to *Saudagar*, *Hum Aapke Hain Koun* is almost elemental in its simplicity, and this is evident from any rendering of its narrative. The narrative seems linearly constructed because it does not span an enormous and uncertain period but its events perhaps take place over a period of about two years. Regardless of these features, the film must be regarded as episodic because the chronology of events is not dictated by the way in which they develop but is simply embedded in the rituals and ceremonies associated with marriage and conjugality. These rituals follow a very strict order, but not the events actually governing the narrative and determining its outcome. Thus, what happens in behavioural or social terms at each of the ceremonies is not different from what happens at the others. In fact, the only event that can be said to 'narrativize' the film is Pooja's death, which creates the single conflict in need of resolution. It is also pertinent to note that this single 'event' driving the narrative is accidental and not the result of any conscious or deliberate act.

Secondly, the narrative makes it amply clear that the family is unaware of the relationship existing between Prem and Nisha because of the manner in which Nisha's marriage to Rajesh is proposed. Yet, in one of the celebratory scenes (Pooja's pregnancy) the women get together and a young woman dresses up as Prem and acts out a romance with Nisha. Also interesting is the fact that what happens in the 'performance' is virtually replicated by Nisha and Prem, and *the imitation of the actions precedes or anticipates the actions imitated*. This serves to cast doubts upon the causal aspects of the narrative and its chronology. As time is virtually stagnant until Pooja's death, the arrangement of this part can be described as an elaborate tableau.

We saw in both *Saudagar* and *Sholay* the inclusion of a preamble or a 'prehistory' that dictated the course of the events in the central narrative, but Barjatya's film seems to avoid this structure. A closer look, however, reveals a different picture. The narrative *has* a 'prehistory' but the innovation of *Hum Aapke Hain Koun* lies in its keeping this constituent sub-narrative completely off-screen. Professor Chaudhury and Kailas Nath, we learn, were friends and their friendship is renewed when the film begins. More importantly, Kailas Nath stepped aside when the woman he loved decided to marry his friend but he has remained a bachelor because he cannot marry anyone else. The character of Kailas Nath is, in effect, doing a double turn. He is partly surrogate father to Prem and Rajesh and partly the disappointed lover who can marry no one else after making way, and who still bears the scars of his disappointment. According to the conventions of dosti in Indian popular cinema, the friendship between the two men is sacred and the proposed family ties are intended to strengthen the relationship. The relationship is strengthened but destiny intervenes with Pooja's death and the ties are threatened. That is why new family ties need to be forged and Nisha is suggested as the instrument. As happens in a host of other films, the events in the narrative's 'prehistory' are crucial in determining the course of the central narrative and the film moves inexorably by this logic.

BARJATYA'S *RAMRAJYA*

The film begins with a cricket match played on the grounds of Kailas Nath's home involving members of his family and household, the family dog performing the task of the umpire. The motif of the cricket match is again repeated after Pooja's wedding to Rajesh and reinforces the image of the happy family. If it is admitted that the film belongs to times where the Indian cricket team rather than the Indian army is invested with the patriotic sentiments of the nation, *Hum Aapke Hain Koun* makes an especially interesting study. The cricket match is not played in uniform and each player wears the clothes that distinguish him socially within the narrative. The hero has a cap that says 'Boy' and Pooja wears one that says 'Girl'. The servants apparently retain their status as servants although the menial clothes they wear are patently unsuited for playing cricket. The servants, however, share the patriotic sentiments required of cricket because when Lallu, the most ubiquitous of them, learns English through Pooja's efforts the paragraph he recites is a paean to the nation and to Jawaharlal Nehru.

Kailas Nath's residence is an enormous space that is always filled with guests and visitors, most of whom are not introduced to us. The space usually includes one token Muslim couple, here Dr and Mrs Khan, who are not asked to do anything more than represent their religion at family gatherings. When a doctor is needed for Pooja, it is someone else who is called in and not Dr Khan. Why Kailas Nath's family gatherings are so crowded with people can only be a matter for conjecture but it does seem to connect with another aspect of the film. *Hum Aapke Hain Koun* has attracted attention for the repeated references it makes to the Ramayana, in particular to the version of the story by Tulsidas which is immensely popular in north India, and to Ram worship. One aspect of the Ramayana that has captured the popular psyche is the notion of 'Ramrajya' or the idea of benevolent rule under which everyone is happy. The Ramayana, as popularly understood, involves episodes in which the people of Ayodhya celebrate occurrences at the royal palace, and the impression of the celebrations is that of vicarious participation by 'the public' in events constituting the private life of the royal family. The crowd assembled within the four walls of Kailas Nath's residence is large enough for us to see aspects of 'the public' in their composition, and the presence of the Muslim couple also makes it nominally secular. Whenever celebrations take place, this crowd also participates vicariously in the happiness of those actually involved, sometimes even acting out their roles as family theatre. The space constituting Kailas Nath's family bungalow has therefore all the makings of a 'Ramrajya', and the overflowing happiness also ensures that the home deserves such a description.

Hum Aapke Hain Koun has been castigated for its vulgar celebration of wealth and the expulsion of the underprivileged from its domain, but a careful viewing of the film makes us wonder how this domain is defined. Apart from the 'underprivileged' not being represented, the film does not even contain street scenes, and no element from the 'real world' is allowed admission, leaving us wondering whether the film posits a world outside the narrative at all. Instead, Kailas Nath's family circle together with his coterie of friends and acquaintances, has the appearances of a microcosmic representation of the nation itself; the nation not as it is but as it could be: in a word, Ramrajya. Sooraj Barjatya's 'Ramrajya' accords all its subjects their rightful places. Masters will be masters and servants will remain servants, although the treatment of the latter by the former will set new standards for benevolence. Together, the two will play cricket, which is perhaps an allegorical way of representing competition and free enterprise under watchful, patriotic eyes.

To conclude, it would be simplistic to claim that all Indian popular films are constructed or arranged in the manner of the three films examined here. The structures of these films, nonetheless, gives us important insights into the construction of narrative in popular cinema. The construction of popular narrative texts also has a bearing on how we understand reality because we tend to construct narratives out of random experiences in order to infuse them with 'meaning'.

NOTES AND REFERENCES

1. To cite a Western critic with some exposure to Indian cinema, Henri Micciolo, 'Unfamiliarity Breeds Contempt', from *Cinema Vision India*, vol. II, no. I, 1982, 'It is widely thought that India ranks at the bottom among the filmmaking nations in terms of quality. The cliché...is that Indian cinema is the worst in the world'. More recently, the same views are echoed by John W. Hood in his introduction to *The Essential Mystery: Major Filmmakers of Indian Art Cinema* (New Delhi: Orient Longman, 2000).
2. The opinion of the kind widely cited is illustrated by this quote from the Bengali actor Utpal Dutt: 'An Indian hero in a blonde wig and in latest Bond Street clothes making love to a heroine who seems to have shopped for clothes in New York last week—that's their conception of Indianness...'; from Roy Armes, *Third World Filmmaking and the West* (Berkeley: University of California Press, 1987), p. 67. Mira Reym Binford, 'The Two Cinemas of India', in John D.H. Dowling (ed.), *Film and Politics in the Third World* (New York: Praeger, 1987), cites art film-maker Kumar Shahani: 'Gratuitous violence, a life dependent on miracles [whether gods or superhumans], change of heart in evil men, and the abuse of women as servile objects of sexual and social exploitation are the cultural products of lumpen-consciousness. Whatever the ostensible or overt themes of these films, their disorganized and anarchic form itself can subvert all hope of determination.' (p. 148.)
3. Sudhir Kakar, *Intimate Relations: Exploring Indian Sexuality* (New Delhi: Penguin Books, 1989), pp. 6–27.
4. Michael R. Real, *Exploring Media Culture* (Thousand Oaks: Sage Publications 1996), pp. 268–9.
5. This also follows from Sudhir Kakar's remarks: 'The prospect of financial gain, like the opportunity for sexual liaison, does wonderful things for increasing the perception of the needs and desires of those who hold the key to these gratifications... [Film-makers] must intuitively appeal to those concerns of the audience which are shared.' Sudhir Kakar, 'The Ties that Bind: Family Relationships in the Mythology of Hindi Cinema', *India International Centre, Quarterly* 8, no. 1 (March 1980), p. 13.
6. Tzvetan Todorov, *The Fantastic: A Structural Approach to a Literary Genre* (Ithaca: Cornell University Press, 1973), p. 33.
7. Vladimir Propp, *Morphology of the Folk Tale* (Austin: University of Texas, 1968), p. 7.
8. Vladimir Propp, *Theory and History of Folklore* (Manchester: Manchester University Press, 1984), pp. 16–21.
9. Peter Brooks, *The Melodramatic Imagination: Balzac, Henry James, Melodrama and the Mode of Excess* (New York: Columbia University Press, 1985), pp. 11–15. Brooks traces the origins of Western melodrama to the French Revolution and its aftermath. According to him, the Revolution attempted to sacralize law itself, the Republic as the institution of morality instead of the traditional

sacred and its representative institutions (the Church, the Monarch). Melodrama is the principal mode of making operative the essential moral universe in a 'post-sacred' era.

10. Interestingly, there is also a traditional explanation for this escapism: '[the films] have deep-rooted foundations in certain traditional rules according to which "drama should be a diversion for people weighed down by sorrow or fatigue or grief or ill-luck; it should be a rest [for the body and the mind]"', *Natyashastra* 113–14. See Lothar Lutze, 'From Bharata to Bombay: Change and Continuity in Hindi Film Aesthetics', in Beatrix Pfleiderer and Lothar Lutze (eds.), *The Hindi Film: Agent and Re-agent of Cultural Change* (Delhi: Manohar Publications, 1985), p. 8.
11. The most influential works are M. Madhava Prasad, *Ideology of the Hindi Film* (New Delhi: Oxford University Press, 1999) and Sumita S. Chakravarty, *National Identity in Indian Popular Cinema* (New Delhi: Oxford University Press, 1998).
12. To illustrate with a few examples, Vinay Lal, 'The Impossibility of the Outsider in the Modern Hindi Film', in Ashis Nandy (ed.), *The Secret Politics of Our Desires* (Delhi: Oxford University Press, 1998), uses Freudian psychoanalysis briefly while discussing Yash Chopra's *Deewar* (1975). Ravi Vasudevan does so similarly with Raj Kapoor's *Awara* (1951) in 'Shifting Codes, Dissolving Identities', in Ravi S. Vasudevan (ed.), *Making Meaning in Indian Cinema* (Delhi: Oxford University Press, 2000). Ashish Rajadhyaksha and Paul Willemen, *Encyclopaedia of Indian Cinema* (Delhi: Oxford University Press, 1995) gives similar readings to *Awara*, *Deewar*, and Nitin Bose's *Deedar* (1951).

    Lacan's influence is usually indirect and felt in studies of Indian popular cinema using feminist theory. See Lalitha Gopalan, 'Avenging Women in Indian Cinema', in Ravi S. Vasudevan (ed.), *Making Meaning in Indian Cinema* (New Delhi: Oxford University Press, 2000), pp. 215–37.
13. John W. Hood, *The Essential Mystery: Major Filmmakers of Indian Art Cinema* (New Delhi: Orient Longman, 2000), p. 3; Chidananda Das Gupta, *The Painted Face* (New Delhi: Roli Books, 1991), p. 54; Ashis Nandy, 'The Popular Hindi Film: Ideology and First Principles', *India International Centre, Quarterly Special Issue* 8, no. 1 (March 1980), p. 90.
14. M. Madhava Prasad, *Ideology of the Hindi Film: A Historical Construction* (New Delhi: Oxford University Press, 1998), p. 48 n. 16.
15. Ashis Nandy, 'The Popular Hindi Film', pp. 89–96.
16. Rosie Thomas, 'Indian Cinema: Pleasures and Popularity', *Screen* 26, nos. 3–4 (1985), p. 130.
17. On some of these distinctions, see Ashis Nandy, 'An Intelligent Critic's Guide to Indian Cinema', revised edition published in *The Savage Freud and Other Essays on Possible and Retrievable Selves* (Delhi: Oxford University Press, 1995), pp. 196–236.
18. Cited in Arthur A. Macdonell, *A History of Sanskrit Literature* (New Delhi: Munshiram Manoharlal, 1958) is Bhavabhuti's play *Malati-Madhava* in which

'the lovers aided in the project by two amiable Buddhist nuns, are finally united. The piece is a sort of Indian *Romeo and Juliet* with a happy ending, the part played by the nun Kamandaki being analogous to that of Friar Lawrence in Shakespeare's play' (p. 352).
19. Drawing from Roland Barthes (*Image Music Text*), Ravi Vasudevan uses the term 'tableau' to describe the construction of Mehboob Khan's *Andaz* (1949). Ravi S. Vasudevan, 'Shifting Codes, Dissolving Identities', pp. 105–6. Vasudevan's argument depends on his detailed analysis/interpretation of one 9-shot segment from *Andaz*. He identifies a single shot with the 'tableau' while my own understanding of the 'tableau' is as a narrative moment, which can be represented by an entire sequence.
20. David Bordwell, Janet Staiger, and Kristin Thompson, *The Classical Hollywood Cinema: Film Style and Mode of Production to 1960* (London: Routledge & Kegan Paul, 1985), p. 12.
21. Ibid, pp. 10–15.
22. Eliot Deutsch, 'Reflections on Some Aspects of Rasa', in Rachel Van M. Baumer and James R. Brandon (eds.) *Sanskrit Drama in Performance* (Delhi: Motilal Banarsidass, 1993), p. 217.
23. S.N. Dasgupta, *Fundamentals of Indian Art* (Delhi: Bharatiya Vidya Bhavan, 1954), p. 43.
24. John Berger, *Art and Revolution: Ernst Neizvestny and the Role of the Artist in the USSR* (Harmondsworth: Penguin, 1969), p. 109. Berger cites an interview with sculptor Neizvestny published in *Soviet Life*.
25. Dasgupta, *Fundamentals of Indian Art*, p. 54.
26. Richard Lannoy, *The Speaking Tree* (New York: Oxford University Press, 1971), p. 54.
27. Roland Barthes, *Mythologies* (London: Paladin, 1973), p. 143.
28. Leo Braudy, *The World in a Frame: What We See in Films* (New York: Doubleday, 1976), pp. 46–7.
29. Also see Anil Saari, 'Concepts of Aesthetics and Anti-Aesthetics', in Beatrix Pfleiderer and Lothar Lutze (eds.), *The Hindi Film: Agent and Re-agent of Cultural Change* (Delhi: Manohar Publications, 1985), p. 25. 'The very looseness and imperfection of the episodic structure makes it possible for a popular film to incorporate the most recent happenings in Indian society, to give shape to the very latest objects of technology, fashions in daily life.'
30. It is useful to cite Ashis Nandy here: '...the issue of plagiarism in such films has been wrongly posed. The story-writer and director of the Bombay film are not brazen thieves who do not care what others think of their theft or who foolishly hope to escape detection. They operate within a consensual system which rejects the idea that the elements of a story are a form of personal property or individual creation.' Ashis Nandy, 'The Popular Hindi Film', p. 91.
31. Arthur A. Macdonell, *A History of Sanskrit Literature* (New Delhi: Munshiram Manoharlal, 1958), p. 354.

32. Robert Scholes, 'Narration and Narrativity in Film', in Gerald Mast and Marshall Cohen (eds.), *Film Theory and Criticism: Introductory Readings*, 3rd edn., (New York: Oxford University Press, 1985), p. 395.
33. Interview with Wimal Dissanayake and Malti Sahai, 'Popular Cinema: Overcoming Prejudices', *Deep Focus* 4, no. 2 (1992), pp. 34–42.
34. For an examination of popular cinema's notion of '*dosti*', see M. Madhava Prasad's analysis of *Sangam* in *Ideology of the Hindi Film*, p. 84.
35. This tendency, or rather the resulting heterogeneous genre, which I am terming a 'conglomeration' has been variously described by other writers as a 'cinema of attractions', a 'bricolage', a 'cinema of interruptions'. See Lalitha Gopalan, *Cinema of Interruptions: Action Genres in Contemporary Indian Cinema* (London: British Film Institute, 2002). Vijay Mishra, *Bollywood Cinema: Temples of Desire* (London: Routledge, 2002), pp. 157–9 speaks (in Metzian terms) of a '*grande syntagmatique*'. Mishra even sees the entire body of Bombay cinema as a single meta-text or narrative syntagm. Each individual movie is a play on the discursive practices that make up the rest of the meta-text. Also see M.K. Raghavendra, 'Generic Elements and the Conglomerate Narrative', *Deep Focus* 4, no. 2 (1992), pp. 21–33.

All Kinds of Hindi: The Evolving Language of Hindi Cinema

HARISH TRIVEDI

While always vastly popular, Hindi cinema has in recent years also begun to acquire high academic respectability. During the 1990s, but especially following the publication of the *Encyclopaedia of Indian Cinema* (1995; rev. ed. 1999),[1] edited by Ashish Rajadhyaksha and Paul Willemen, which consolidated and canonized this form of grassroots entertainment into a field of academic study as perhaps only an encyclopaedia can, there has followed a spate of academic monographs and collections of essays on the subject which have approached the subject from a wide range of theoretical and analytical perspectives. The principal impulse here has been similar to that behind Cultural Studies which has made the phenomena of popular and mass culture the subjects of academic enquiry, while the rise of Film Studies and, in this particular case, also Post-colonial Studies, has also contributed to the upsurge of engagement with this long neglected, and indeed derided, subject.

Ever since the beginning of 'talkies' in India in 1931, Hindi cinema had by and large remained an object of educated contempt but now, suddenly within the last decade, it has become a worthy and even 'sublime' object of highbrow academic enquiry. Indeed, in a spectacular reversal of fortune such as is a cliché of Hindi cinema, this untouchable has been turned into the high priest of the temple of Indian dream and desire.² Among the various approaches adopted to this infinitely multifarious field, there is however one conspicuous absence, indeed an uncanny silence, regarding the medium of Hindi cinema, the Hindi language. One possible reason for this may be that though the films are in Hindi, the discussion is now all in English, often produced by non-Hindi-speaking researchers often working not in India but in Western academia and necessarily oriented to an Anglophone readership. Because of this basic disjunction, the last thing to have attracted any sustained attention is the nature of Hindi in Hindi cinema.

Another possible reason may be that there is of course a view that cinema has a language of its own (or even that cinema is a language) which is not verbal but visual. This view was most resourcefully propounded by Christian Metz in *Film Language: A Semiotics of the Cinema* (English trans. 1974) and *Language and Cinema* (English trans. 1974), where he attempted, as he himself said, 'to get to the bottom of the linguistic metaphor' in order to see how far the mode and syntax of cinema resembled the signifying system of what are called natural languages; and he concluded, not entirely illuminatingly perhaps, that while cinema was not a *langue* (language system) it was nevertheless *langage* (language). However, this line of argument is now seen to have marked a phase of film theorization in which cinema seemed to be in an acute disciplinary need to establish its distinctiveness from other cognate art forms, especially narrative fiction. As Robert Stam has said: 'For Metz, the question "Is film language?" is inseparable from the question "What is specific to cinema?"'³ Such anxiety for self-definition now having passed, even a determinedly experimentalist film-maker such as Mani Kaul, who treats narrative as only an incidental and relatively insignificant element of film-making, can say (following Giles Deleuze) that:

films shouldn't be considered a language. Film is not a language because there is no semantic order in it. Things don't have the same meaning in it as they have in a language. If you take a shot of a carpet, what does it mean? It is not a word. So there is no need to unnecessarily call film a language, the way people [do] in every seminar.⁴

In any case, even if cinema is a *langue* or *langage,* or both or neither, that does not take away from the indisputable and plain unmetaphoric fact that, at the same time, the language of Hollywood cinema is (American) English, that of French cinema French, and that of Hindi cinema Hindi. Leaving aside the abstract, self-reflexive, and in the present context diversionary question of cinema *as* a language or the language *of* cinema, one might still usefully engage with the objective and empirical manifestations of language *as used in* cinema.

In this essay I propose to take an initial step towards exploring this primary element of Hindi cinema, its constituent language, without which it may still be all kinds of things to all kinds of viewers but would lose its claim to be *Hindi* cinema. I do so by examining some major presuppositions about the Hindi of Hindi cinema, the received wisdom as it were, which may be summarized as follows. One, the language of Hindi cinema is not really Hindi but Hindustani (an uneasy and unequal mixture of Urdu and Hindi with more of the former than the latter) if it is not outright Urdu. Two, this Urdu or Hindustani, in contrast to the Sanskritic Hindi sought to be propagated after Independence as the official language of the Indian nation-state, has achieved a wider popularity and currency throughout India, and has done more towards making Hindi an effective national language than could all the apparatuses of the state. Three, Hindi cinema articulates the popular or subaltern culture of the nation like no other medium of collective expression and consumption. While readily granting that there is more than the proverbial grain of truth in all these hypotheses. I seek to subject them to the kind of questioning that alone could guarantee and vouchsafe their validity.

THE ENTITLEMENT OF URDU

It is widely believed that, in a significant misnomer, the language of Hindi cinema is not Hindi but in fact Hindustani. There would be few (or at least fewer) problems with this formulation, however, if 'Hindi' were not at the same time polarized to mean Sanskritic Hindi and if 'Hindustani' were not taken to mean a language closer to Urdu than to Hindi. For, if Hindustani were indeed the more readily understood stratum of language common to both Hindi and Urdu and situated midway between them, it would not be such a contentious issue whether we called this language Hindi or Hindustani or Urdu.

However, Hindustani has always been a controversial and vexed term, especially since it began to be propagated as a secular-nationalist desideratum in the 1930s, at about the same time, incidentally, that the first Indian 'talkies' began to be produced. To start with, there never was an already existent, autonomous, and distinguishable language called

Hindustani, as freely admitted by probably the most fervent champions ever of Hindustani, Mahatma Gandhi and Premchand, both of whom were champions of Hindustani second and advocates of Hindu–Muslim harmony first. To complicate matters, Hindustani had, ever since the early decades of the nineteenth century when the British gave this term currency, carried the taint of being considerably closer to Urdu than to Hindi; so much so that Christopher King, in the glossary of his book on the tussle between Hindi and Urdu, *One Language, Two Scripts* (1994), explained 'Hindustani' as meaning, simply and primarily, 'Urdu.' To say that the language of Hindi films is not Hindi but Hindustani would thus be to walk more than half way down the path to saying that it is in fact Urdu.[5]

Indeed, one or two persons actively associated with the making of Hindi films have suggested that Hindi films should be more accurately called Urdu films. Reportedly, Sahir Ludhianvi once caused a controversy by asking why Hindi films were not certified as Urdu films as all of them were in Urdu anyhow.[6] Now, Sahir (1912–80), one of the most prolific and successful lyricists of Hindi films from the 1950s to the 1970s, already had something of a reputation as an Urdu poet before he began to write for films, and an early big break came for him when his poem 'Chakle' (Brothels) was, at assistant director Raj Khosla's suggestion, incorporated into the film *Pyaasa* (1957) by Guru Dutt. The refrain of this poem was '*Sanakhwan-e-taqdis-e-mashriq kahan hain?*' (Where are the worshippers of the holiness of the East?), but this had now not only to be merely simplified but virtually rewritten (with a corresponding shift in meaning) to become '*Jinhen naaz hai Hind par vo kahan hain?*' (Where are they who are proud of India?) before it could be used in the film, because (in Khosla's words) 'no one would have understood the difficult Urdu of the original.'[7] This instance is fairly symptomatic of the gap between Urdu and the language of Hindi films, and while Urdu writers such as Sahir may have gone on writing courtly and compounded poetry in Urdu to please themselves, they were obliged to add generous quantities of water to the wine of Urdu when it came to writing for the masses who watched Hindi films.

Perhaps the most elaborate and engaging case for calling the language of Hindi cinema Urdu has been made out by the novelist and historian Mukul Kesavan. Through a fond evocation of the entire feudal, decadent, nawabi world of 'Urdu, Awadh and the Tawaif,' Kesavan argues that there exists a 'singular relationship between Hindi films and Muslim-ness' which is not only reflected in films with Muslim characters and themes (the so called 'Muslim socials') but 'has determined the very nature of this cinema', and that the 'most obvious example' of this 'Islamicate' phenomenon is the dominance and persistence of Urdu in Hindi cinema. As evidence, he offers titles of twenty films that are all in Urdu ('the list is endless'), and cites lines from songs to demonstrate that the 'screenplays and lyrics of Hindi films are written mainly in Urdu.'

However, this plea for the recognition of Urdu as the true medium of Hindi films begs many questions. To begin with the simpler and more readily verifiable matter of titles of films, Kesavan's sample seems unrepresentative as it is obviously carefully culled, and Kesavan then fudges the issue by conceding in a footnote that he has 'no quarrel with those who would claim them [these twenty titles] for Hindustani rather than Urdu...'[8] If Hindustani is not simply Urdu but some kind of an in-between language with a basic vocabulary of say even 500 words which are understood equally readily by speakers of Sanskritic Hindi as well as of Persianized Urdu, the claims Kesavan makes for Urdu would be substantially eroded. Thus, of his sample, while *Alam Ara*, *Mughal-e-Azam*, *Qayamat Se Qayamat Tak*, and possibly also *Farz* and *Bawarchi* may by a liberal reckoning be granted to be Urdu, *Awara*, *Sahib Bibi Aur Ghulam*, *Khamoshi*, *Safar*, *Namak Haram*, *Sholay*, *Ishq Ishq Ishq*, *Waqt*, *Bazi*, *Masoom*, *Deewana*, *Aaj Ki Awaz*, and *Dushman* comprise words of common Hindi–Urdu and may be called Hindustani if they are not to be called without qualification Hindi. (All the thirty-five words in Kesavan's twenty titles are to be found in a concise Hindi dictionary such as R.S. McGregor's *The Oxford Hindi–English Dictionary*, except two: *ara* and *azam*.)

A fairer finding would be obtained perhaps by looking at a wider or at least a more random sample. To begin again (aptly enough) with *Alam Ara*, the first Hindi talkie, and to take an equally small but random sample, the titles of the next nineteen Hindi films listed in chronological order in the *Encyclopaedia of Indian Cinema* are: *Devi Devayani*, *Draupadi*, *Shirin Farhad*, *Ayodhya Ka Raja*, *Indrasabha*, *Jalti Nishani*, *Madhuri*, *Maya Macchindra*, *Radha Rani*, *Sati Savitri*, *Sati Sone*, *Shyam Sundar*, *Zalim Jawani*, *Karma/Nagan Ki Ragini*, *Lal-e-Yaman*, *Meerabai/Rajrani Meera*, *Miss 1933*, *Puran Bhakt*, and *Yahudi Ki Ladki*. Of these twenty titles, thirteen are clearly Hindi, *Jalti Nishani* would probably qualify as Hindustani, *Miss 1933* is English, and only the remaining five titles are Urdu and 'Islamicate'. On the other hand, seven of the thirteen Hindi titles comprise entirely Sanskrit words which are current in Hindi while five others, such as *Ayodhya Ka Raja* or *Maya Machhindra*, are predominantly Sanskritic and thus a far cry from the 'Islamicate'.[9]

To go for another sample equally at random, of the first twenty titles of Hindi films listed in the index of M. Madhava Prasad's book, *Ideology of the Hindi Film* (1998), possibly three are in Urdu (if we count as Urdu two films each entitled *Andaz* and one entitled *Dastak*), five are in Hindustani (*Aandhi, Beta, Deewar, Dhool Ka Phool,* and *Dil Ek Mandir*), one is in English (*An Evening in Paris*), and the remaining eleven are in Hindi (*Aakrosh, Abhiman, Anand, Ankur, Anubhav, Aradhana, Ashirwad, Bhumika, Bhuvan Shome, Damini,* and *Dharti Ke Lal*), with all but two being in *shuddha* Sanskrit/Hindi, and the other two also containing a clear Sanskritic element (*Bhuvan Shome*, a proper name, and *Dharti Ke Lal*).[10]

For the larger sample of Prasad's entire index which contains forty-six titles, along with say the 143 Hindi film titles to be found in the index of Sumita S. Chakravarty's book *National Identity in Indian Popular Cinema* (1993),[11] twenty-six titles are in Urdu, twenty-five in English (including six titles partially in English), forty-nine in Hindustani, and eighty-nine in Hindi. What is more, in Prasad and Chakravarty put together, even if we were for extreme argument's sake to concede all Hindustani titles to be Urdu and club them together with Urdu titles, these would still be fewer (seventy-five) than those in (Sanskritic) Hindi (eighty-nine). Also, in what is probably the largest 'Filmography' appended to any book on Hindi cinema so far, in Vijay Mishra's *Bollywood Cinema*, 236 of the 239 films listed are Hindi films and the count among them along the above lines is thirty-seven titles in Urdu, forty in Hindustani, twenty in English, and 137 in Hindi (including fifty-three Sanskrit/ic).[12] Of course, the numbers given here will vary a little with the linguistic disposition and discrimination of the particular enumerator, but they will not vary by, say, more than five per cent. These then, broadly, are the linguistic facts of the matter.

Nevertheless, there is perhaps a simple psychological explanation for Kesavan's gross misperception, in which he is far from being alone. Perhaps the Urdu titles stick and expand in memory because they are the more striking for being fewer, and for being therefore, in most viewers' perception, a trifle exotic. Another related subliminal reason for remembering and cherishing the Urdu-'Islamicate' elements in Hindi films in our current national discourse may be the secular predilection to regard such evidence as a manifestation of our 'composite culture'. There is perhaps also a supporting historical reason: even if the proportion of Urdu titles was not any greater in the early decades of Hindi cinema (as demonstrated by the entries in the *Encyclopaedia* for the initial years of Hindi films), it is perhaps true that (Sanskritic–) Hindi titles have become more numerous and prominent in the decades after Independence and Partition, thus reflecting a general shift in language use. Kesavan himself cites an interview in which 'the mainstream film-maker' Subhash Ghai explained that he had given a film of his the (*shuddh* Sanskrit) title *Khalnayak* (1992) because it was 'apt' and because 'we've been hearing such difficult words on Doordarshan's Hindi *samachar* [TV news] bulletins and in serials like *Mahabharat* [so] that I think our vocabulary has improved'. However, what Kesavan relegates to an endnote as an exception and as a 'straw in the wind' may now actually be mainstream usage, and it also shows how the much-maligned *sarkari* (or official) Hindi has attained a degree of popular circulation.[13]

It is for these understandable, sentimental, and worthy reasons that, notwithstanding all the facts that can be adduced to the contrary, the impression persists in certain quarters that the language of Hindi films through much of their history has been Urdu or at least Hindustani. However, so far as the weight of objective and verifiable evidence is concerned, there can be little doubt that it is indeed Hindi, and perhaps surprisingly Hindi that is often in a high Sanskritic register, which has been the vehicle of these films ever since they began to be made. Rajadhyaksha and Willemen seem to be entirely justified, therefore, in identifying the language of these films in their *Encyclopaedia* straightforwardly as 'Hindi', while allowing at the same time the label 'Hindi–Urdu' to a small number of films 'to suggest that we are dealing with a Hindi film making extensive use of Urdu, usually for the lyrics.'[14]

URDU WRITERS, HINDI WRITERS

This is the more remarkable, for it is undeniable that a considerable proportion of Hindi films up to the 1970s were written by Urdu writers, many of whom had a previous or parallel reputation as literary writers in that language, including Saadat Hasan Manto, Ismat Chughtai, Khwaja Ahmad Abbas, Sahir Ludhianvi, Majrooh Sultanpuri, Rahi Masoom Raza, Kaifi Azmi, and Sardar Jafri. While some of them wrote scripts and screenplays, most of the writers named above wrote 'lyrics' or songs, that unique and highly popular component of Hindi cinema.

The notably, even disproportionately, numerous presence of Urdu writers in Hindi cinema is usually ascribed to the fact that Urdu writers were prominent also in Parsi theatre, the form of popular entertainment from which Hindi cinema almost directly derived its semiotic, verbal, and musical idiom. It is also pointed out that Urdu writers were equally prominent in a later and rather different movement, the Progressive Writers' Association (PWA, established 1936), and in particular the Indian People's Theatre Association (IPTA, established 1943), both of which overlapped with the early development of Hindi cinema. However, rather than explain the phenomenon, such historicization just pushes it further back, for the question to ask then would be: how was it that the Parsi theatre or the PWA and IPTA had such a high proportion of Urdu–Muslim writers to begin with?

Here too, this broad picture needs to be differentiated and nuanced. While the standard-bearer of Parsi theatre dramatists is widely acclaimed to have been Agha Hashr Kashmiri, it is perhaps not always adequately acknowledged that hardly less prominent or prolific than Agha Hashr were two other writers from a distinctly different background, Pandit Narayan Prasad Betab and Pandit Radheshyam Kathavachak. In any case, commercial considerations dictated that all three writers addressed broadly the same audience in a language that ranged widely from Persianized Urdu to Sanskritized Hindi but which mostly occupied the middle ground of wide intelligibility. In a famous dictum on the subject, Betab in the prologue to his enormously successful play *Mahabharat* laid down the pragmatic policy on the subject:

Na theth Hindi na khalis Urdu, zuban goya mili-juli ho.
Alag rahe dudh se na misri, dali dali dudh men ghuli ho.
(Neither straight Hindi nor pure Urdu, it should really be a mixed language. The milk should not be kept separate from the sugar, each lump of which should dissolve in the milk.)[15]

In any case, from the evidence available, it appears that the language of the same playwright could swing from one extreme to the other to suit the theme and the historical/mythological period and *mise en scène*. For example, as Lakshminarayan Lal has demonstrated in his valuable study of the Parsi theatre, Agha Hashr Kashmiri himself could range from the fairly Persianized Urdu in his play *Rustam va Sohrab*, with a line such as '*Agar tum Maadar-e-Iran ke farzand hote to main kaneez bankar tumhari khidmat men apni zindagi...*[breaks off]' to the distinctly Sanskritized Hindi of his play *Bhishma-Pratigya*: '*Daya-daya! Jis stree ke pas roop hai hriday nahin hai, seva hai prem nahin hai, putra ki lalsa hai kintu putra ki mamta nahin hai—uske pas daya?*'[16] (Unfortunately, there is no way of illustrating the wide variance in the registers used through the translation of these citations into English, here as well as in some other instances below). As each Parsi theatre company employed several writers and scripts evolved through collaborative effort, such wide linguistic range would have been easier to achieve.

In his extensive and richly documented if somewhat unanalytical and 'under-theorized' book, *Cinemai Bhasha aur Hindi Samvadon ka Vishleshan* (1998; *An Analysis of the Language of Hindi Cinema and its Dialogues*), Kishore Vasvani offers the most detailed account so far published of the language of Hindi films from the silent era up to the 1980s. In *Raja Harishchandra*, which was probably the single most frequently performed Parsi theatre play with over 4,000 performances over the years at various venues (including Porbandar where the young Mohandas Gandhi watched it and was deeply moved and influenced),[17] and which predictably was turned into the first silent film made in India by Dadasaheb Phalke in 1913, the title-cards were in two languages, English above and Hindi below. As cited by Vasvani, the Hindi version had the following on the first two and the last two cards, respectively:

—*Gramin praja ke* [sic] *vinati se Harishchandra raja shikar ko jate hain.*
—*Kinhi striyon ki karunavani sunkar shabdako* [sic] *taraf raja ka jana...*
—*Imandari* [sic] *kartavya palne ke liye rani ka vadh karte vaqt Shivaji ka sakshatkar hona. Aur Rohitashva ka jivit hona.*
—*Harishchandra ke* [sic] *satyapariksha men uttirna dekhkar Vashishtha ke samne mukut uske hath men dena.*

The language here is clearly more Sanskritic Hindi than Urdu, and of the ninety-five words used in all the ten title-cards taken together, according to Vasvani's count, eight words are in Urdu, one in Marathi (*saangata*) and all the rest in 'Sanskrit and Hindi.'[18]

Another interesting fact to consider in this context is that in the early decades of Hindi cinema, it was not only Urdu writers but also a number of Hindi writers who were attracted to the new medium, just as they had been to the Parsi theatre. At least three Hindi novelists of the front rank left home and high literature to go and work for various cinema companies for varying periods in the infancy of the new medium: Premchand, Amritlal Nagar, and Bhagwati Charan Verma. All three had a literary reputation in Hindi at least as high as any of the Urdu writers named above had in Urdu literature, and besides his undisputed place as the greatest novelist and short story writer in Urdu as well as Hindi, Premchand was also to go on to preside over the first convention of the PWA held in Lucknow in 1936. While they were themselves involved in writing for films, both Premchand and Varma had one each of their major novels, *Sevasadan* and *Chitralekha* respectively, made into films, and, incidentally, it was Varma who, as the script-writer for *Jwar-Bhata* (1944), suggested the name Dilip Kumar for its new hero Yusuf Khan.[19]

The story of the participation in films of these Hindi writers—and a host of other younger writers such as Narendra Sharma, Pradip, Shailendra, Neeraj, and Kamleshwar—may serve to complement and counterbalance the better known facts of the corresponding participation by the Urdu writers, but it perhaps merits being told in some detail elsewhere. It may be sufficient here to note the salient fact that the major Hindi writers soon became disgusted with what they felt to be the crass commercialism and vulgarity of the Hindi films of their times and the utter insignificance of the role of the writer in them. Both Premchand and Varma left the world of films sooner than later (Premchand in fact within a year), prizing their artistic integrity above financial gain, to return as sadder and wiser men to resume their literary careers though, ironically, Varma at least had to continue to bear the stigma of having once written for films.[20]

If the Urdu writers continued to flourish in the world of films, one possible reason for it may have been that they were the inheritors of a somewhat different and more pliable tradition of literary patronage, and of literature being regarded as entertainment, and perhaps knew better how to bend with the wind. (Alternatively, of course, the more avowedly radical of them may have wished to take it upon themselves to mitigate the deplorable state of affairs through their participation; to subvert the system from within, as the phrase goes.) In any case, the presence and then prompt withdrawal of major Hindi writers from Hindi cinema can be seen to have represented a wishful alternative line of development for Hindi cinema, which remained unfulfilled and therefore remains unsung.

SONGS AND DIALOGUE

Songs and so-called 'dialogue' have such a highly significant place in Hindi (and Indian) cinema that they need to be discussed as special categories. Songs in some quantity in almost each film are a unique feature of Indian cinema and the most prominent emblem of its much talked about non-realism, as contrasted with the wholly prosaic realism of Hollywood. Not only have songs marked the emotional (or, literally, melodramatic) high points of Hindi films but they have also often been exempt from the narrative burden of films, standing apart in an aesthetic space of their own with its even more non-realistic conventions. For the past several decades, for example, songs have often been shot in exotic foreign locales that bear no relation to the story, with large supporting choruses materializing out of thin air amidst foreign hills and meadows without any felt need to explain how they got there. The hero and the heroine themselves change their clothes during a song almost from shot to shot, with perhaps greater frequency and predictability than that with which the soul, according to the Bhagavadgita, changes its bodily raiments.

In terms of production and circulation too, songs have been fairly autonomous of the film in which they occur. They are often written, set to music, and sung well before the shooting of the film begins, and then 'picturized' with a range of directorial skills acknowledged to be quite distinct from those required in shooting narrative scenes with dialogue. Songs are released in cassettes and CDs some time before the film itself is, with the 'music rights' sold separately from the rights to distribute the film, and their popularity or lack of it often bears little relation to the success or failure of the film itself. Ever since talkies began, Hindi film songs have been fondly remembered and sung by huge numbers of film-goers at all kinds of social occasions, and one of the most popular forms of group entertainment now, whether on picnics or on long journeys, is the game of film *antakshari* in which each team has in turn to sing a film song beginning with the last syllable of the song sung by the other team, in a kind of musical tag; some version of this game is also a perennial attraction on several TV channels. Even when alone, countless Indians are haunted by film songs in their most private moments, with an apt line or two always floating up to the top of the mind to sum up and vicariously articulate any given emotion. (In a nice spin on this, a song in the film *Saath Saath* (1982) asked: '*Ham jise gunguna nahin sakte/Vaqt ne aisa geet kyon gaya?*', i.e. Why did the times sing a song/Which I cannot hum to myself?)

Far more widely and intimately perhaps than any kind of pop music in the West, Hindi film songs have constituted the emotional imaginary of mainstream Indian life, across class and degrees of intellectual sophistication. Rickshaw-wallahs, long referred to at least metonymically as the target audience of commercial Hindi films, have always sung them, and when a tonga-wallah carrying passengers on a deserted road late one evening in Brahmapur, in Vikram Seth's *A Suitable Boy*, is moved to begin singing '*Ek dil ke tukre hazaar hue...*', one of the passengers promptly sheds his class inhibitions to join him.[21] A semi-literate young woman in the village Shivpalganj in Shrilal Shukla's classic Hindi novel *Rag Darbari* composes (with the expert help of a female social worker) a love-letter which comprises entirely bits and phrases of popular Hindi film songs, while in a neighbouring village at a 48-hour devotional singing marathon, many of the most popular *bhajans* (hymns) have been set to tunes of film songs.[22] The song from *Shree 420* beginning '*Mera juta hai Japani...*' has been adopted virtually as the theme-song of his own hybridized life by Salman Rushdie as well as for his hero Saleem Sinai, and is again evoked at the beginning of *The Satanic Verses*,[23] while the 'subaltern' cultural historian Sudipta Kaviraj has with remarkable intellectual resourcefulness expounded the many implications of what he calls a 'Song of the City'—'*Zara hatke zara bachke, yeh hai Bombay meri jan*' (Step aside, my dear, and watch out; you are in the city of Bombay)—which he first heard as a child in a remote and holy town in Bengal and which has stayed with him ever since, though he has never seen the film in which it occurs nor indeed, by his own admission, many other Hindi films.[24]

These free-floating songs of Hindi films have also enjoyed a kind of linguistic autonomy of their own. They have often been the most 'Urdu' part of Hindi films, using as they often do a limited and conventionally familiar vocabulary of romance: *ishq, mohabbat, dil, vafa, judai, tanhai, gham* (i.e. love, love, heart, faithfulness, separation, loneliness, sorrow) and perhaps a dozen more words of similar intent and register, which are, to speak osmotically, faded flowers from the garden of Urdu poetry. As Madhava Prasad has observed:

> The songs adopt a literary style which has a predilection for certain recurrent motifs: the *mehfil, shama, parwana, chaman, bahar, nazaaren* [sc. *nazaare*], and so on [i.e. private gathering, candle, moth, garden, spring, beautiful sights]. This repertoire of images is drawn from the frozen diction of romantic Urdu poetry.[25]

This basic Urdu/Hindustani vocabulary has become the vehicle of the discourse of love in Hindi films, possibly because the vocabulary of love in Hindi poetry, which could have provided an alternative source, was always tied up allegorically with the love of gods, mainly Krishna, and was thus not readily available for secular and particularly 'vulgar' commercial use. Such a divine constraint is caught with delectable irony in a film song which has for its refrain: '*Yadi aap hamen aadesh karen/To prem ka ham Shi Ganesh karen*' (If you kindly permit me to do so/ Shall I make an auspicious start to love by invoking the name of the god Ganesha). In contrast, with all its predictability and narrow range, the Persian-derived vocabulary gave to the Hindi film songs, especially those from the 1940s and the 1950s, a kind of transgressive charge as well as a derivative unreality that quite matched the escapist, fantasy plots of the films.

As with songs, the dialogue too of Hindi films, especially from the so called 'golden period' (variously dated 1931–50 or 1931–60 but in any case ending a decade or two before the rise of either Amitabh Bachchan or of the new or parallel cinema),[26] was so stylized and rhetorically stiff as to give the English word 'dialogue' a peculiar and specialized meaning in the Hindi language, as in the popular phrase: '*Kya dialogue mar rahe ho?*' (i.e. why are you spouting 'dialogue'?). Though naturally to a lesser extent and only selectively, dialogues of Hindi films could prove memorable and repeatable like the songs, and the great actors who achieved stardom before say 1970, such as the trinity of Dev Anand, Dilip Kumar, and Raj Kapoor, each cultivated their own particular style of 'dialogue delivery' which remained largely unchanged from film to film and was perceived to constitute the better part of their acting.

Most notably, Dilip Kumar spoke in a measured grave tone with impeccable Urdu *talaffuz* (enunciation), to the extent that early in his career he was even entrusted with the responsibility of 'dialogue-director', i.e. of tutoring other actors how to speak, presumably because they came from various other linguistic backgrounds and did not know how to utter some peculiar Perso–Arabic sounds not to be found in Indian languages other than Urdu, and sometimes represented in Hindi with a dot under the consonants, for example f (and not ph), gh (and not g), q (and not k), and z (and not j).[27] Raj Kumar, whose principal claim to fame was perhaps his dialogue delivery, was a shade more deliberate and theatrical, and there were charges against him as well as against Dilip Kumar and others that during shooting they often stole the 'dialogue' to be spoken by lesser actors if they found it particularly stirring.[28] On the other hand, there were actors who had much else going for them but could not deliver a simple line. Manto recounts how an actor couldn't deliver the simple line '*Maine Peshawar ka paani piya hai*' (I have drunk the water of Peshawar) even after many takes, altering it in the process to versions such as '*Maine Peshawar ka peshab piya hai*' (I have drunk the piss of Peshawar), etc.[29]

In the early days of Hindi talkies, as actors, directors, writers, and technicians from far-flung parts of the country flocked to it to make a career for themselves, the language of Hindi cinema often sounded not much like Hindi at all or even Urdu or Hindustani. As H.S. Saxena, a veteran connoisseur of cinema as well as of Hindi, has observed, the dialogues of the Hindi films of the late 1930s and 1940s were in a language that was 'a cocktail of Persianized vocabulary, Marathi syntax, and Bengali pronunciation'.[30] The Persianized vocabulary, as has been seen, had constantly to be toned down in order to make it commonly intelligible, with even an avowed champion of Urdu such as Sahir Ludhianvi being obliged to write songs which 'mixed Hindi and Urdu [and] were marked by their simplicity of expression.'[31] Altogether, thus, even in the songs, which remained the most conventional, stylized, and artificial components of Hindi films linguistically speaking, it was not quite Urdu that was used so much as a simpler and more demotic language which had the fragrance or the flavour of Urdu. In his recent hit song 'Chhaiyan chhaiyan' in the film *Dil Se* (1998), Gulzar captured this distinction to a nicety when he wrote, '*Ho yaar mera khushboo ki tarah/ Ho jiski zuban Urdu ki tarah*' (May my lover be like a fragrance/

And his/her language rather like Urdu): that is to say, not quite Urdu but suggestive of Urdu and redolent of it.

MUGHAL-E-AZAM

In common regard, the high point of the old kind of high Urdu dialogue delivery in Hindi was attained in *Mughal-e-Azam* (1960, but begun in 1951 and nine years in the making), especially in the scenes of confrontation between the great Mughal Emperor Akbar, on the one hand, and his rebellious son Prince Salim and the maid with whom he had fallen in love, Anarkali, on the other. 'The film is remembered mainly for [Kamal] Amrohi's dialogues', notes the *Encyclopaedia of Indian Cinema*, and it evidently helped that Prithviraj Kapoor, who played Akbar, had actually begun his acting career with the Parsi theatre and had never quite lost its quavering, stentorian, pre-microphone tone and manner, while Salim was played by Dilip Kumar, the great dialogue-deliverer himself. The lofty rhetorical tone was set in the opening scene with a voice-over spoken by 'India', no less: '*Main Hindustan hoon. Himalayaa meri sarhadon ka nigahbaan hai. Ganga meri pavitrata ki saugandh. Taarikh ki ibtida se main andheron aur ujalon ka sakhi hoon...*' (I am Hindustan. The Himalayas are the sentries of my borders. The Ganga is the pledge of my purity. From the beginning of history, I have been a witness to darkness and light), a point of interest here being that as soon as it begins to roll, the high Urdu needs to be inflected with a contextually apt Sanskritic phrase such as '*Ganga meri pavitrata ki saugandh*' (The Ganga is the pledge of my purity).

In other key scenes too, the Persianized Urdu alternates with the simpler and more easily communicable Hindi. In one of the most celebrated and repeated lines of the entire film, Akbar says to Anarkali, '*Salim tujhe marne nahin dega aur ham tujhe jeene nahin denge*' (Salim will not let you die, and I shall not let you live), which with all its antithetical balance is as simple as Hindi can get, just as Salim's speech of defiance to his father, for all its rhetorical climactic structure, is in diction easy enough to follow: '*Taqdeeren badal jati hain, zamana badal jata hai, mulkon ki taarikh badal jati hai, magar is badalti duniya men mohabbat jis insan ka daman tham leti hai voh insan nahin badalata*' (Destinies change, times change, the histories of nations change; but, in this world where all is subject to change, a person who has known love does not change).

Anarkali's cry of defiance, in a famous song, is even more simply phrased; indeed, neither Hindi nor Urdu could get more basic than '*Jab pyar kiya to darna kya*' (I've fallen in love; why should I fear!)

Vasvani points out that the various characters in the film are dictionally differentiated; for example, while Akbar says '*isteqbal*' for welcome, his Hindu wife Jodhabai says '*swagat*'.[32] Though the film did have a little more than its fair share of high Urdu words and phrases such as '*zille-ilahi*', '*azeemshan*', '*kaneez*', and '*iltija*', its rare attempts to elevate the diction into the realm of the recondite toppled over into unintended comedy. One such instance was Akbar's repeated use of the word '*Takhliya!*' meaning privacy, which he peremptorily uttered whenever he wanted to dismiss all present in order to be alone, but so precious and pure was this word of Arabic that, as Rahi Masoom Raza (who himself wrote the dialogue for over 300 Hindi films beginning in the mid-1960s) recounts, many of the viewers thought Akbar was each time asking for '*Takiya*', i.e. a pillow.[33]

Mughal-e-Azam was one of the most high-Urdu films ever made, as may be thought to accord with its grand imperial Muslim theme, if we overlook the inconvenient little historical detail that Akbar himself and his court could not have spoken Urdu because the language was born only about two centuries after Akbar's reign. However, *Mughal-e-Azam* probably also marked the end of the high-Urdu strand even in a Hindi film with Muslim subject-matter, and in general a turning away from literary Urdu to both more *tadbhav* (indigenous) and *tatsam* (Sanskritic) varieties of Hindi. As has been shown above, a stream of what may be called Hindu–Hindi (i.e. Hindi thought suitable to mythological, historical, or social Hindu themes) had run parallel to Muslim–Urdu (i.e. Urdu thought suitable to historical or social Muslim themes) throughout the development of Hindi films, right since *Alam Ara* and *Devi Devayani* (both 1931). What is more, these two streams had often mingled in the same films, as of course had Hindus and Muslims through a shared history of a thousand years. Even *Mughal-e-Azam* had an utterly Hindu–Hindi song-and-dance set-piece depicting the festival of Holi: '*Monhe panghat pe Nandlal chher gayo re*' (Krishna came and teased me at the village well).

Moreover, beginning in the 1960s, cinema audiences comprised an ever diminishing proportion of persons who had before Partition learnt some Urdu in school as their *doyam zuban*, i.e. second language, and a correspondingly higher ratio of younger viewers who were now learning Hindi in school, often with an element of Sanskrit forming a part of the Hindi syllabus, and had grown up with the formal Hindi of the Akashvani and Doordarshan (the state-run radio and television) circulating all around them as a part of their daily lives. In any case, the Urdu fraction of the language of Hindi films had perhaps always been a part of their lack of realism. In a comic exaggeration of the artificial world of older Hindi films, Javed Akhtar, one of the leading dialogue-and-song writers of Hindi cinema in recent years, has said:

> We have many states in this country, all of them are Indian states, but each has its own different culture, tradition and style...Gujarat...Punjab...Rajasthan, Bengal, Orissa or Kerala... And so Hindi cinema has its own culture... Hindi cinema has its own myths. It even has its own architecture: grand houses that have a grand stairway leading into the living room!... You see the father coming down these grand stairs wearing a dressing gown with a pipe in hand. He stands on the steps and says pompously: '*Ye shadi nahin ho sakti*' [This marriage will not take place].[34]

Up to the 1960s, it was not only films that featured the old decadent ambience of the *tawaif* and courtly society (which Kesavan evokes) but also films which depicted the contemporary upper class urban society such as Akhtar sketches in above, which had a notable proportion of urbane Urdu. Indeed, this Urdu was perhaps as much a part of what Akhtar calls the unrealistic culture and the myth of Hindi cinema as the grand staircase.

KINDS OF HINDI

(a) DIALECT HINDI

However, not all Hindi films featured either a *kotha* (a prostitute's house) or a grand staircase. Ever since *Achhut Kanya* (1936), many films had been set in villages, and particularly after the coming of Independence, a number of progressive films were made in the social-realist or the neo-realist mode, most notably *Do Bigha Zamin* (1953) and *Mother India* (1957). Some of these films had their rural characters speak in *khari boli*, i.e. standard urban Hindi, but the language of many other rural films sought to approximate to some kind of realism and moved away from urban Hindi to a kind of constructed Hindi dialect.

This often had elements of Avadhi, Braj, and occasionally Bhojpuri in it without actually being any of these dialects, and has served to authenticate all representations of village life in Hindi cinema, from *Ganga Jumna* (1961) through *Teesri Kasam* (1966) to *Lagaan* (2001).

Besides these films set in villages, a far larger number of films, including some with an exclusively urban setting, also included some songs which were not in Urdu (which had always been an urban language) or in standard Hindi but in dialect. These came in several varieties of which one, for example, was the bhajan or song of devotion and prayer, which had a traditional Braj or Avadhi resonance (in continuance of the Bhakti movement in Hindi poetry of the medieval period) and became quite a staple of the Hindu family melodrama, no less than the ghazal or the *qawwali* was of the (far less numerous) Muslim socials.

Another kind of popular film-song in dialect was the folk song, or more often a somewhat rewritten version of a folk song, which achieved a new peak of popularity in the later films of Amitabh Bachchan, in which he often played a low-class character living in Bombay who however originally 'came from' a rural north Indian background and still valued and adhered to the popular practices of that part of the world. A notable instance of this kind of song was '*Khaee ke pan Banaras-wala...*,' (When one eats a pan of the Banaras kind... *Don*, 1978). More remarkably, in another Bachchan film, *Silsila* (1981), which had an upper-class cosmopolitan setting with the lovers sprinting through the tulip fields of Holland, a folk song in dialect about adultery was aptly inserted: '*Rang barsai bheegai chunar-wali, rang barsai.*' The fact that Bachchan chose at the peak of his stardom to sing some of these songs himself added both to their popularity and to Bachchan's own authenticity as an actor who had actually grown up in the Hindi heartland, and was indeed, as he sang, a '*chhora Ganga kinare wala*' (i.e. a lad from the banks of the Ganga).[35]

Another category of songs in dialect were those with a classical or semi-classical structure, for the good reason that in the so-called Hindustani (i.e. north Indian, as distinct from southern or 'Karnataka') classical music, the words in all the *bandish*es (compositions) had always been in Braj. Many songs sung in early Hindi films by K.L. Saigal (1904–46) fall into this category; for example, '*Dukh ke din beetan naahin*' (*Devdas*, 1935). When the songs were high classical, as in the scenes of confrontation between Akbar's court musician Tansen and his young challenger Baiju Bawra (*Baiju Bawra*, 1952), famous classical singers such as D.V. Paluskar and Amir Khan were brought in to sing them ('*Aaj gaavat man mero jhum ke*'), as was Bade Ghulam Ali Khan in *Mughal-e-Azam*. The point that such classical or semi-classical songs had always to be in dialect was sweetly clinched in a scene in *Milan* (1967), in which Sunil Dutt is teaching Nutan to sing a song beginning '*Sawan ka mahina pavan kare sor*', and she repeats it twice as '. . . *pavan kare shor*', upon which he reprimands her: '*Shor nahin, baba, sor, sor.*' (Not '*shor*', my dear, it is '*sor*', '*sor*'. The point being that '*shor*', which means a loud sound or din, is the urban Urdu/Hindustani form, while '*sor*' is the indigenous dialect form.)

The emergence of dialect as one of the many voices of Hindi cinema attained its most remarkable manifestation with the production of a number of films entirely in Bhojpuri, a dialect or variety of Hindi spoken in eastern Uttar Pradesh and the adjacent areas of western Bihar. (Bhojpuri also remains, as it happens, the lingua franca of all *girmitiyas*, i.e. bonded, labourers who had been sent out a hundred years ago or more to work on the sugar plantations in other British colonies as distant from India, and as far apart from each other, as Trinidad and Fiji). Eighteen Bhojpuri films were produced in the 1960s, nine in the 1970s, as many as 90 in the 1980s, and 28 between 1991 and 1995.

These films were predominantly pastoral–romantic, with the sweetness of the dialect reaching across even to viewers who did not fully understand the dialect. The first, foundational film of this sub-category was also one of the most popular, with its title-song, '*Ganga maiya tohe piyari charhaibo, sajana se karde milanavaa, ho Ram*' (1962; I shall offer you a yellow sari in gratitude, Mother Ganga, if you bless me with a reunion with my husband), combining aptly the simple devotional with the erotics of separation (*viraha* or *birahaa*). However, the popular surge of Bhojpuri films has now virtually subsided, possibly because Bhojpuri is not large enough or distinct enough from standard Hindi to have its own viable constituency.[36]

(b) SANSKRITIC HINDI

While one kind of movement away from Urdu/Hindustani was towards dialect, another point of departure saw the induction of a markedly increasing proportion of *tatsam*, or Sanskritic, Hindi. A marker of this change was the new confidence with which the Hindi poet and prolific film-lyricist Pandit Narendra Sharma (whom Bhagwati Charan Varma had brought along with himself to the Hindi film world) felt able to insert into *Bhabhi Ki Churiyan* (1961), a song of his celebrating sunrise with the refrain '*Jyoti-kalash chhalke*' (The auspicious water-pot of light overflows), which is broadly reminiscent in both imagery and diction of the hymns to Usha in the *Rig-veda*, and which, incidentally, the foremost Marxist literary critic in Hindi, Ram Bilas Sharma, thought to be the best modern Hindi lyric.[37] In a way, this was the other side of the coin of what had happened to Sahir's Urdu lyric in *Pyaasa* only four years earlier, with the difference that Sharma's Sanskritic lyric could go into the film quite unaltered.

However, the defining moment here perhaps was the advent in the 1970s of the new/art/experimental/parallel cinema in Hindi. Shyam Benegal, who has endured as the leading light of this movement, gave to his first four feature films in Hindi one-word titles which were entirely Sanskritic: *Ankur* (1973), *Nishant* (1975), *Manthan*, and *Bhumika* (both 1976). No director in the history of Hindi cinema had come on so Sanskritically strong so consistently, and his terse and abstract eponymous gravity caused as much of a *frisson* as the engaged seriousness of the new subject-matter and his treatment of it. The dialogue in these films did not use markedly Sanskritic Hindi (for two of them in fact had rural settings and used versions of the local dialects) but the titles were apt indicators of their realistic, high serious orientation. What is remarkable in this context is the fact that this (at least eponymous) Sanskritization of Hindi films was brought about by new wave directors nearly all of whom by birth and upbringing were not Hindi-speakers. Besides Benegal, they included, notably, Kumar Shahani (*Maya Darpan*, 1973; *Tarang*, 1984; *Khayal Gatha*, 1988; *Bhavantarana*, 1991) and Govind Nihalani (*Aakrosh*, 1980; *Ardha Satya*, 1984; *Drishti*, 1991), and perhaps the only thing in common between all these pioneering films was their Sanskritic titles.

How was it that these new non-Hindi directors apparently favoured more Sanskritic Hindi than the traditional Hindi-speaking directors? Part of the explanation lies perhaps in the fact that through much of the first half of the twentieth century, at least since the Lucknow Pact (1916) which brought the Congress and the Ali brothers together to pursue shortly afterwards the common agenda of Non-Cooperation and Khilafat, Hindi and Urdu had been sought to be brought together not for reasons of any literary or cultural commonality but for the external and expedient political reason that this was perceived to be one vital way of uniting Hindus and Muslims in a joint political programme. The attempt in the 1920s and the 1930s to forge and promote a common language called Hindustani was thus a part of this broader endeavour but ultimately remained a utopian nationalist desideratum rather than anything approaching ground reality. When challenged to show a single book written in this in-between language, Premchand, the greatest literary champion of Hindustani, had disingenuously answered, 'if such a language already existed, where would be the need for an institution such as the [Hindustani] Academy?' and Gandhi, the greatest political promoter of Hindustani, had similarly conceded: 'But what is Hindustani? There is no such language apart from Urdu and Hindi...There is no such written blend extant.'[38]

On the other hand, nearly all the other major Indian languages, including even the four Dravidian languages, had a proportionately larger Sanskritic word-stock, especially in the literary register, than did modern Hindi which had cohabited more with Urdu or at least been obliged to be more its bedfellow than any other Indian language. Even in the early years of Hindi cinema, various directors and writers from Bengali or Marathi or Tamil had produced films in two languages, their own as well as Hindi, with Sanskritic titles such as *Bandhan, Nartaki* (both 1940), *Amrit, Raj Nartaki* (both 1941), *Bharat Milap, Meenakshi, Vasantasena* (all 1942), *Mahatma Vidur, Ramrajya, Shakuntala, Shankar Parvati* (all 1943), etc. and whenever such films had a different title in the other language, it was usually even more Sanskritic than the one in Hindi.

In the 1970s then, what the non-Hindi new wave directors did was to give Hindi another unwitting push towards recognizing its Sanskrit matrix which it shared in common with the vast majority of other Indian languages, and which in turn was principally what separated it from Urdu. Shortly afterwards, even Urdu- or Panjabi-speaking makers of mainstream, commercial Hindi films moved towards adopting more Sanskritic titles and dialogue, in recognition of the fact that the old linguistic ground beneath their feet had shifted.

(c) BAMBAIYA HINDI

Yet another major innovation in the language of Hindi films began in the 1970s, and for the sake of convenience, this too, like the popularity of folk songs, can be hung on the tall peg of Amitabh Bachchan— probably the most phenomenally successful figure in the history of Indian cinema. This was the increasing use of what is variously called *Bambaiya* or *mavaali* or *tapori* Hindi, the hybrid Hindi spoken by the low class of character inhabiting the seamier side of that industrial– commercial metropolis who walks on the border-line of law, makes his own destiny, and is a robust, irreverent 'rebel', often out to avenge by any means the wrongs done to himself or his family, and to resist wider social injustice. The language spoken by such a character was an improvised mixture of the many languages heard on the meaner streets of Bombay with elements of a more specialized underworld argot, and had earlier been used to occasional comic effect, in phrases such as '*khali pili khallas*', or '*Apun ko kya mangta saab—kuch bhi nahin*'. Now however, with the emergence of the Bachchan subaltern character, this unsophisticated language, miles, even worlds, removed from any courtly elegance, took on an aggressive, rough, and even brutal edge.

In what is probably the most extensive study of the 'Figure of the "Tapori"' to be published so far, Ranjani Mazumdar characterizes the language of the *tapori* to be 'a combination of English, Gujarati, Marathi, Hindi, Tamil and various other linguistic resonances', though the only example she cites, from the film *Rangeela* (1995), falls well short of illustrating such a wide range. Rather more persuasive is her argument that the *tapori* language 'embodies a polyglot culture that does not fix itself within [the] traditional Hindi–Urdu conflict', and that this new language serves 'to contest the power of a unitary language' (i.e. 'Urdu–Hindustani'), and to expose 'the vanity of élite linguistic formations'.[39]

To illustrate this language from one of the first films to deploy it to consistent effect, *Amar Akbar Anthony* (1977), we get sentences such as the following:

Ye valela batli bhi phor daal! Dekhtaich nai(n). (So, go on now and smash this bottle, too! Don't you have eyes?)
Koi apne ke takkar ka mafik ka larki milna mangta na. (But let me meet some girl first who will be my true match.)

Tere ko bola hai, daaru nai(n) peene ka, fikar nai(n) karne ka. (I've told you, haven't I: don't drink, and don't worry.)
God promise, ham sach bola hai. (I swear by God I'm telling the truth.)[40]

Since the heyday of Amitabh Bachchan, this language has remained the vehicle of similar characters played by a whole succession of villain–heroes and, more significantly, it has been the authenticating dialect, so to say, of some trenchantly realistic and 'meaningful' films which offer a critique of contemporary society through an exposè of its underworld, such as *Satya* (1998) and *Chandni Bar* (2001). However, the *tapori* language has occasionally gone beyond such a function, to be used even in a romantic situation where it suggests a macho curtness, as famously in the song '*Aati kya Khandala?*', a phrase which is so far removed from even an informal, colloquial register of Hindi that the simplest way of saying it in normal Hindi may be by expanding it to what in comparison may seem like high courtesy: '*Kya tum mere saath Khandala chalogi?*' (i.e. will you come with me to Khandala?)

All the various kinds or strands of film Hindi distinguished above, from watered down courtly Urdu to rural dialect to pan-Indian Sanskritic Hindi to the underworld Bambaiya Hindi, together constitute an astoundingly rich resource of expressivity. The discussion above has focused, if only by necessity, on the more visible and memorable elements of Hindi films, such as their titles or particular lines from songs and dialogue, but a detailed analysis of the script of any reasonably successful Hindi film (which, incidentally, is hardly ever available in print!) will demonstrate the lively, idiomatic, and apt use of a large range of registers to individuate characters, accentuate the dramatic elements of various situations, and sustain the dialogic interaction between characters in a suggestive and nuanced manner.

One further area of investigation in this context would obviously be whether the use of language in Hindi films is gendered in any significant manner. While the question of gender has attracted wide attention in studies of Hindi films, it has been addressed principally in thematological terms of female stereotypes, patriarchy, marriage, family, victimhood, desire, gaze, purdah, rape, revenge, etc., with the female 'body as text' as the focus of much analysis. The language spoken by women characters, especially in terms of how it may be different from that spoken by the men characters, seems not to have been an issue for discussion so far, except perhaps for Malati Mathur's passing observation that in some boy-meets-girl situations, the girl is from a higher class and speaks in English, whereupon the boy often surprises her by replying to her in English. It may however be argued that the situation is perhaps equally common in Hindi films where a rich English-speaking boy meets an 'innocent' village belle 'unspoilt' by much education, as for example in the film *Taal*. In both such cases, class perhaps overrides gender.[41]

SHOLAY

One of the major delights of the film *Sholay* (1975), one of the biggest hits in the history of Hindi cinema, was the virtuosity of the several different kinds of Hindi aptly deployed in it by the most celebrated team of dialogue writers in Hindi films, 'Salim–Javed' i.e., Salim Ali and Javed Akhtar. One, but only one, instance of such use that resounded on the lips of film-goers throughout India for years afterwards was the scene in which Amjad Khan, playing the dacoit Gabbar Singh, berates and then shoots dead some members of his own gang for having fled like cowards in an encounter with the police. '*Sarkar kitta inam rakkhe hai ham par*,' (What is the reward the government has set on my head?), he asks rhetorically in full swagger, with just a trace of dialect, and then tantalizingly plays Russian roulette with the three members of the retreating party. He shoots one by one at the first two, draws a blank each time, and as the tension mounts while he aims at the third, he asks, '*Ab tera kya hoga Kaliya*?' (And what's going to become of you, you darkie?) He shoots, and it is a blank again!—whereupon he overrides chance and shoots at each of the three again, killing them. The *Kaliya* line, with its thrillingly cynical playfulness, became probably the best-known quotation from this film or any other for many years; a mock-existentialist question widely and merrily repeated by film-goers all over India in all kinds of contexts.

By its very success, this Gabbar Singh episode overshadowed several other passages of equally apt dialogue in the film. For example, in a speech marked by deliberate 'fine excess', Hema Malini, playing a tonga-driver named Basanti, seeks in her first scene the custom of Amitabh Bachchan and Dharmendra by delivering an exuberantly comic, apparently uninterruptible, breathless monologue in which she asks them not so much to ride with her as to go and get lost if they didn't wish to.

All Kinds of Hindi

Haan Babuji, kahan jaoge? [...] Arre, kya tonga nahin dekha pahle kabhi? [...] Dekho, mujhe bephijool [sic] *baat karne ki aadat to hai nahin, chalna hai to bolo na chalna hai...*

(So, gentlemen, where do you want to go? [...] Hey, haven't you ever seen a tonga before? [...] Look, I'm not in the habit of carrying on a conversation unneedlessly [sic], so if you want to come ride with me why don't you just say so...)

As Dharmendra and Bachchan try to get a word in edgeways to say that they do indeed wish to ride in her tonga, she continues regardless:

Nahin chalna hai to theek hai, koi baat nahin, ab Basanti se koi dushmani to ho nahin jayegi. Tum baahar nikle to maine socha ki tonga karoge to pooch liya, koi jabardasti ka sauda to hai nahin, baithe baithe nahin baithe nahin baithe...

(If you don't want to come with me that's quite all right; it's not as if Basanti is going to hold it against you. As you came out [of the railway station] I thought you might need to hire a tonga so that's why I asked you but it's not as if I'm going to force you to strike a deal, for it's fine by me if you sit in my tonga and fine if you don't.)

This is a virtuoso scene, insomuch as it is not at all necessary to the plot, which indeed it comically and 'unneedlessly' retards. Bachchan himself later has a delightfully written scene with Hema Malini's *mausi* (aunt) in which he is supposed to plead Dharmendra's suit for Hema Malini's hand but ironically ends up thoroughly blackening his friend's character. Thereupon Dharmendra gets drunk, climbs atop a high water tank (a water tank in a village with no running water?—but never mind), and threatens to commit suicide, singling out especially the unrelenting *mausi* for the blame. His speech culminates, as speeches of semi-literate Indians under intoxication and grave emotional stress sometimes do, in a kind of pidgin:

Dekh lena gaon-wallon... When I dead, police coming, police coming, Burhia going jail. In jail, burhia chakki peesing and peesing and peesing and peesing.[42]

That is to say, the old hag *mausi* will go to jail for causing his death and be sentenced to long-term rigorous imprisonment during which she will be set endlessly to perform the customary penal task of stone-grinding grain, '*chakki peesna*' indeed being Hindi slang for going to jail (as is 'porridge' in English).

In her lively if somewhat wide-eyed account of the making and the unprecedented success of the film *Sholay*, Anupama Chopra relates that Polydor issued not only a record of the songs of the film but, a month after the release of the film, also another 'fifty-eight-minute record of selected dialogue'. A little later, they followed it up by releasing as many as fifteen separate EPs of dialogues of different episodes from the film.

By now, watching *Sholay* in the theatre had become a little like a Karaoke experience. The entire audience would be mouthing the dialogue with the characters. Some had even memorized the sound effects, down to the last flipped-coin sound.

Chopra reveals how the dialogue for the water-tank scene cited above was actually scribbled at the very last minute by the procrastinating Javed Akhtar in a car as he was leaving the location and being driven to the airport and then, while an assistant was sent to check him in, in the car-park with the bonnet of the car serving for a desk.[43]

IN SEARCH OF A HINDI FILM-SCRIPT

Oddly enough, this incident seems fairly representative of how a Hindi film gets written. The story of a large number of Hindi films is so hackneyed, formulaic, and yet amorphous that no real need is felt to write it down. When a producer or director approaches the actors of his choice to cast them in his film, he apparently goes and simply narrates the story to them, often in a colloquial mixture of Hindi and English. Dialogues are often written scene by scene, and not only the director or the speaking actor but almost anyone who happens to be around on the sets feels free to offer emendations. On top of such ad hoc-ism is the unabashed derivativeness of much Indian film-making; if the Hindi film happens to be a copy of (or 'inspired by') a certain Hollywood film, it is likely to be marked by an implausibility of character and situation which the half-hearted attempts of the writer and the director can do only so much to mitigate.

Rahi Masoom Raza, Urdu poet, Hindi novelist, and a former academic with a PhD degree who had taught Urdu at the Aligarh Muslim University before turning to writing dialogues for Hindi films in the mid-1960s, and who went on to win the *Filmfare* award for the best dialogue-writer three times, once described his job and its many constraints in the following terms:

I write dialogue. Just look at my plight. The sets that have been put up are pure fantasy. The look and make-up of the characters is Indian but the soul foreign, for the whole sequence has been lifted from some foreign film and been inserted in this story. What kind of dialogue can I write? Where shall I find the language to fit this impossible hodge-podge? That is why the dialogues of our films sound so artificial and the truth of the matter, sir, is that though he may win awards for it, it is seldom the dialogue-writer who writes the dialogue. In fact, everyone but the dialogue-writer has a right to fix the dialogue written by him. Some do it without humiliating the dialogue-writer and some others precisely so as to humiliate the dialogue-writer... We do not demand of the actor that he should speak what has been written; rather, we demand of the writer that he should write what the actor wishes to speak! And that is why the writer is required to be constantly in attendance on the sets with his file tucked under his arm.[44]

Even a marquee name, the dialogue-and-song writer Javed Akhtar (who with his co-writer Salim became the only Hindi film-writer to have his name featured on film posters, after Pandit Mukhram Sharma in an earlier era and Ramanand Sagar for example on the poster of *Barsat* (1949)) has recounted how not only is it common for him and other song-writers to write words to tunes already composed by musicians but that he has even been obliged to write Hindi words to fit the lip-synch of actors who had already sung a particular song in an earlier Tamil version of the film, which reduced him to having to choose words that matched, for example, the labials already employed in the original song.[45]

As if all these complications were not enough, it is often the case that the production team involved in making a Hindi film includes technicians, including major functionaries such as the camera-man and the sound-recordist, who may not know much Hindi. Javed Akhtar himself has claimed that he does not know Hindi, by which would-be shocking assertion he seems mercifully to mean no more than that he writes his Hindi in the Urdu script, which is then transcribed by an assistant in the Hindi, i.e. Devanagari script because, unlike himself, as Akhtar explains, 'most people read Hindi.' Akhtar adds, for good measure, that '[m]ost of our play-back singers...don't know the language properly'.[46] Nor, in fact, do many actors who have come to Hindi films from other languages, and before being able to master the language, some of them have needed to be dubbed. Similarly, A.R. Rahman, currently the top-ranking music director in Hindi films, actually knows very little Hindi but prolifically provides tunes for songs he himself doesn't understand; indeed, his lack of the language does not stop him from occasionally singing a Hindi song himself.

All this is reminiscent of Woody Allen's film *Hollywood Ending* (2002) in which Allen himself plays a film director beset by mounting problems. When someone asks him, 'But why have you hired a camera-man who speaks only Mandarin?' he answers, 'Because in these parts [i.e. Hollywood] it's hard to find a camera-man who speaks only Cantonese.' The truth is that what is the height of comic absurdity in Woody Allen appears to be a common and mundane enough reality in the making of Hindi films. In such circumstances, it may seem a miracle that any effective Hindi gets spoken or sung at all in Hindi, and yet it does, on the whole, in film after film week after week. Even many mediocre films, which can be faulted for their plot, camera-work, and direction generally, often throw up lines of dialogue and an odd song or two which help redeem the film or at least go on to live an autonomous life of their own, while good films are hardly ever let down by their dialogues or songs.

IN HINDI BUT NOT OF HINDI?

Judging by its language, Hindi cinema has over the decades shown a vitality, variety, and even virtuosity which is truly remarkable and which, partly because of the pan-Indian range of writers, directors, actors, and singers who contribute to it, quite overflows the bounds of the standard or literary language of the north Indian Hindi heartland. The pan-Indian polyvocality which may have seemed to be an odd and unsettling commodity in the early days of the talkies has now come to be seen as a source of enrichment and has flowered into a relative strength of Hindi films.

However, the eclectic quality of Hindi cinema, especially in linguistic and cultural terms, has also been the cause of some anxiety and discontent. Jabri Mall Parekh, an academic and Hindi film-critic, has ruefully complained that Hindi cinema really does not belong to or reflect the social and cultural life of the Hindi-speaking community.

One could ask: whom do Hindi films represent? Do they represent the linguistic community which has come to be called the Hindi *jati* [community]? Or do they represent the linguistic community which holds itself apart from Hindi and calls its language Urdu, but which supporters of the concept of the Hindi *jati* insist on seeing as incorporated within it? Can Hindi cinema too be regarded as regional cinema in the same sense as the Bengali, Marathi, Tamil or Malayalam cinemas are? Can Hindi cinema be seen to be representative of the cultural identity of the Hindi-speaking area as other regional cinema is?[47]

Indeed, an interviewer recently put to Amitabh Bachchan the astounding idea that Bachchan was 'the first person from north India who had come to prominence as an actor' in Hindi films, and though Bachchan initially demurred, he could not come up with any names other than those of the minor actor Motilal, the music director Naushad, and the writer Javed Akhtar who had also come from the Hindi-speaking area. 'Yes, I agree that most actors have come from Panjab, South India or Bengal.'[48]

This may seem a very odd state of affairs indeed; so strange as to be barely credible, and beyond the parameters of even Woody Allen's zany imagination. However, one may read the situation somewhat differently to suggest that going as much by its makers as by its viewers, and by its medium as well as its message, Hindi cinema has a truly pan-Indian character. If Hindi cinema is India's national cinema, that may be precisely because it is not 'representative' of or chauvinistically dominated by a particular region. It transcends the so-called Hindi belt to embrace all of India, to say nothing of its popularity beyond. Actors, directors, and singers from the many languages of India have gravitated to Hindi and sought a makeover to Hindi in order to achieve nation-wide recognition, and these have included, to name at random only a variety of mainstream directors, V. Shantaram (from Marathi), Bimal Roy (from Bengali), and Mani Ratnam (from Tamil). They have come over not for the money alone, for even Satyajit Ray, certainly the most widely honoured Indian film-maker ever with ultimately an Oscar for lifetime achievement, who was deeply rooted in a Bengali (and more specifically, Bengali literary) sensibility, having made nearly all his Bengali films out of Bengali books, was eventually tempted to make a couple of films in Hindi, *Shatranj ke Khilari* and *Sadgati*, both based on classic short stories by Premchand.

NRI HINGLISH, GLOBAL ENGLISH

Reflecting its role and status as a national repository, flag-bearer, or lightning-conductor, Hindi cinema in its current post-colonial, liberalized phase manifests yet another linguistic turn: to 'Hinglish', i.e.

a code-switching mixture of Hindi and English words in the same sentence. Over the past decade or so, any number of successful 'NRI' films have been made which have foreign locales not only as inert backdrops as earlier but as places where characters from Hindi films actually visit or live, even outside the magic–realist world of Hindi film songs. This reflects an upper-class cosmopolitan Indian mobility which has become a staple subject-matter of Hindi films, much as the villages were half a century ago—except that the villages have now vanished from the Indian imaginary, as Ashis Nandy has argued.[49] If the 'real' India not so long ago lived in its villages, as Gandhi said, a highly visible and glamorous fraction of it now lives abroad, at least on the evidence of numerous recent Hindi films. Such a phenomenally increasing presence of upper-class Hinglish-speaking Indians who are shown to shuttle between the East and the West and who, for all their Westernization, still mouth feel-good sentiments in praise not of Bharat or Hindustan (à la '*Phir bhi dil hai Hindustani*' of *Shri 420*) but of 'India' (as in '*Yeh mera India/Mathe ki bindiya*' in *Pardes*) forebodes a change in the very character of Hindi cinema and its potential viewership. In an article entitled 'Bollywood: Next Generation', Madhu Jain observes how in such NRI-oriented films:

India is looking more like a mini-Europe or United States... The tastes of the international Indian audience have had an impact on Bollywood, determining the choice of the stars, stories and music of the film. Overseas is the new Eldorado for Indian producers.[50]

It is not only Hindi films set partially abroad which have characters speaking in 'Hinglish'. The recent surge of patriotic anti-colonial films set in India, such as *1942: A Love Story* (1994), the five versions of the Bhagat Singh story all made within 2001–2, and the enormously successful *Lagaan* (2001) which made it to the shortlist of five nominations for the Best Foreign-Language Film for the Oscar awards, have British characters speaking in either English or in ungrammatical anglicized Hindi and some Indian characters speaking in Hinglish. Though *Monsoon Wedding* (2001), which won the Golden Bear at the Venice Film Festival, is set entirely in Delhi and all its characters are upper-middle-class Indians, including some NRIs, it had more than sixty per cent of its dialogue in English and the remaining part of Hinglish/Hindi dialogue subtitled in English for the benefit of NRI as well as Western audiences.

Beyond hybridized Hinglish, English by itself has become the sole medium of several films made in India with an entirely Indian cast of characters, such as *Hyderabad Blues*, *Rockford*, and *Bollywood Calling*, all directed by Nagesh Kukunoor; *Bandit Queen* (released in both English and Hindi under the same English title) directed by Shekhar Kapoor; and *English August* (based on the novel in English of the same title by Upamanyu Chatterji) directed by Dev Benegal. At the same time, some Indians have also directed a few mainstream Hollywood films in English, such as *Elizabeth* by Shekhar Kapur, *The Sixth Sense*, which starred Bruce ('Diehard') Willis, was one of the biggest grossers of the year in the United States and won an Oscar nomination for the best director for M. 'Night' Shyamalan, and *Vanity Fair* by Mira Nair, with Reese Witherspoon in the lead role of Becky Sharp.

Even on home ground, Hindi cinema is now acquiring a new, élite variety of Hindi in Hinglish, which could perhaps be seen in terms of cultural classification as being situated right at the other end of the social spectrum from the Hindi rural dialect discussed above. It now finds itself obliged to share its traditional space with films being made in global English by Indian directors both in India and in the West, on both Indian and non-Indian themes. The Indian film industry, spearheaded by Hindi films, has long stood as the one major alternative and challenge to the global hegemony of Hollywood. Now, however, with Bollywood (as the Hindi film industry is increasingly called) looking to orient itself more and more to upper-middle-class themes and audiences both within India and in the Indian diasporic communities in the West, and with Indian directors and actors seeking to achieve an international breakthrough in the West (rather on the pattern of Indian writing in English having broken through a couple of decades ago with Salman Rushdie), Hindi cinema appears set to undergo increasing globalization, possibly even to the extent of no longer remaining either India's national cinema or even Hindi cinema. However, this deeply transformative phenomenon perhaps requires a fuller exploration elsewhere.

NOTES AND REFERENCES

No essay I have ever written has evoked such enthusiastic participatory involvement from pre-publication readers, both academic and non-academic. For filling gaps in my knowledge, rescuing me from grievous errors of fact/fiction, and suggesting further lines of enquiry, some of which I would have liked to pursue had this essay not already been as long as *Sholay*, I thank my brother Raghav, my sons Pranjal and Mudit, my old teacher H.S. Saxena, and, among expert colleagues and friends, Rupert Snell, Vijay Mishra, and Rachel Dwyer. I also thank both the editors of this volume for their patience and their discriminating (and widely varying!) comments on a draft.

1. Ashish Rajadhyaksha and Paul Willemen, *Encyclopaedia of Indian Cinema* (1995; new rev. ed. New Delhi: Oxford University Press, 1999); hereafter referred to as *Encyclopaedia*.
2. See, for example, Ashis Nandy (ed.), *The Secret Politics of Our Desires: Innocence, Culpability and Indian Popular Cinema* (Delhi: Oxford University Press, 1998), Vijay Mishra, *Bollywood Cinema: Temples of Desire* (New York: Routledge, 2002), and the other studies cited below.
3. See Robert Stam, *Film Theory: An Introduction* (Malden, Mass.: Blackwell, 2000), p. 109, and also Metz's essay, 'The Imaginary Signifier' (1975), in Robert Stam and Toby Miller (eds.), *Film and Theory: An Anthology* (Malden, Mass.: Blackwell, 2000), pp. 408–36, where Metz attempts to distinguish cinema from literature, including theatre, by propounding what has become known as 'apparatus theory', i.e. the effect on the perception of the viewer of the material, technical, and physical aspects of watching a film.
4. 'Undivided Space: Mani Kaul in Conversation with Udayan Vajpeyi', in *Hindi: Language Discourse Writing* 2:4 (Jan. –March 2002), p. 140.
5. See Christopher R. King, *One Language, Two Scripts: The Hindi Movement in Nineteenth Century North India* (Bombay: Oxford University Press, 1994), and for a divergent view, my 'Hindi and the Nation' in Sheldon Pollock (ed.), *Literary Cultures in History: Reconstructions from South Asia* (Berkeley: University of California Press, 2003), especially the section 'Inventing Hindustani: Gandhi and Premchand', pp. 975–83.
6. Cited in Rahi Masoom Raza, *Cinema aur Sanskriti* (Cinema and Culture) (New Delhi: Vani Prakashan, 2001), p. 28. According to the table of films classified by languages in the *Encyclopaedia*, pp. 30–2, not a single film was certified by the Central Board of Film Certification as an Urdu film between the years 1931 and 1985 (presumably because none sought such certification), and only seven films were so certified between 1986 and 1995, whereas the number of Hindi films so certified between 1931 and 1995 stood at just under 8,000. However, a spot check revealed that in the main entries, the *Encyclopaedia* describes *Mughal-e-Azam* (1960), *Mere Mehboob* (1963), and *Pakeeezah* (1971) all as Urdu films, so there is apparently some inconsistency here.
7. Nasreen Munni Kabir, *Guru Dutt: A Life in Cinema* (1996; Delhi: Oxford India Paperbacks, 1997), p. 82.
8. Mukul Kesavan, 'Urdu, Awadh and the Tawaif: The Islamicate Roots of Hindi Cinema', in Zoya Hasan (ed.), *Forging Identities: Gender, Communities*

  and the State (New Delhi: Kali for Women, 1994), pp. 244–7, 256. See also in the same volume Fareed Kazmi, 'Muslim Socials and the Female Protagonist: Seeing a Dominant Discourse at Work', pp. 226–43, in which however there is hardly any discussion of the language of these overtly and almost exclusively Muslim-content films.
9. *Encyclopaedia*, pp. 253–8.
10. M. Madhav Prasad, *Ideology of the Hindi Film: A Historical Reconstruction* (Delhi: Oxford University Press, 1998).
11. Sumita S. Chakravarty, *National Identity in Popular Indian Cinema 1947–87* (Delhi: Oxford University Press, 1998).
12. Mishra, *Bollywood Cinema*, pp. 271–6.
13. Kesavan, 'Urdu, Awadh and the Tawaif', in Zoya Hasan (ed.), *Forging Identities*, 1994, p. 257.
14. *Encyclopaedia*, p. 11.
15. Quoted in both Lakshminarayan Lal, *Parsi–Hindi Rangmanch* (The Parsi–Hindi Stage) (Delhi: Rajpal and Sons, 1973), p. 104, and in Somnath Gupta, *Parsi Theatre: Udbhav aur Vikas* (The Parsi Theatre: Rise and Development) (Allahabad: Lok Bharati, 1981), p. 246, with the delectable difference that Gupta begins, '*Na khalis Urdu na theth Hindi...*'.
16. Quoted in Lal, *Parsi–Hindi Rangmanch*, pp. 93, 122.
17. M.K. Gandhi, *The Story of My Experiments with Truth* vol. I, trans. Mahadev Desai (Ahmedabad: Navjivan Trust, 1927), pp. 24–5. Gandhi wrote, 'This play —*Harishchandra*—captured my heart. I could never be tired of seeing it. But how often should I be permitted to go? It haunted me and I must have acted Harishchandra to myself times without number. "Why should not all be truthful like Harishchandra?" was the question I asked myself day and night.'
18. Kishor Vasvani, *Cinemai Bhasha aur Hindi Samvadon ka Vishleshan* (The Language of Cinema and an Analysis of Hindi Dialogues) (New Delhi: Hindi Book Centre, 1998), pp. 133–4.
19. For the principal facts, see Amrit Rai, *Premchand: His Life and Times*, trans. Harish Trivedi (1982: rpt. Delhi: Oxford University Press, 1991), and Bhagwati Charan Varma, *Dhuppal* (Fluke) (New Delhi: Rajkamal, 1981). On the matter of some older Muslim/Urdu-speaking actors adopting Hindu/Hindi names for the sake of greater commercial acceptability, compare Waheeda Rehman, 'I Didn't Let Guru Dutt Change My Name', interview with Chandan Mitra, *Alliance Darpan*, (Feb.–March 2003), pp. 8–14. For the reverse case of Om Prakash Bhandari who, in the belief that a lyricist for Hindi films must have a Muslim/Urdu name, chose to write as Qamar Jalalabadi, see Ramesh Kumar Singh, 'Main to Ik Khwab Hoon', *Janasatta Ravivari*, (9 Feb. 2003), p. 4. As a case of the wheel coming full circle in contemporary times, compare the case of the aspiring actor Fardeen Khan who has dropped the 'Khan' from his name, as he explains, so as not to be confused with too many other actors named Khan.

20. Savaging on ideological grounds Varma's saga of nationalist politics, *Terhe Merhe Raste* (Zigzag Ways, 1946), the eminent Marxist Hindi critic Ram Bilas Sharma began by recalling that Varma was 'a former script-writer for Bombay Talkies'. 'Preface' by Sharma to Rangey Ragahv, *Seedha Sada Rasta* (The Straight and True Path) (1967; rpt. Delhi: Radhakrishna, 2002).
21. Incidentally, in the Hindi translation of *A Suitable Boy*, the translator Gopal Gandhi expands upon the original here to supply the names of the film, the lyricist, and the singer—*Pyar Ki Jeet*, Qamar Jalalabadi, and Mohammad Rafi respectively—thus exploiting the shared cultural recall of the Hindi reader which, as Vikram Seth probably rightly judged, would not have been available to the English-language reader. *Koi Achha-sa Larka* (New Delhi: Vani Prakashan, 1998), pp. 45–6.
22. Shrilal Shukla, *Rag Darbari* (1968; rpt. New Delhi: Rajkamal 1988), pp. 208–9 and 206, respectively.
23. Salman Rushdie, *Imaginary Homelands: Essays and Criticism 1981–1991* (London: Granta Books, 1991), p. 11, and *The Satanic Verses* (London: Vintage, 1998), p. 5.
24. Sudipta Kaviraj, 'A Song of the City', unpublished paper.
25. Prasad, *Ideology of the Hindi Film*, p. 45.
26. See, for example, Yves Thoraval, *The Cinemas of India* (New Delhi: Macmillan, 2000), where the 'golden age' of 'Hindustani' cinema is dated '1930s–60s' on p. 68 and the heyday of Hindustani 'from the 1940s to the '60s' on p. 69.
27. Dilip Kumar interviewed by Javed Akhtar, *India Today Sahitya Varshiki* (India Today Annual Literary Number), 1993–4, pp. 178, 185.
28. Raj Kumar interviewed by Vinod Tiwari, *India Today Sahitya Varshiki* (India Today Annual Literary Number), 1997, p. 159. See also the detailed insider account of the writing and delivery of dialogues by a minor dialogue-writer, Harmal Singh, in his *Filmen Kaise Banti Hain* (How [Hindi] Films Are Made) (Jaipur: Rajasthan Patrika Ltd., 1996).
29. Saadat Hasan Manto, *Meena Bazar* (Hindi ed.; New Delhi: Rajkamal, 1962), pp. 87–92.
30. H.S. Saxena, formerly Reader in English at the University of Allahabad and Vice-President of the Allahabad Film Society, personal communication, 8 Jan. 2003.
31. Nasreen Munni Kabir, *Bollywood: The Indian Cinema Story* (London: Channel 4 Books, 2001), p. 176.
32. Vasvani, *Cinemai Bhasha*, p. 199.
33. Rahi Masoom Raza, *Cinema aur Sanskriti* (Cinema and Culture) (New Delhi: Vani Prakahsan, 2001), p. 43.
34. Nasreen Munni Kabir, *Talking Films: Conversations on Hindi Cinema with Javed Akhtar* (New Delhi: Oxford University Press, 1999), p. 36.
35. Amitabh Bachchan was born and spent his early childhood in Allahabad, where his father, the popular Hindi poet Harivansh Rai Bachchan (1907–

2003), taught English at a school and then at the university; some of the folk-songs his son sang were in fact credited to him. For the poet Bachchan's own account of how he first came across two such songs, '*Rang barsai bheegai chunarvali...*' (*Silsila*, 1981) and '*Holi khelain Raghubira Avadh men...*' (*Baghbaan*, 2003), which were sung during his childhood in the lanes of Allahabad during the festival of Holi, see his essay 'Rang Barsai Bheegai Chunarvali, Rang Barsai...' in *Bachchan Rachanavali* (The Collected Works of Bachchan), (Delhi: Rajkamal, 1983), vol. 6, pp 458–64.

36. Shatrughna Prasad, 'Bhojpuri Filmen: Hindi Filmon ke Darshakon ko Bantata Hai [sic]', (Bhojpuri Films: They Divide Hindi Viewers) in *Vartaman Sahitya*, special issue on 'Sadi ka Cinema' (Cinema of the Century), (Aug.–Dec. 2002), pp. 398–9.
37. Ranajit Saha, *Yuga-sandhi ke Pratiman: Rabindranath se Ramvilas tak* (Patterns of an Age in Transition: From Rabindranath to Ramvilas) (Delhi: Granthalok, 2002), p. 287.
38. Both cited in Trivedi, 'Hindi and the Nation', pp. 979–80.
39. Ranjani Mazumdar, 'Figure of the "Tapori": Language, Gesture and Cinematic City', *Economic and Political Weekly*, (29 Dec. 2001), pp. 4873–4 and 4877.
40. The three eponymous characters in this film, who are Hindu, Muslim, and Christian respectively, are each sought to be differentiated through their language. Thus, Anthony is also given some bursts of dazzling, show-off English, the blind old man (their father) says in fairly *tatsam* Hindi, '*Akbar, aaj teri bhakti aur Baba ke chamatkar se mujhe aankhen milin*', while Akbar is portrayed as an Urdu poet ('Akbar Ilahabadi'—but with no resemblance to a very different satirical poet (1846–1921) of that name and he uses words and phrases such as '*khwabon ki shahzadi*' and '*furqat*'. Incidentally, at one point in the film, a character writes a secret note in the Urdu script '*kyonki yehan kisi ko Urdu nahin aati*', i.e. because no one around here knows Urdu!
41. For a sample of feminist studies of Hindi films, see Shoma A. Chatterji, *Subject:Cinema Object:Woman: A Study of the Portrayal of Women in Indian Cinema* (Calcutta: Parumita Publications, 1998), and Jasbir Jain and Sudha Rai (eds.), *Films and Feminism: Essays in Indian Cinema* (Jaipur: Rawat Publications, 2002), which includes 'Courting: Hindi Film Ishtyle' by Malati Mathur, pp. 59–64.
42. Vasvani in his *Cinemai Bhasha* too quotes some of the dialogue cited in this section, pp. 234 and 237.
43. Anupama Chopra, *Sholay: The Making of a Classic* (New Delhi: Penguin Books India, 2002), pp. 170, 174, 172, and 108, respectively.
44. Raza, *Cinema aur Sanskriti*, p. 36.
45. Kabir, *Talking Films*, pp. 13–14.
46. Ibid., p. 49.
47. Jabari Mall Parekh, 'Hindi Cinema banaam [vs.] Hindustani Cinema', *Kathachitra: Cinema ka Hindi Traimasik*, no. 1: Oct.–Dec. 2002, pp. 90–1.

48. Sumant Mishra, 'Amitabh Bachchan se Baat-Cheet' (A Conversation with Amitabh Bachchan), *Kathachitra*, no. 1 (Oct.–Dec. 2002), p.16.
49. Ashis Nandy, *An Ambiguous Journey: The Village and Other Odd Ruins of the Self in the Indian Imagination* (Delhi: Oxford University Press, 2001).
50. Madhu Jain, 'Bollywood: Next Generation', in Lalit Mohan Joshi (ed.), *Bollywood: Popular Indian Cinema* (London: Dakini Ltd, 2001), pp. 305, 335.

The Comic Collapse of Authority: An Essay on the Fears of the Public Spectator

D. R. NAGARAJ

PART I
THE BEGINNING OF THE JOURNEY:
THE MODE OF THE NOBLE MELANCHOLY

INTRODUCTORY

Comedies are like crows. Judging by the image of the crow from the vast literature on India by seafarers from the West, the sight of ordinary crows meant the end of the journey over rough seas; they, the crows, were the signs of a landfall, a statement of hope. In this story of Indian films that deals with the experience of the great disintegration of authority, which may be expressed as the collapse of major values, comedies mean the end of an anxiety-ridden voyage on the violent seas of social change. Comedy is the sign of hope; it suggests that the community has acquired sufficient strength to handle the crisis of change with confidence. Laughter is the crow which symbolizes the end of the hegemony of anxiety.

This essay treats popular films as Jatakas, astrological charts, of the Indian viewer (public spectator). No other art genre mirrors the psyche of Indians as does the popular film: the cinema hall is a temple, a psychiatric clinic, a parliament, and a court of law, and, of course, these in themselves are for them a great source of entertainment. This conviction has given me the comic courage to write a serious treatise on comedy.

ROMANTIC LOVE AND CINEMATIC FORM

The theme of collapse or disintegration of authority is not new in the history of Kannada cinema. I define authority both within civil society and in the discourses of the nation-state as the assertion of certain values in the areas of family, public life, and religious identities. A selective merger of the civil society and statist discourses within the context of certain values produces authority and the spectator instantly recognizes them. One should be careful in using the concept of the public spectator, which is an offshoot of the notion of public sphere, and has a strong element of élitism, separating the self of the analyser from the mass of filmgoers by making them a public out there.[1] More than that, the concept seeks to posit a crude unity between art experience and the public discourse on values. By consciously avoiding these two dangers, it should be possible to use this category meaningfully.

In the first phase, the theme of collapse of authority is invariably explored in the mode of noble melancholy, and, then, in the next phase, the mode of comic collapse is born.[2] The collapse is hung around the neck of the spectator as an albatross, to draw on the famous English poem 'The Ancient Mariner'; the crow appears a little later in the voyage. In the meanwhile, however, a sea-change has occurred in the value system of the public spectator. Between these two modes there lies a bloodless revolution. This chapter proposes to explore this phenomenon.

It appears that the Kannada-speaking public cannot either mourn or celebrate any disappearance of old values or the arrival of new ones with unalloyed enthusiasm. It ought to be an experience of interdependent origination. I am not being ironical here. In other words, the birth of a new realm of experience or a value is accompanied by the death of another equally important value system. To illustrate this point, one can analyse the emergence of romantic love in Kannada cinema: it was born against the backdrop of the disappearance of the joint or extended family.

The history of Kannada cinema had its era of romantic idealism in the years 1950–70, and in those colourful decades the theme of the birth of romantic love was explored in the context of sweeping changes in Karnataka society. Interestingly, the sociological research of M.N. Srinivas was anchored in those years. His famous concepts of analysing social change, Sanskritization and Westernization, were also a product of the societal experience of that time. Speaking in a cinematic metaphor, it meant that the lilting tunes of love songs were intertwined with the elegy sung by neglected parents. However, the latter cannot be exaggerated beyond a tolerable limit, the limit being constantly negotiated between the internal pressures of the newly evolving form of popular cinema and the changing values of the society.

At this stage it is also useful to study the treatment of the theme of romantic love films in contrast to the contemporary ethos in literature. Interestingly, in the popular romantic cinema, the birth of love is seen as a major spin-off of the emergence of a new kind of individualism. The historical process of individuation is seen to occur in the universe of romantic love; in terms of cinematic form it meant the predominance of near-idyllic and pastoral images. One could not escape the irony of presenting the vast cityscapes too in the mould of pastoral space. However, in Kannada literature those were the years of the modernist Navya literary movement with its great emphasis on the existential becoming of the protagonist who is defining himself in terms of defying the taboos of society and tradition. What was the cool breeze of romantic love for the heroes of the popular cinema, who were also in the process of becoming modern individuals, was the heat of lust for the protagonists with a highly developed modernist sensibility in literature. The modernists had just discovered a new continent of sex, and they were quite adventurous travellers in that interesting terrain of the physicality of the body. They were nothing if not overtly sexy and sexist. Compared to these penis-conscious heroes, the new lovers of the Kannada cinema were rather too coy and coquettish for comfort.

The heroines of the day were outrageously draped, mostly in saris but occasionally in salwar kameez and, yes, in trousers as well. Enough care was however taken by the cameraman to offer sexist shots that would cater to the desires of the male viewers. It was both bold and sly within certain permissible limits of the public taste. The Navyas in literature were defining and describing tradition as oppression, whereas the makers of popular cinema were far more ambivalent in their attitude towards traditional culture, in which the emotive content of songs inhered. Precisely because of this the works of the film-makers of this generation of romantic idealism are richer and more tension-ridden than the products of a clearly articulated generation of radical and realist writers.

That tradition was the source of their themes and material, and the modern genre of cinema was the area of their creativity, had put the film-makers in a double bind. Therefore, their struggle with the new genre to make it yield traditional meanings has produced some of the most outstanding works of art not only in Kannada but also in Indian cinema as a whole. In this multifaceted struggle, which took a clear shape in the films of the 1950s and onwards, the first effort was to deal with the master narratives of the collapse of the joint family.

The multi-layered mode of the popular cinema that can accommodate both elegies and celebratory songs was a product of this effort. At once the popular film-makers celebrated the arrival of the new and mourned for the old in the popular cinema at the primary level of its meaning. However, subtle tensions pervaded the text at a much deeper level. It is true that some of the greatest classics of south Indian cinema such as *Devdas*, in continuation of the Bengali original, celebrated the tragic disintegration of the love-ridden hero. They presented the modern lover as tender, fragile, and unworldly; he was also incapable of sublimating his passion into something else. The lonely figure of the jilted lover, haunted by hostile forces, is an archetype of the popular film. The pain of separation was given equal space with the joy of union. On the whole, the tone of unrequited love was stronger than that of love consummated: to use the motif of a famous Hindi film song, 'the moon is only half, our union has also remained half'. The lovers loomed larger than life on screen demanding total attention and sympathy. However, there was this other stream which presented the father as more fragile than the lover.

THE CONFLICT BETWEEN THE *PREMI* AND THE *GRUHASTHA*: B.R. PANTHULU AND RAJ KAPOOR

A classic of the 1950s, *School Master* (1958), a Kannada film directed by one of the leaders of modern cinema, B.R. Panthulu, can serve as a work that registers all the subterranean currents of meanings involved in the making of the mode of noble melancholy.[3] A whole generation or two of Kannada speakers are influenced by this film whose songs evoke strong associations and memories to this day in the Kannada diaspora; this is partly because it captures the values and emotions of the generations who left their home towns in search of better careers.

The film's popularity can only be accounted for by its well-tuned synthesis of conflicting values, in which adversaries are handled not so much with artistic care but a deft and strategic submergence of tensions in the form of popular melodrama.

School Master is the first film in Kannada that explored the theme of disintegration of larger societal values that had their roots in tradition. Interestingly, Panthulu, who was trained in the professional theatres of south India, was scarcely enthusiastic about portraying the tales of individuals. Whenever he attempted to do so, he ended up doing something else, generally with the characteristic story of society as a whole. In many ways, he invites comparison with Raj Kapoor, not on the basis of their commonality but in the way that differences between the two surface in the treatment of the theme of romantic love. A discussion on the differences between the two will also help to build a differential understanding of popular Indian cinema; the contrast centres around their engagement with tradition.

Raj Kapoor was an enthusiastic modernist who endorsed the revolt of the young against stifling traditions; for him the best creative space was in the values created by modernity. He celebrated the arrival of the new that nurtured a profound fear of the old.

The narrative viewpoint in Raj Kapoor's films was a product of the director's identification with the young male lover, which could also accommodate the heroine who is created by the adoring gaze of the male public. Raj Kapoor sought to create a magical world of love with enchanting songs and dances. Indeed, efforts have been made by Raj Kapoor's biographers to bring in an element of personal authenticity by creating an almost one to one relationship between the love stories in his films and the women in his private life.[4] The idea was to reinforce the conviction among the public that the cinematic myth merged with the reality of Raj Kapoor's private life. In other words, commercial cinema invariably attempts to eradicate the distinction between the private and the public life of the cinema-goers. On this basis alone is the political role of the film stars carefully built, a subject to which we shall return later. To draw the contrast between Raj Kapoor and Panthulu more sharply, the former creates his films from the viewpoint of the young lover but the latter does so from the view of the liberal family man with deep roots in tradition. It was a classic case of conflict between the *premi* (lover) and *gruhastha* (householder).

The powers of the form can however be quite cruel. Though Panthulu has all the makings of a liberal *gruhastha*, popular cinema shapes his creativity. To make an extreme statement, the form in cinema is so powerful that it literally, not only cinematically, dictates terms to the film-maker. The film-maker is made by the film form. Against this background, the narrative self of the film is split into two halves, which are constantly interacting with each other. The dialogue between these two often assumes quite interesting forms, giving the film extraordinary energy. Panthulu is forced—and he becomes a willing prisoner of what is being imposed upon him—to celebrate the genesis, growth, and expansion of romantic love. Raj Kapoor tells his story from the viewpoint of the educated urban middle-class individual but the village and the small town in Panthulu demand codes of recognition. Raj Kapoor has to iconize his codes of love in order to generate the greatest energy to celebrate the new courtship which can have unsettling implications for the institution of the family; he has to be the priest of the new love. The family that asserts itself in the end in Raj Kapoor's works is a new incarnation that has retained only a thing or two from its previous birth. Panthulu is aware of the fact that the form of the popular cinema is compellingly in favour of modern values. His dilemma becomes all the more moving because he is caught between the charming powers of the form and the compulsions of tradition.

In *School Master* there are several *upakatha*s or subplots; they serve the director usefully at two levels. First, these subplots help Panthulu to conceal the real purpose of exploring the nature of romantic love. Second, they place the crises that are created by love in the larger context of change. These subplots then make Panthulu both ambitious and cunning, in the Joycean sense of the terms. When an artist is placed in an oppressive situation, guile is one of the strategies of survival. *School Master* begins as a tale of a lower middle-class schoolteacher and his three children: a tale of idealism and of nation-building; and the nation is built in classrooms. Only later in the film does the theme of romantic love surface. It is the story of a simple village schoolteacher and his lifelong struggle, shaped by his conception of himself as a teacher charged with responsibilities towards a village, to instil values of filial loyalty and nation-building both within his family and in the wider society. His trials and tribulations furnish the film with its themes.

Panthulu's family consisted of his wife, two sons, and a daughter. The schoolmaster and his wife made many sacrifices to educate their two sons, and to marry off their daughter with a hefty dowry which was to be paid after Panthulu's retirement. Both the sons were well-educated, found good jobs, and were married to girls from good families. When the father retired all the children arrived at the parental home, expecting to share the retirement emoluments; but that money had already been spent to clear their loans incurred to educate the two sons. Instead, now the sons had to take care of their parents: the father settled down with the elder son and the mother with the younger one. While this separation from each other was itself difficult to come to terms with, Panthulu and his wife soon found themselves being treated like servants by their daughters-in-law. In the meanwhile, the house Panthulu built in the village is auctioned to recover unpaid loans. A former (orphan) student of the schoolmaster, whom the teacher had set on the right path, bought the house. When he signed the document with the very pen his teacher had gifted him at his graduation, Panthulu recognized his former student. The schoolmaster was overjoyed to see a student who embodied the values that he had believed in, even if his own children had rejected those.

In the opening scenes of the film, the schoolteacher is shocked to see the degradation of the school; its children have even forgotten to say prayers in the morning. Also, the school has its share of good, bad, and indifferent teachers with a villainous feudal lord as the political head of the village. The task of building the school–nation begins in right earnest and the first step in that direction is to say prayers. What is the fate of a school–nation which cannot say its prayers? Teach the talented children of the school the song '*Swami devane Loka palane te namostu namostu te*' (O lord who is the protector of the world, salutations to you, salutations to you). It has since become the regular prayer in many schools in the Old Mysore region of Karnataka. Curiously, though Panthulu is imaging the process of nation-building, he does so not by directly picking up a political theme but by focusing on the institution of formal education.

This minimalist mode inevitably has its excesses, and there is a scene of the schoolchildren literally building a house for their teacher. The accompanying song '*Bannirai navella guruseve maduva*' (Come, let us serve the teacher), has also become immensely popular. The purpose of all these sentimental scenes is to establish the primacy of the institution of gurudom. However, a larger formal tactic is also at work: by bringing the guru to the centre, the film seeks to smuggle in some clandestine material from the margins of the text. Interestingly, the guru has many elements in common with King Lear, but he falls on bad times not because of his vanity; others in society are responsible for the downfall of this estimable individual. The pathos generated by the fall of the guru is used to hide fears about the nature of romantic love and its impact on filial loyalty on which the institution of the traditional family is built. Therefore the major crises occur in areas other than the fall of gurudom. In any case, in the end the fallen guru is restored to his formal glory, at least notionally, by one of his former students. An ordinary schoolteacher is made iconic.

Panthulu places the importance of gurudom in a larger web of relationships and value systems. The real authority of the guru is seen together with other equally vital ideals of the joint family: filial loyalty and the intense idealism entailed in building a nation. Death and disease in any of these realms also signal danger for the rest. Only a liberal *gruhastha* can weave these dangers organically together: Panthulu does not fit the bill with perfect ease; tensions mark the form of the film throughout. Here too the limits of Panthulu's sensibility surface naively, somewhat marring the otherwise ideational maturity of the form: while the degeneration of other institutions comes from within, the forces that threaten gurudom come from the outside. Here too the formal logic of the popular film has played an important role in so shaping the director: it is quite difficult to lyrically narrate the tale of a hero who becomes internally corrupt and causes his own downfall. The central feature of the popular melodrama is its unassailable strategy of placing the incorruptible hero in the context of hostile and degenerate external forces. In the midst of the raging storms of change the hero stands alone in his unrelenting posture, evoking both admiration and fear for the lunacy of history which brought these forces into being.

Panthulu does not look at romantic love with any intolerance, for such distrust would have undercut the director's ability to maximize the use of the cinematic language of song and dance of the popular cinema. The form of the popular cinema, which was in its formative stage in these decades, had in-built romantic scenes of love. Not all that surprisingly, even in those mythological and devotional films, love scenes appeared regularly, defying logical consistency in the development of the story. Heroes before taking to renunciation were given every opportunity to indulge in erotic pleasures, as this was a necessity not so much for the protagonist but for the public. In other words, the popular film released a new form of social energy called romantic love. India as a nation lived that experience as no other society did; it was and is obsessed with love in fantasy rather than, as in the West, in reality. *School Master* seeks to understand this craving which has made the nation in its cinema halls. It is not patriotism that has made India into a nation but the tree-hopping lovers of its films. *School Master* understood this need for love and has presented the public with a couple of delightful songs of love, which are far from being songs of innocence.

The song '*Radha Madhava vinoda hasa yaru mareyada prema vilasa*' (One cannot forget the love of Radha and Madhava) soon, and quite expectedly, became a hit with Kannadigas. Structurally, however, Panthulu constructed the story in such a way as to suggest that the birth of romantic love had led to the weakening of familial loyalties.

POWERS OF THE FORM AND THE WILL TO DISSENT

At this stage of the discussion, a discussion on the imperatives of the form of the popular cinema becomes inevitable. In the case of Panthulu, the sociology of the form of cinema is in direct conflict with the sensibility of the film-maker who has his moorings in the values of a different world. It can be safely said that the cinema in India became extremely important for its enthusiastic portrayal of the values of romantic love and its muffled scream against tradition. This was an excessive statement of desire set against the forms of morality of an old order. The so-called irrationality of the form, with its a-realist use of songs and dance, in the popular cinema is an assertion of the historically rebellious against the over-rigid values of a society in the areas of gender and caste segregation. Songs and dance are the logical expression of a different notion of morality: they are the ultimate expression of transgression.

To put it differently, transgression is an essential component of the popular cinema; it alone brings popular cinema into being.[5] Whatever might be the self-definition of the popular cinema in India, it came into being only as a rebel form, notwithstanding its often professed commitment to conservatism. The cinema, right from the outset, has played a major role as an extreme modernizer. The popular film has certain historically 'progressive' elements built into it. In this sense, there cannot be any backward-looking commercial films: even in the overtly conservative films made on themes such as superstition and religious miracles, there is virtually always a modern angle to them. The technology of the genre is never neutral and it yields only to a stiff resistance on the part of the most intransigent traditionalists. The near-idyllic locations for picturization of love songs offer a statement against tradition where spaces are symbolically ordered. Only modernity makes use of the out-of-bound spaces to indicate or suggest a non-spiritual mode. The parks, trees, hills, rivers are used in a secular cause, whereas in pre-modern art forms such symbolic spaces were the exclusive prerogative of divine lovers. The familiar figures of Radha–Krishna are unconsciously evoked by the visual language, but it is important to note that this *parakiya* or foreign mode of love was a source of irritation for conservatives in Hindu cultural memories. Here the modernist meta-language of the cinema utilizes cultural memory against tradition.

To return to Raj Kapoor, it is self-evident, for the reasons cited earlier, that he had no such problems in taking sides in a battle against tradition. Apart from the tree-jumping hero and the heroine, all the other characters in the story are insignificant. The traditionalists, those opposed to love, are washed away in the magical flood of song and dance; it is the vibrant lyricality of the victor. (Because of its confidence in the victory of the historical forces of modernity over other life-styles, the form can even afford the luxury of interchanging the joy of the victor with temporary defeat.) The fear of the old and defeat can substitute for jubilant celebration: the interchangeability of these two divergent experiences constitutes the hallmark of the Raj Kapoor brand of popular cinema. Panthulu cannot be so confident of himself, for his view of change might be acceptable to a large section of the public but the form would stiffly resist it. If he were a novelist, it would have been possible for him to write a work from the perspective of the forgotten father. At this historical juncture, the novel can comfortably nurse a rebel writer in its interstices, one who is out of sync with the formal requirements of the genre. Art forms gradually give up their dogmatic clinging to their original meanings, and are gradually separated from the semantic places of their birth and achieve autonomy. However, during the period we are discussing, that is the 1950s and 1960s, Panthulu was compelled to negotiate with the internal pressures of the form of the popular cinema, and could not but realize that they also exercised pressure on meaning. Can one possibly tell the story of an old schoolteacher who is neglected by his own children in an entertaining way? The film being the genre of an epoch which is in constant search for limitless joy and desire, a search unleashed by the phase of modernity in history, Panthulu decides not to directly attack the institution of romantic love. Romantic love is the lifeline of the form he is working with. Instead he sees it as the growth of selfishness in the personality of young lovers.

Lovers, for Raj Kapoor, have a surreal intensity about them. Panthulu makes them just acceptable as a structural necessity. In other words, within Panthulu there is a tension between the primary language of the *vachya*, the literal meaning of the cinematic image, and the *vyangya*, the implied meaning of the perspective from which the film is built. The enthusiasm of the image is checked by the scepticism of the episteme, and, precisely because of that the public of that generation do not recall *School Master* for its portrayal of romantic love. For them it is a tale of the fracturing of a family; the public too assumes a sense of guilt. The eloquent Panthulu maintains an enigmatic silence about the causes of this disintegration.

FORMAL PAMPERING OF THE MODERN AND A BALANCING OF OPPOSITES

Panthulu's silence is basically about the kind of privileging that the historically 'progressive' enjoys with the form. We should consider this silence as part of the larger debate about the relationship between world-views and art forms in their moments of historical origin. For instance, the novel has a great many difficulties in accommodating pre-modern experience in its internal space: a problem that acquires many interesting dimensions vis-à-vis the cosmologies of castes.[6]

It is possible to entertain a question of a purely hypothetical nature about the options that were available to the director at the moment of the film's making. Was it possible to project the schoolmaster as a slightly perverted and outlandish man? The answer would have to be in the negative, for that goes against the very grain of the popular cinema. Beyond a point, the Indian public is wary of approving a simple-minded opposition to the family old guard. Even Raj Kapoor would not do it. This points to the existence of a very interesting structure in the popular cinema: the balance of opposites, and one need not construe it as any necessary opportunism on the part of the form. It presupposes a far more mature understanding of the nature of conflict in human life and history. The notion of irreconcilable opposites is not at all acceptable to the public in India, and this has forced the film form to conform to their likes and dislikes. The form has its own internal compulsions, a legacy of the historical moment of its birth, but it also has to be responsive to the needs of the community.

The notion of a merger of opposites is so central to the form of the popular cinema that even divergent film-makers such as Raj Kapoor and Panthulu can only offer variations on it, which of course defines their individuality without breaking the basic structure. Even the formal requirements of the classical epic with their insistence on *ashtadasha varnana*, the eighteen themes of description, appear more generous with deviance than the popular cinema. Even the partisan posture that an artist tends to strike is well within the control of the form, which supposes an equilibrium of emotions. It is allowed to bend the rules of the form within permissible limits; no film-maker, however bold s/he is, can behave like God. It is the form that is God and all else, including even the most arrogant, can only be His instrument. S/he who breaks these laws will end up as an 'art' film-maker, forever banished from the community of popular films.

STRATEGY OF INTERNAL TRANSLATION: THE TIGER IS ONLY A CAT

This raises the question of the limited choices available to an artist when s/he is working with the popular form in the cinema. To make such limited choices more creative, the most talented among them resort to an interesting strategy: I would define this as the strategy of internal translation. Genuine works of art are created within this mass of run-of-the-mill commercial cinema by such internal translation. For instance, in *Bobby* (1973), Raj Kapoor had to translate the cruelty of tradition as the heartlessness of a particular family. Similarly, Panthulu translates the disappearance of the notion of filial loyalty, a by-product of the birth of romantic love, as a form of private selfishness on the part of the individuals involved. Only by such internal translations are both the individual identity of the film-maker and the collective structure of the popular film preserved. Only if the intolerance of the casteist traditional society is presented as the heartlessness of a particular family will the film-maker have a case to denounce parental authority. However, in the process the narrative viewpoint of the film also becomes a trifle too jaded and ideological to be able to understand the positions of the family; the negative capability disappears.

To take the discussion on this process of internal translation further, it depicts the characteristics of historical change and institutional behaviour with all their rigid codes, as the particular behavioural patterns of individuals. Internal translation fights any kind of typology that makes history paramount; it even offers to translate history as nature. For instance, the question of class in Raj Kapoor's films is an interesting subject to explore. The callousness of the rich is quite a favourite area for emotional scenes in Raj Kapoor's films but he never presents such callousness as the essential quality of the rich. Being rich is a matter of ostentatious life-style and conspicuous consumption, attractive material for the cameraman who can create an ambience that evokes both jealousy and admiration on the part of the audience. It is true that the physiognomy of social characters in Raj Kapoor's films bases itself on a certain kind of essentialism in the variety of human nature, and the idea of presenting a class character with inerasable qualities would not have met with his approval. It can be too dangerously close to the Marxist typology, even though of a vulgar kind.

Internal translation is also a mechanism for exploring, if not of resolving, some unstated fears about the logical conclusions of the method that the narrative is employing to delineate the given theme in the context of social change. It gives enough formal place for a dark interplay of uncertainties about the nature of history and social change. This becomes evident when Panthulu attempts to translate and transcend his own fear about the consequences of the birth of romantic love as the inborn selfishness of a few beings; but he also indirectly conveys to the public his worst fears about love, which creates many subtexts in the film. In his heart of hearts, the schoolteacher knows that the change is real and his children may never return to him and his wife. He refuses to face the truth because he feels his wife will be unable to confront it. Ironically too, his wife suspects this to be true about her husband.

The unconventional social, or to be precise, sexual, mores of the leading characters are translated by the popular cinema as a mythical re-enactment of a holy ritual. Unmarried boys and girls cannot be seen together making love in a lonely forest guest-house in the dead of a winter night—let us recall the famous scene of the Hindi film *Aradhana*—but the couple is made to walk around the fire: here the imaginative attempt is to legitimize the unacceptable. The bonfires of desire have to be translated as the sacred fire of a vedic wedding, and Rajesh Khanna and Sharmila Tagore simulate the *saptapadi*, the seven steps of a marriage ritual. The ancient ritual of *gandharva vivaha* is repeatedly invoked. Similarly, underworld goons are translated as mythical *asuras* or demons. Only recently have they begun to be presented as neighbourhood boys in league with the nasty politician.

Let us now return to *School Master*. As the film slowly unravels its story, a tale of total disintegration envelops the spectator. All his beliefs die a tragic death: the ideal of the building, the reality of familial loyalty, and the sacred bond between parents and children all gradually collapse. The schoolteacher, hero of the film, can scarcely digest the interconnectedness of these epochal changes in the lives of the men and women around him and their organic link with history, whose sole quality is to roll ruthlessly onwards. Panthulu is however certain that the schoolteacher is bound to evoke sympathy from the public in whom the echo of the values of the old world is yet to fade, but he also avoids overstating his case for the forgotten parent. In other words, the form of internal translation allows a free play of all the unresolved tensions of the narrative: a twilight zone of half-perceived truths, half-digested realities, and reluctantly acknowledged changes is created.

The idea of an unalterable human essence is at the core of the strategy of internal translation, and the ideal of the eventual triumph of human goodness informs its mood, which is optimistic. The melodrama operates on the basis of the playful interaction between pessimism of the mind and optimism of the will. This formal strategy of internal translation qualitatively differentiates the good ones from others which too deal with more or less identical themes.

Many Kannada films have dealt with the subject of the disappearance of the base values of pre-modern society such as the joint family and filial loyalty. There are dozens of such works, but one can cite, for instance, two well-known films of the 1960s—*Kulavadhu* (1963), which had the theme of an intolerant traditional family and *Chandavalliya Thota* (1964), which dealt with the death of the joint family. The presence of the process of internal translation makes a film a 'multidimensional melodrama' and its absence makes it unidimensional.

The multidimensional melodrama has many significant characteristics in common with its counterpart in the West, though the cultural pressures of the indigenous community have brought about many significant changes in its form. Therefore, the original melodrama is virtually unrecognizable in the Indian milieu. The necessity for internal translation arises from the overdetermination of a whole range of factors, some of which have been discussed earlier. This strategy has a striking similarity with a common folk practice. The folk taboo on naming the evil rests on a technique closer to the construction of a simile. It creates many subtexts within the master text, which reflects a much deeper anxiety of naming a thing directly. The act of naming makes the subject vulnerable to the attack of what is being avoided. In the villages of Karnataka, the folk practice is not to call a snake a snake; it is referred to as a worm. The candle is not just extinguished, it is 'increased'. Human beings do not die; they are made over to the Lord above. Tigers become cats. A belief creates its own aesthetic strategy, and each reinforces the other.

This strategy is in striking contrast to the psychological mechanism discussed by Freud in his *Beyond the Pleasure Principle*, where the mind returns to a dark and tragic experience only to achieve mastery over it. The intensity of the original experience is re-lived. The folk method is to reduce the stature of the undesirable presence through a particular way of describing it. That mode of description is an attempt to metaphorically control reality. In this scheme of things, metaphorical control is everything. When a snake is translated as a worm, it fuses a belief with a way of metaphor-making. Though it is difficult to chart the passage of this technique to the form of the Indian popular film, it can be certainly traced to the forging of this genre by freely borrowing from indigenous theatre traditions. The founding parents of Kannada popular cinema were men and women from theatre, who had learnt a great deal from the folk merger of belief and metaphor. This mode of naming something differently has become more sophisticated by immersing itself in the meta-strategy of internal translation.

The mono-dimensional melodrama does not translate its tensions internally; simple endorsement or opposition to a particular type of meaning constitutes its form. The emotions of *shoka* (sorrow) and *karuna* (pathos) overwhelm the public and high mimetic acting of the variety perfected by the Tamil thespian Shivaji Ganeshan has provided the necessary model of acting for all others in the south to emulate. The Kannada film *Chandavalliya Thota* (1964) is no exception to this.

The central strength of *School Master* is its conviction that our society has fallen on bad times. This is worth mourning in grand fashion, and the cinematic form attempts to reactivate the will to build a nation. The theme of 'great disintegration' is grand enough to inspire seafarers to undertake a difficult journey on the ship of melodrama and melancholy. It has also recognized the fact that a change in the public sphere will have its own reverberations in the private sphere; the contrary is equally true. The recognition of this merger of horizons has contributed to the evolution of the popular cinema as the most authentic genre of public art in India. It abolishes the boundaries between the private and the public by interiorizing the former and by transforming it into an individualized experience. The politics of Kashmir is reborn in the shape of *Roja*.

CODA

To put back the grand narrative of Kannada cinema on its tracks, I suggest that in its phase of romantic idealism, four master themes—nation-building in its minimalist modes, the birth of romantic love and the consequent disappearance of the joint family, Kannada nationalism, and the celebration of the bhakti model of religious life—were the basic ingredients of all the popular films.

The popular film was a product of the consensus that was emerging in the make-up of the spectator, and it was based on these four themes. In these areas, over the next three decades, the form of the popular film further divided itself to give birth, with an astonishing self-reflexivity, to a new genre of comedies that mocked the death of those values that had created such wonderful works of art. The consensus that had served as the bedrock of creativity also suffered a fracture which cannot be easily repaired.

The 1980s saw the beginning in films of self-mockery of the public sphere. Religious practices of being were savagely satirized by comedians, and their comic disrobing was all the more powerful as its targets were powerful godmen like the Saibaba of Puttaparti. Religious authority was no longer sacred or feared, and nation-building itself became a euphemism for self-serving actions. The monolithic form of the popular cinema was split into several sub-genres; some conformed to the basic rules of the original game, some transgressed, and some doubly so. The spectator had matured sufficiently as a community to receive modes of comedic representation of the degeneration of several of its cherished authoritative values. The dissolution of the authority of romantic love was one such extremely entertaining theme. Thus began the era of new comedies not only in Kannada but also in other south Indian languages.

PART II
THE BIRTH OF THE ACTOR–GOD AND THE NEW COMEDY

The genre of full-length comedy did not exist in Kannada till the 1980s. The reason for its absence is not hard to explain. The form of the popular film itself was seen to be complete as it had all the *navarasa*s. Both *sringara* (erotic) and *hasya* (humorous) were integral, almost fatally linked to the form of the popular film. The humorous parts were either a comedy of manners or a situational comedy; usually it was a judicious blend of the two. Sometimes the comic scenes were quite crude and amounted to virtual slapstick. In social films, comic scenes were either events caricaturing the ultra urban or the Western from the point of view of the villager. The innocent manners of the villagers were also the butt of many jokes. Both were readily available for the making of comedy. A very fashionable and trendy girl from the city making fun of an innocent village lad and subsequently falling in love with him later was the standard fare. The village bumpkin, too, had sufficient scope to reciprocate when he arrived in the slightly absurd city. On the whole, however, the city was generally held as being evil and the village was portrayed as representative of innocent virtue. In such stories, hypocrisy and moral innocence met each other and the ensuing comedy was not free of judgemental laughter. Even when full-length comedies appeared in the 1970s, it was humour carved out of eros. Raj Kumar's *Lagna Patrike* (1967) in Kannada is the best example of this variety.

Satires are an altogether different matter and a specific, dogmatic position on major issues in history is essential to produce it. Only arch conservatives, or radicals, or utterly dismissive cynics can create effective satires. Also, new satires or new comedies need a selective split in the community of the public spectator. They also represent the breakdown of the larger consensus that had produced master narratives of the bygone era of romantic love and nation-building idealism.

The 1980s saw many films that cannot be described as comedies though they had famous comic actors in leading roles: Dwarakish was one such enterprising man. There was change only in the profile of the hero: instead of a handsome face there was a comic person in the lead. The structure remained more or less the same with greater emphasis on the prankish acts of the hero. The journey from the sublime to the farcical had to pass through the ridiculous parading as the heroic. Kannada cinema, quite inevitably, had also to pass through this intermediate phase. Once a new genre was born in the space of cinema, it established for itself the right to coexist with other older or yet to be born genres.

Since the 1970s, south Indian cinema has slowly but steadily developed the cult of the actor–god phenomenon.[7] It was a deliberate attempt, at one level, to wipe out the crucial distinction between art and reality, and at the other, cinema-generated myth and history. A semi-planned and semi-spontaneous plan was adopted by the super-heroes of the south—Raj Kumar in Kannada, M.G. Ramachandran (MGR) in Tamil and N.T. Rama Rao (NTR) in Telugu—to adopt mythical roles on a major scale. Myth-making had reached unbelievable proportions and it would inevitably reach the public. Myth had reached such excessive heights that it had to become real or try to envelop the real. M.S.S. Pandian has described this phenomenon in his interesting study as the 'image trap', a description that only partially explains it.[8] In the case of MGR, it was an attempt to fuse different dimensions of an individual's existence; the real persona of the actor was emptied to transmit totally surreal and iconic codes.

The hero was transformed into an icon and politics became an exercise in mythifying the present. In contrast to this, Raj Kumar's iconicity was differently effected; here the project was to build him into a super-ethical hero. Smoking, drinking, and other vices were taboo in his films. In this sense, the iconicity of the triad of superstars in three languages of the south took three distinct directions: Raj Kumar, the moral model; MGR, the political demi-god; and NTR, the religious hero. The third had a vast repertoire of mythological films in which he had played the role of Krishna, who appeared on earth to redeem the people. I am not suggesting that it was only these films that brought NTR to power; I am just linking these to the project of presenting him as an *avatara* of the present times in the Telugu country. Similarly, MGR answered the deep need of historical myth-making at the core of modern Tamil consciousness.[9]

This was the genesis of the political role of the superstars of south Indian cinema.

Already by the early 1970s, the archetypal hero of the Indian cinema had to dissolve himself, as he had gone beyond all limits of normalcy and idealism. Heroes of other kinds were to be born. In the Hindi cinema, he took the shape of an angry young man, superbly personified in the emergence of Amitabh Bachchan, where exaggerated clowning and anger were the principal characteristics of the leading role.

The new comedy was the most effective way of subverting the process of iconicity that had eradicated the distinction between the cinema-goer and the political being in the eyes of the spectator. One answer of the popular cinema to the phenomenon of the 'great disintegration' was to bring the hero out of the cinema hall to history. The idealist cinema of the 1950s and the 1960s depicted a great many imperfections, including many charming infirmities of the hero. He too was human notwithstanding his larger-than-life virtues. Doing away with the hero's infirmities for the consumption of the spectators was an effort to make the latter passive and surrender their political initiatives to the superhero.

It had to become an internal problem of the form: the new comedy became self-reflexive about the grand themes that commercial cinema had explored in the 1950s. This was because, in the mind of the spectator, the new comedy assumed that he was both wary and tired of the will to build a nation in public life. Perhaps starry-eyed idealism had become an utter impossibility and a cynical view of things could provide a new beginning. Whatever the reason, the self-reflexive mode of the Indian cinema at once became a mirror to the spectator as well as a critique of its own formal history. The new comedy was born under the intelligent yet deeply cynical conviction that nothing rotted sooner than styles of cinema-making.

Not all the new comedies have this quality of self-reflexivity in them; on the contrary, it is their apparent innocence on this question that has differentiated them from mere spoofs. Self-reflexivity is a knife that can cut both ways in the history of art forms. The difference between spoofs and comedy is that the spoofs, because of their self-reflexivity, blunt the edges by sacrificing both passion and simplicity.

As a classic example of a spoof, one can take M.S. Sathyu's *Chitegu Chinte* (1978) in Kannada which sought to make use of the aesthetic technique of trivializing its targets at all levels, including the history of the cinema. Every frame of this film revelled in the self-reflexive mode, weaving in satirical modes of history, past and present. The film seeks to demolish all forms of representations in democratic politics and the popular cinema, thus assuming a judgemental tone that is dismissive of all forms of populism. Not all that strangely, the film equated democratic politics of the mass variety with the film form which has the mass spectator as its constituency.

If intellectual arrogance of a vague leftist persuasion were to choose a form for its self-expression, then, surely, the spoof would be the most favourite candidate. From the very outset, this genre denies the spoof-maker the structural elements of the popular film. The re-imagination of the great or important moments of public or cinema life is from the perspective of contempt. New comedy depends on a code of intimacy with what is being comically interrogated, a position which the spoof cannot assume. The spectator is expected to reconstitute the entire image by re-translating it into the original: the artistic principle of the double is taken to an absurd extreme. The mimicry itself becomes the prisoner of the thing that is being sought to be demolished. Sathyu aims at ridiculing Jayaprakash Narayan, MGR, and a whole range of events and men, but in his very intensity he tags along with them. Nothing subordinates like obsessive spoofing in the film form; it is Prometheus bound all the way.

CROWS IN THE BEDROOM: *SCHOOL MASTER* TURNED UPSIDE DOWN—*GAURIGANESHA*

When melodrama turns upside down, farce is born. This statement is fully applicable to *Gauriganesha* (1989), a farce that turns *School Master* on its head. What was mourned as the death of the bond of love between children and parents from the perspective of the latter came to be repeated as a farce related with cynical laughter. Here it is the father who abdicates the responsibility for his child. *Gauriganesha* portrays the death of romantic love, a deadly sin committed by the forward youth of the present times.

A detailed synopsis of *Gauriganesha*, directed by Phani Ramachandra, a well-known director of comedies in Kannada, will lay bare the mechanism of this dual collapse. I do not wish to delve into the question of the 'origin' of the story of *Gauriganesha* because the question of 'originality' is not crucial to this discussion, though the wholesale lifting of plots from one language into another is quite common in the Indian film world. They even have an interesting word, 'remake', for this.

Lambodara, an unemployed youth, is the leading man of the film who has all the charming traits of a confidence-trickster. He is witty, handsome, and, yes, a good samaritan. He lives in a lower-middle class *chawl* and never has enough money to pay his rent regularly. That he is forced to live the life of a con-artist has not diminished his love of life; on the contrary, it has only enhanced his resourcefulness. Visiting state hospitals to ensure a free bed and breakfast has become a matter of routine with him. Such a life has provided him with a beautiful nurse as a girlfriend. The important thing is that, defying the expectations of the spectator, the con-hero and his heroine have no romantic love songs picturized on them. They do not have a love life worth depicting. Such an absence of a love life even for the hero is quite central to the meaning of the film. The film spends the first forty minutes trying to establish the totally amoral nature of the leading man, but he is invariably treated with warmth and affection. Lambodara's role is brilliantly played by Ananth Nag, who incidentally is famous for his love films. The film seeks to exploit the cinematic past of the hero because the public expects its favourite hero to engage in erotica, but he ducks it. The narrative viewpoint of the film refuses to judge the hero in moral terms, for later in the plot he will hold up a moral mirror to other important people.

In one of Lambodara's stays at a government hospital, before being ejected from it, he chances upon the personal diary of a young girl who has died of a heart attack. As she was an orphan, Lambodara pretends to be her brother and clears away all her personal effects which include her journal. An almost unbelievable autobiographical story emerges from the pages of the girl's diary, and Lambodara himself is a little shocked to read it. She has provided gory details of the men who had crossed her path in life. Various men, rich and influential, including her former lecherous boss, appear just as they really were. A couple of them are under the impression that they have slept with Gauri, a myth which Lambodara will later use with deadly ingenuity. Actually, it was one of Gauri's pleasure-loving friends who had substituted for her under the cover of darkness. The most crucial episode of the plot comes much later in the form of a marriage of convenience suggested to Gauri by a young man who wanted to escape the matchmaking designs of his parents. A pseudo-wedding is arranged but the 'bridegroom' is made to leave in the middle of the whole farcical show. On that fateful night, the friend who usually doubled up for Gauri, sleeps in the bridal chamber, in a desire to enjoy the comforts of a five star hotel. A friend of the 'bridegroom' forces himself, in a drunken stupor, on the girl and sleeps with her. The bridegroom is killed in an airplane accident; his friend suffers a deep sense of guilt about his drunken debauchery, for he is under the illusion that he had slept with Gauri. Only the two girls know the secret about what had actually occurred during that murky night.

Lambodara decides to continue the story. It is so filmy, he mutters to himself, that it deserves a talented man like Phani Ramachandra, who is in fact the director of *Gauriganesha* (the film). Here for the first time, the self-reflexive motif enters the film and stays throughout it at a discreet level.

Lambodara writes to three people: Gauri's former boss, now in the US; Anand, who had sex with the bride who is also away in Calcutta; and lastly, to the parents of the fake bridegroom, who has died in an air crash. The contents of the letter are moving: Gauri has given birth to a child and has died, thus forcing her poor brother to raise the parentless kid. He has conjured up two fathers and a guardian family for a phantom child, such was Lambodara's criminal genius. Can they come and take the child? Obviously, he has convinced all the three that the male child belongs to them alone. They are made to own up the guilt but they cannot raise the child. Would Lambodara be gracious enough to raise the child himself, and for this money would be no problem whatsoever. The money-extortion machine swings into action and Lambodara milks them happily every month for the maintenance of the non-existent child. So far so good.

The real trouble for Lambodara begins when the two fathers and the grandparents decide to descend on Bangalore to visit the child. That all the three visits take place simultaneously is sheer coincidence, a factor to which we shall turn later. Lambodara is not one to be scared of such a calamity; he manages to bring home an over-smart little boy, Ganesha, from one of the orphanages in the city. The first encounter between Ganesha and Lambodara is both interesting and hilarious, as the self-reflexive mode caricaturing Indian film history comes to the fore. Ganesha has been a great film buff. His every move and dialogue reek of film history, thus providing the viewer with a great deal of mirth. All the melodramatic moments of reunion between the father and the child are converted into amusing, farcical scenes because of the self-reflexivity of the form. Ganesha even asks Lambodara: 'How should I do it? In slow motion? In fast moving style?', thus taking away any traces of real emotion from the plot.

Finally the secret is out much to Lambodara's embarrassment and chagrin, but he is not one to accept defeat easily. He turns against them all and challenges each one on his hypocrisy and threatens them with exposure. They quietly disappear from the scene after having been in the dock of Lambodara's court of cynical and ruthless morality, begging him to leave them in peace. After the farce is over, Ganesha sets out to return to his original home, the orphanage, only to be stopped by the tearful Lambodara; he adopts him as a son. Only in the end is a positive portrayal of a new kind of filial bond stressed, thus retaining a firm place in the spectrum of the popular film.

The film works on some of the major themes that go into the making of the moral–psychological life of the film spectator. Lambodara feels only some sense of shame, but others are forced to really experience guilt; the conflict between shame and guilt provides the film with a perspective to balance the lapses in morality, both of Lambodara and the fictitious parents. The authority of values such as romantic love, family bond, and sexual morality of the middle-classes are all stripped bare with barbed satire.

The structure of *Gauriganesha* illuminates the internal link that exists between melodrama and farce: the mode of repetition has a central place in the farcical subversion of tear-jerker structures. In a melodrama, the technique of repetition is born as an internal necessity of the emotional lives of the leading roles: for instance, in Raj Kapoor's *Mera Naam Joker* (1970), repetitions of the scenes of the clown being let down by women and sentimentality submerge the structural aspect and make it invisible. In a farce it becomes a sheer necessity of the plot: each emotional encounter has to be repeated three times, as Ganesha has two fathers and grandparents in addition. After a while, the spectator forgets the deliberate quality of the plot and enjoys the episodes for their own sake. The structural nature of comic descendence becomes quite apparent here; each element of the plot ought to reach its ultimate excess. The plot unfolds itself at such a comically furious pace that the fated accident becomes essential at the end. The spectator too waits for the explosion of the climax. In a farce, the public craves for the final crisis, in a melodrama they are desperate to avoid it. *Gauriganesha* does not adopt the detective technique of bringing any new material to judge the people it is focusing on; nor is it interested in portraying them as unusual people. It takes the position that these are ordinary men and their ordinariness goes against them.

The film focuses on the 'harmonious' nature of the men in the dock; compromise is not their second nature but their first. They can even afford the luxury of wallowing in guilt when it assumes the comforting form of harmless affection for a child. They can use the latter to house the guilt without allowing the eruption of any major crisis to dislocate their lives. Their career is the first and the foremost priority in their lives, and they can sacrifice anything for it including ethical responsibility for their own acts of commission and omission. Lambodara has no career to build and therefore appears more authentic than all of them put together. This ethical point of view makes use of the split between the craving for upward mobility and the values of caring and familial authority. The fathers come to their own arenas of parental responsibility as tourists; the depth of their pleasure is matched by the degree of their concern. The film seems to argue that their capacity to plumb the depths of love is severely limited by such callous indifference towards adherence to certain basic values. The absence of romantic love is translated as a crippling inability to enjoy the pleasures of life.

In the scenes of the encounter between Lambodara and the putative relations, the basic flaw and lack of strength in their characters is further underlined. The con-artist has no remorse about his unethical stratagems and, ironically, his detractors, too, cannot muster sufficient anger to shake him up. Clearly, the film supposes, and rightly so, that the sympathies of the public will lie with Lambodara, not with his victims. *Gauriganesha*, at the level of motifs, works to subvert those of the *School Master*, but retains the same characteristic of not directly referring to the phenomenon of the disappearance of romantic love and its consequent impact on the youth.

What works as a matter of emotional truths in the melodrama is transformed by the intricacies of the plot. The over-complicated story line usually conceals the rawness and directness of the subject-matter at hand; it indicates life overwhelming aesthetic text, not its absence. Against this background, it should be noticed that *Gauriganesha* rests its fragile plot on a series of improbabilities; any logical examination of the story is self-defeating. The mode of comic transcendence has become a reality precisely because of the constant negotiations between the improbable and the plausible in the plot. This requires further discussion because it is crucial for a recognition of the codes by the spectator. In melodramas such as *School Master* such codes work on the very surface because the plot grows on the strength of the entirely possible and real.

Gauriganesha is possible only in the context of a cinema tradition; it represents comic reversal of both the meaning and the structure of the popular melodrama. Such fusion is organic to generate its meaning, for it assumes that the spectator lives his or her life only in films. The spectator was earlier fed on the rich diet of romantic love, but in these times of historical change, that cherished love of the upward mobile classes has suffered a fatal blow. It has suffered a comical death.

The mode of noble melancholy, employed during the exploration of the 'great disintegration', seeks to woo the public in order to move them to witness the tragic collapse of the authority of certain values.

That the farcical mode leans to a great extent only on the melodramatic mode but stays away from any kind of inter-textual relation with the epic or mythological tradition of Indian films points further to its exclusive rootedness in the structure which it mocks. Ridicule is a form of greater attachment in the history of the cinema. To use a category from Bharata's *Natya Shastra*, the *bija* or the seed of the comic farce is placed in the melodrama, but the two take divergent routes to explore the same idea. Fantasy, which has assumed the form of coincidence of the plot, here plays a more interesting role than it does in fantasy films per se.

Coincidence is quite a common property of comedy; comic situations born of disharmony have also been quite common in its history. Comedy is, essentially, a state of disharmony. The excessive use of the technique of coincidence creates a formal state where there exists no dividing line between itself and fantasy. According to Western theory, fantasy represents the 'privileged viewpoint'; in comic inversions of melodrama, too, it presents the same as far as its physiognomical attitudes towards its characters are concerned. In *Gauriganesha*, however, the coincidence is elevated to the status of the 'original sin', from which all subsequent events follow, the sin being the callous attitude towards both romantic love and marriage. The basic ethical core of the film expects that at least one of these two should be respected.

FANTASY AS THE META-LANGUAGE OF THE CAMERA AND THE AMUSED PUBLIC

Indian cinema offers other comic visions too that are not committed to the authority of either romantic value or marriage. Balachander's famous film *Manmatha Leelai* (1976) offers itself as a vital contrast to *Gauriganesha*, though the former also deals with the theme of the moral collapse of marriage. The hero is a handsome man, elegantly played by Kamala Hasan, who is a saree-chaser; his charming clumsiness enhances his attractiveness to women. Usually, when 'serious' films explore the theme of the collapse of the institution of marriage, a third man or woman is brought to the fore to explain the crisis. The burden of wedlock is so heavy that it requires three to carry it. In this case, there is not one woman but literally scores of them constantly threatening the marriage. Even today, the mainstream popular cinema is yet to accept the reality of separation or divorce; a romantic aura is built around such stories, which generally deal with temporary separation, and finally the two are united to save the marriage. *Manmatha Leelai* has no use for these façades; according to it, marriages are romantically made only in films, and are therefore equally vulnerable to collapse under the attack of Manmatha, the Indian god of sex. *Manmatha* observes no boundaries in marriages; in fact, the common understanding that informs both the films is that sex is more real than romantic love.

The meta-language of Balachander's film works in cartoon-like images; what can appear to be cinematic gimmicks, are quite central to the meaning of the film. The hero is caught literally with his pants down in many of his escapades, and the camera causes him to whine like a puppy. He hops around like a dwarf. The directorial attitude, too, in *Gauriganesha*, treats the hero with some indulgence laced with a slight disdain but is basically one of affectionate banter. Here fantasy is translated as the commentary by the camera; the director makes imaginative use of both camerawork and editing.[10] The judgemental tone operates in *Gauriganesha* at the level of the plot; in *Manmatha Leelai* it makes fun of the man for his beguiling weaknesses. The collapse of marriage and the lack of fidelity in it are presented as the *leela*, play of Cupid; the tone of mourning is absent. *Gauriganesha* is more ideological and rooted in old world values than the Tamil comedy; for Balachander, the behaviour of his hero constitutes only a lapse, but for Phani Ramachandra it is 'guilt' over the abandonment of certain sacred values in the milieu of the family. This accounts for the absence of palpable tension in the narrative tone of the Tamil film, and also for its excessive presence in the last scenes of the Kannada work. Titillating touches to the narrative of the former make it more attractive for a sex-hungry public. The concern of the conservative over the collapse of the institutions of love and marriage has led to the making of a farce in Kannada, while in Tamil a more liberal and modern outlook regarding these has given birth to a comedy.

THE GREAT DISINTEGRATION AND AMBIVALENCE TOWARDS THE PUBLIC SPECTATOR

The films that we have so far discussed are characterized by a marked ambivalence towards the spectator. In fact, the chief characteristic of the popular film in India is that it is shaped by a suspicion that the viewer might harbour values different from the primary *vachya*—literal meaning—that it is attempting to present. Transgression of the given, it is feared, might be the actual preference of the public when choosing among the limited choices available in the area of social change. The public themselves are internally divided and have multiple ethical and aesthetic choices: this aspect has driven the ambitious film-maker to split one spectator into two halves. One part, the *vachya*, caters to the assumed monolithic public and says certain things that have a greater prospect of finding acceptance in the loudest possible way, and the other, the *vyangya*, engages itself in a clandestine form of communication with the public. The *vachya*, or literal meaning, is always for public consumption; by contrast, the *vyangya*, or implied meaning, is for the initiate, and the two are intertwined with each other in vying for the viewer's attention. The Indian film public has a multiplicity of masks; an arch conservative in the domestic arena in matters of private morality and family values might prove to be a passionate radical in the cinema hall endorsing the collapse of the same tradition.

Generally, the practice of film theorists in India is to assume a well-integrated public spectator, in whom there exists a unity in matters relating to the private and public domains. This means the rejection of the film experience as a special realm. This essay argues that there exists a film spectator who is radically different from the public, although the two persona are continually interacting with each other: the film buff is being continually wooed by the *vachya* text of the form. The popular film assumes that its *rasika*, or connoisseur, is always prepared for transgression; otherwise the variety that one sees in the Indian cinema cannot be explained. The notion of consensus moves the film-maker to believe that the *rasika* is prepared to accept anything or every thing; consensus also entails the merger of opposites as they are conceived of together by the public and the popular film: politics versus humanism, harmony and conflict, love and hate.

The creation of the subtext lies in the popular film's effort to look for a hidden partisan who is prepared to take sides provided the statement of the problem is also defined discreetly; it is akin to a clandestine visit to a brothel by a conservative middle-class man. The partisan takes the form of transitory emotions and meanings and the constant is always the sea of the consensus: the traditional Indian poetic notions of *sthayi* and *sanchari* are more apposite in describing this process. The notion of consensus is problematic in many senses; it is the source of comfort for both the political radical and the status quoist. The consensual attitude discourages any effort to specify the culprit in the *vachya* form; hence the use of the mode of internal translation, an aesthetic strategy I have discussed earlier. Violation and transgression are made to look alike; here lies the political danger of the excessively consensual film form. This debate assumes special significance if one has to discuss the portrayal of the disintegration of the authority of communal harmony in films.

Communal harmony was a part of the unconscious in Indian society; it was one of those unthought of realms of everyday life that moulded both the fabric of social relations and symbolic representations of higher spiritual truths. Even when the problem of the communal divide came to the fore, it was not treated as unbridgeable. It was seen and defined as a problem of the society; the wound and the healing were both situated within the matrix of social relations and their memory. Now, however, for the first time in Indian history, communalism is coming to be seen as a total crisis enveloping civil society and the state. Communal harmony was one of the foundation stones of the making of the nation-state and the political community that was created as its corollary. In other words, it was seen as a political necessity. The way discourses of the state and the civil society played with each other in the area of communal harmony made it a value of authority in the eyes of the public. The political transformation of social reality was total.

In the pre-nation state days, the rift between the two religions was seen against the backdrop of the goal of spiritual liberation, and even a cursory study of poets and mystics from both Hinduism and Islam would substantiate this reading. Not that the Hindu–Muslim conflict was absent in pre-colonial times, but the means of understanding it were by and large social and religious.[11] The role of the state was clearly identified and articulated as insignificant. The passage of the theme of communal harmony from social to the political necessity of the modern Indian state has reproduced itself as a public ideal. Fears of the state have engulfed civil society; civil society, as a product of political will, is born to the exclusion of other vital memories relegated to the background. When civil society becomes a creation of the secular will of the state, all the previous realities undergo a radical change of character. The society that had survived communal tensions in the past was a total society, and the role of the state in its cultural forms was marginal, not decisive. The security-conscious state, with its intelligence, law and order maintenance apparatuses, and anti-terrorist squads, treats every breach of the peace as a deadly strike at its fragile ego. Hurting the ego of the state is seen as an attack on the larger fabric of society: the virtual disappearance of the line that divides the people and the state explains the massive presence of defence forces in the popular cinema which deals with 'anti-national' forces. Whatever the state touches is turned into fear and anxiety and that is, sometimes, gold for the commercial cinema. Here the state is not a military and security complex but a state of mind; to be more precise, a mode of handling the theme of national disintegration. The excessive presence of soldiers in the Indian cinema has always been a statement on the absence of political will on the part of the people to rise to the expectations of the state and its creation—political society.

JOURNEY OF COMMUNAL HARMONY IN THE MODE OF NOBLE MELANCHOLY

All the other authoritative values of the film spectator have found themselves mirrored in the mode of comic dissolution. However, the theme of the death of communal harmony has just begun the first phase of its formal journey; the mode of noble melancholy has found powerful expression in Mani Ratnam's *Bombay*. The link between *Roja* (1992) and *Bombay* (1994) needs further exploration because the latter signifies the shifting of the film-maker's focus from a statist perspective to the society's, though with a heavy emphasis on political identity. In *Bombay*, too, the consensual mode has reasserted its hold on the popular imagination, albeit in a more imaginative and unconventional way. In *Roja* the consensual mode was almost absent and the political nature of violence was highlighted at the cost of silencing other viewpoints that might have given a lie to the statist stance of the film. *Roja* was a statement of political ecstasy and agony; the deliberate identification of the heroine with nationalism was only one of the ideological devices of the film. The violence that spills over in *Roja* is violence of nationalistic necessity on both sides, but the director retains his choice to remain on Roja's side. In *Bombay*, Mani Ratnam has become more nuanced and subtle and has sought to distance himself from the simplistic endorsement of the Indian state. He seeks to make *Bombay* a statement on the basic nature of human violence and the capacity for love: a tale of two forces in eternal conflict.

The film, *Bombay*, from the very outset, attempts to distance itself from the task of contextualizing the problematic. *Bombay* is only a symbolic site, built on information accumulated amongst the public—a site where perennial clashes occur.[12] Mani Ratnam uses all the information at his and the spectators' command and transcends it. *Bombay* is built on the technique of turning information, that is indeed quite specific, into timeless wisdom. What is given in the form of information is bartered for wisdom. The stand-in for Bal Thackeray in the film is shown as being remorseful about communal violence, although in real life the man remains unrepentant: this juxtaposition creates its own harmony. Mani Ratnam adopts the strategy of de-temporalizing the context of violence, hence the passion for provocation, and then, of course, a sense of self-denial. The constant is personified in the film, the transitory outside the real life and history, and the two put together try to woo the public.

The strength of *Bombay* lies in its clear-eyed perception of the mind of the spectators, both Hindu and Muslim, that the will to violence resides concealed amongst both communities. The public need not have participated in the orgy of violence, but that fact does not take away the passive will to knife the Other. The entire strategy of the narration of *Bombay* derives its passion, which is reflected in its editing and music, from the conviction that it is only holding the mirror to the annihilationist tendency of the entire public. Of course, the film also assumes that there exists an undying humanist energy and love of peace that will eventually assert themselves.

Bombay transforms the information that the public has on the problematic of communal violence both into codes of recognition and of the iconic; the information that is being fed to the public in the form of news, photographs, and other sources of information including gossip is used as the basic material through which the film works. In this sense, *Bombay* has nothing which cannot be reduced into information; fiction is only secondary, as a peg on which information is sifted into different codes. Codes of recognition are created out of the heartless and violent acts of the faceless masses and some identifiable characters; they are intended to facilitate the recognition that each one of the spectators would have behaved in that way. However, the de-contextualization of the problematic is achieved through the creation of iconic codes; every crime and violation of human values is imaged as the assertion of the natural over the societal. The iconic code is created by lifting the mass media material to the status of primordial archetypes, fire, for instance, becomes one such image. Fire is a multidimensional archetype: the fire of love, the source of passion capable of uniting humans. Fires of hate, on the other hand, can transform human beings into monsters. There appears a metaphysics of violence when ordinary information is iconized. The matches fail to ignite in one crucial scene of the film, and this is an attempt to introduce some anthropomorphic element into the world of natural symbols. Through such dramatic events, the narrative somewhere tries to hint that eventually even violent human beings will come round to accepting peace and harmony. The ordinary is elevated to the status of the iconic code, and thus the director assures the identification of the public with the symbolic logic of the film. The particular is the source of political judgement and the narrative viewpoint of the film rejects it deliberately; here, curiously, lies its vulnerability. The total truth of communal violence is that both the warring communities equally share the blame for it: such is the narrative logic of the film. By trying to invoke the notion of common humanity the film refuses to take a political stand on the problem of violence, thus situating itself in the area of convergence of the state and civil society. Agony and fear become the central emotions of the film, thus making it a part of the psyche of the trinity. What remains in the narrative are forces, nothing but forces; everything becomes a matter of forces.[13]

The inability of our popular cinema to produce a film in the mode of comic dissolution shows how fear-ridden our public has become about exploring the nature of this crisis. The spectator has shown sufficient maturity and energy to withstand the crisis in other forms of authority. The spectator can handle the tumultuous changes that have enveloped the bedrooms of the public, corridors of temples, and political authority with a surprising degree of self-reflexivity which can also digest the related tensions and trauma. However, where public themes are involved with the legitimacy of the state, a deep-seated fear about probing its comic dimensions has pre-empted the possibility of comic vision. Political authority is seen as an immoral structure which has lost its credibility but the larger legitimacy of the state is respected. The fear of the state, it is assumed by the popular films, is also shared by the public. The problem of the representation of the Muslim and the threat to the integrity of the nation-state are merged to produce a film such as *Roja*; the overall tone of palpable tension remains by and large unaltered.

The tensions raised by films such as *Bombay* are to a degree unbearable. If the mode of melodrama dissolves itself to produce comic and farcical visions of the collapse of the authority of communal harmony, then, surely, the signs of self-healing of the public will become visible. The growth of comedy is no longer a matter of the internal history of the cinema but also an indicator of the rising resilience of the community. That is how history is shaped by the dictates of fiction.

WAITING FOR THE CROW...

The death of secularism is still a raw wound; it has become a forbidden zone for satire and humour. The state and the civil public entertain modes of melodramatic grief to explore this experience of the collapse of communal harmony. When communities assume largely political identities ignoring other streams, the self-reflexivity of the kind that produces comedy is seriously damaged. Jokes on sardarjis are out, caricaturing other communities has become politically incorrect. As the ideal of communal harmony is a subject of the state, and of course of the centre too, it has found some common interest in the making of Indian society into a modern political community; comedy finds itself bound by fear of both these forces. Can anyone produce a comedy on the demolition of the Babri Masjid? The 'heroism' of those who sought to project this demolition as a great historical act of correcting a historical wrong certainly has a comic ring to it. Farces are born in a community when symbols are substituted for reality; the Buddhists and Vaidikas ridiculed each other about their laughable excesses. The Babri Masjid and Ram Janma Bhoomi controversy has all the ingredients necessary for the production of a comedy or a farce. Comedies are born to ridicule the psychology of war or the will to violence or when the air is thick with the smell of blood, as was the case with Aristophanes's play *Lysistrata*. The comic vision is also employed to laugh at the self-righteous belief in the correctness of one's ideas; intoxication of this kind can give birth to intolerance. The medieval Sanskrit farce *Matta Vilasa Prahasana* mocks at such intoxication, both physical and ideological, though the play was unfair in its portrayal of the Buddhists. All these examples signify the self-confidence of a community that is capable of laughing away its agony. However, why expect all this only from cinema? The answer, to use a Kannada proverb, is that the popular film is like a band of thieves who arrive at a village fair even before it has begun. Other art forms, with all their timidity and wisdom, will arrive later. The crows are always the first; others descend on the scene later.

India awaits a comedy, a crow at that, on the death of secularism. What is mocked in death is bound to live in the guts of living history.

Editors' Note: The editors would like to place on record their immense gratitude to Prithvi Datta Chandra Shobhi for his editorial assistance in bringing this chapter to publication.

NOTES AND REFERENCES

1. For a statement on the public sphere, see Jurgen Habermas, *The Structural Transformation of the Public Sphere* (London: Polity Press, 1989).
2. I have used the category of the mode of melancholy, which is an improvization on one of the Jaina narrative modes, *vikshepini*, and this is different from the use of melodrama in discussions of Western cinema and popular arts. For two interesting statements on the genre of melodrama, see Peter Brook, *The Melodramatic Imagination: Balzac, Henry James, Melodrama and the Mode of Excess* (New York: Columbia University Press, 1985), and Christine Gledhill (ed.), *Home is Where the Heart Is: Studies in Melodrama and The Woman's Film* (London: British Film Institute, 1987). I have also drawn on Ulrike Sieghlor, 'Imaginary Identities in Werner Schroter's Cinema' (PhD thesis, University of East Anglia, 1994). For a discussion on the Jaina notion of *Vikshepini*, see my *Sahitya Kathana* (Heggodu, Karnataka: Akshara Prakashana, 1996), pp. 201–10 (in Kannada). Also see Jagadish Chandra Jain, *Prakrit Narrative Literature* (Delhi: Munshiram Manoharlal, 1981).
3. B.R. Panthulu's *School Master* (1959) is one of the important films in the history of Kannada cinema. I have taken the dates of films from Ashish Rajadhyaksha and Paul Willemen, *Encyclopaedia of Indian Cinema* (Delhi: Oxford University Press, 1995).
4. Even popular biographies of Raj Kapoor attempt to reinforce the image of him as lover-rebel who fights tradition. See Bunny Reuben, *Raj Kapoor: The Fabulous Showman* (Delhi: National Film Development Corporation, 1988).
5. As Ravi Vasudevan sums up the dominant theoretical trend regarding attitudes towards popular culture: 'in the literature on popular culture there has been a tendency to conceptualize it as a field of resistance to the dominant culture'. See his 'Shifting Codes, Dissolving Identities: The Hindi Social Film of the 50s as Popular Culture', *Journal of Arts and Ideas*, nos. 23–4 (1992), p. 52. Also see Colin Macabe (ed.), *High Theory/Low Culture: Analyzing Popular*

Television and Film (Manchester: Manchester University Press, 1988). For a larger discussion on the theme of transgression, see Peter Stallybrass and Allen White, *The Politics of Transgression* (London: Meuthen,1988).
6. For a discussion of the relationship between cosmologies of the caste system and the novel, see my *Flaming Feet* (Bangalore: South Forum Press, 1993).
7. *Gauriganesha* (1989) is a film directed by Phani Ramachandra; it was also a box-office hit.
8. The making of the superstar cult has been analysed by Indian scholars; for some case studies see M.S.S. Pandian, *The Image Trap* (New Delhi: Sage Publications, 1992); for a study of the Tamil star Rajnikanth, see J. Michael Kennedy, 'Reading of the Popular Text' (PhD thesis, Jawaharlal Nehru University, Delhi, 1992), particularly Ch. III, pp. 71–112. For an analysis of Telugu's Chiranjeevi, see S.V. Srinivas, 'Devotion and Defiance in Fan Activity', *Journal of Arts and Ideas*, no. 29 (1996), pp. 67–83. For an analysis of the Jayalalita phenomenon of Tamil Nadu, see M.S.S. Pandian, 'Jayalalita: "Desire" and Political Legitimation', *Seminar*, no. 401 (1993), pp. 31–4.
9. The entire politics of Tamil Nadu in the last century and this revolves around the centrality of Tamil glory in history. For studies of different facets of the phenomenon, *see* Robert. L. Hardgrave, 'The D.M.K. and the Politics of Tamil Nationalism', *Pacific Affairs* 37 (1965), pp. 396–411; also his *The Dravidian Movement* (Bombay: Popular Prakshan, 1965); and, with Anthony C. Neidart, 'Films and Political Consciousness in Tamilnadu', *Economic and Political Weekly* 10, nos. 1–2, pp. 27–35. Also see Marguerite Ross Barnette, *The Politics of Cultural Nationalism in South India* (Princeton: Princeton University Press,1976); M.S.S Pandian, 'Tamil Cultural Elites and Cinema: Outline of an Argument', paper presented at the Study Week on 'Making Meaning in Indian Cinema', IIAS, Shimla, October 1995.
10. To discuss the ideology of the camera, I have drawn on, of course by transforming it, Edward Brannigan, 'The Point of View Shot', in Bill Nichols (ed.), *Movies and Methods* (Calcutta: Seagull, 1993), Indian edn., pp. 672–91.
11. Ashis Nandy analyses the misreading of history by modernist-'religious' fanatics in his 'Twilight of Certitudes: Secularism, Hindu Nationalism and other Masks of Deculturation', reprinted in his *The Romance of the State and the Fate of Dissent in the Tropics* (Delhi, Oxford University Press, 2003).
12. For an insightful discussion of *Bombay*, see Ravi Vasudevan, '*Bombay* and Its Public', *Journal of Arts of Ideas*, no. 29 (1996), pp. 44–65.
13. Gilles Deleuze, *Cinema2: The Time-Image* (London: Athlone Press, 1989), pp. 139–40.

The Voice of the Nation and the Five-Year Plan Hero: Speculations on Gender, Space, and Popular Culture[1]

SANJAY SRIVASTAVA

This chapter seeks to make some comments on how, over the previous four decades or so, a particular female singing voice, with its specific tonality and modulation, became an expression of gender identity in India. Also, given the interactional nature of gender, this discussion is also concerned about the cultural politics of Indian masculinity. The intention is to explore the stabilization of gender identities through specific elements of Indian modernity: a nationalist discourse in which 'woman' as a sign has fluctuated between the poles of the mother and the sexually dangerous being; cinematic representations of Indian culture; the relationship between the performer and the audience in Indian music; the cultural production of space; the relationship between the Indian provincial and metropolitan cultures; the discourse of centralized economic planning; and the relationship between orality and literacy in popular culture.[2] These topics are explored through the career of India's most famous 'playback' singer, Lata Mangeshkar.

LATA, FEMININITY, AND THE SPACE OF THE NATION

This discussion is not concerned with whether Lata's voice is 'good', 'bad', 'authentically' Indian or otherwise, but rather, with the tendencies that come to gather about her singing style and attribute to it the characteristic of 'good', and 'authentically' Indian–feminine. Also, what follows is not an argument about *causality*[3] and, although the discourse of nationalism looms large, this should not be taken to mean that projects of modernity can simply be reduced to it. Clearly, nationalist ideology is only one of the grids upon which post-colonial modernity is based.[4] Therefore, while I primarily concentrate on pleasure as a nationalist project, it clearly does not exhaust inquiry into the topic.

During the last and the current century, Indian popular music has, in the main, been connected with films, and whilst in the early films many of the songs were sung by the actors themselves, during the 1940s this practice gave way to 'playback' singing where the actor's singing voice was provided by someone else. Therefore, as is well known, in India singers are not necessarily stars in themselves and, till quite recently, commercial music was sold in the market under the banner of the film with which the songs were associated. Singers cultivated little public presence, and rather than the personality of the singer, it was their voice that functioned as a sign. This situation has only recently begun to change, and even then can't be compared to the situation of Western pop music. Public awareness of singers and their songs was, in the absence of a culture of performances (as existed, for example, in the case of Nautanki artistes[5] and poets),[6] generated and maintained through a vast circuit of published and other means.[7] Among the former might be included film-magazines such as *Madhuri*, and *Filmindia*, the latter first published in 1935 by Baburao Patel, and song-books produced (also from the 1930s onwards) by the music academy and publisher, Sangeet Karyalaya of Hathras, Uttar Pradesh. Song-books in particular were avidly collected by fans across India.[8]

One of the most recent, and perhaps most ambitious, contributors to this circulating body of knowledge and appreciation is the Kanpur-based Har Mandir Singh 'Hamraaz', an employee of the State Bank of India, who is the publisher of the periodical *Listener's Bulletin*, and the compiler of the *Hindi Film Geet Kosh* (Hindi Film-Song Digest), a four-volume project on Hindi songs for the period 1931–70. The *Bulletin* (earlier known as *Radio News*) was founded in 1971, and is characteristic of the singular passion that often attaches to Hindi cinema and its many aspects. Begun as one person's desire to establish 'an easy mode of communicating with music lovers all over India and abroad',[9] the periodical whetted Hamraaz's appetite for the impressive *Hindi Film Geet Kosh* project. The process of compiling the digest is itself instructive of the constitution and consolidation of the community of film-fans. Hamraaz, therefore notes that he had always been a fan of the 'Hindi film songs of fifties [sic] and earlier decades', and began collecting information on songs of the period from the age of sixteen or seventeen (that is, around, 1967–8). However, given the paucity of the kind of information he was seeking—names of lyricists, singers, and record numbers, for example—he was frequently frustrated in his endeavours.

Around 1970, Hamraaz wrote to a film magazine seeking information about songs from the magazine's readers. This elicited a response from a 'Mr K.D. Sharma of Kota (Rajasthan) [who] wrote back that he faced the same problem as I did'.[10] Eventually, Mr Sharma provided Hamraaz with a copy of Firoze Rangoonwala's book *Indian Filmography* 'and observed that the films...were listed according to year of censorship and that the category, names of films, their directors, and artistes were given all right but what music lovers desired to viz., [sic] the songs, the lyricists, the singers, disc numbers, etc. were not there'. The *Hindi Film Geet Kosh* began, then, as a quest to benefit all 'music lovers'. During the process of collecting information for the compilation, Hamraaz travelled to a number of places in India, and many with their own private archives came to his aid:

Mr Vijay Singh Chandel of Agra and Mr N.D. Prakash 'Patialvi' of Patiala... Mr Ratanlal Kataria of Kekri (Dist. Ajmer)...Mr P.K. Nair [of the Pune based National Film Archives]...Mr B.V. Dharap [also of Pune]...Mr B.N Chatterjee of Bhopal (now residing in Nagpur)...Mr P.S. Jadeja of Rajkot and Mr Suleman Kherani at Jamnagar who had hundreds of rare song booklets of films of yester-years...Mr Harish Raghuvanshi of Surat...Mr Veerbhadrasinh Jhala of Narwar (Distt. Ujjain, M.P.)...'[11].

It is this circuit of men (and in terms of public activities, it is gendered) and their passions, collections, and compilations that for long have constituted the sites of interaction and dissemination of filmic culture such as songs.

Of course, in addition to the films, records, and published material, there was another important site that catered to the community of connoisseurs of the Hindi film song: radio. So, for example, in his biographical note, Har Mandir Singh 'Hamraaz' recalls that during his adolescence he was an avid listener of the 'Vakya Geetanjali' programme on Radio Ceylon (now Radio Sri Lanka):

They would announce a meaningful sentence of 7 or 8 words and would ask the listeners to send in Hindi film songs beginning with each word. It was my desire to participate in the various programmes of Radio Sri Lanka particularly the VAKYA GEETANJALI that set me on the path to noting down in exercise books the relevant particulars of all the film songs I liked.

It was through these various ways that a relatively invisible playback singer such as Lata Mangeshkar acquired a public presence, with her biography becoming a fragment of the broader knowledge and discussion that surrounded the reception of her filmic songs.

Lata Mangeshkar was born in 1929 in Indore, and as a child both she and her sister Asha Bhonsle learnt music from a series of accomplished musicians. Lata recorded her first song in 1942, and since then has, reputedly, sung in 18 Indian languages. One source estimates that by 1991 she had recorded around 6,000 songs,[12] while journalistic accounts speak of a substantially greater corpus. Among female playback singers, then, Lata's voice has dominated the Indian popular music scene. Also alongside this dominance, she established a specific vocal style which, in conjunction with the factors I will discuss below, became recognized as an aesthetic marker of 'modern' Indian female identity. Also, if 'vocal style (aside from the language) is the single most important marker of aesthetic identity',[13] then it can be argued that Lata's singing voice has instituted a very specific identity for Indian womanhood; one that has almost no precedence in traditional forms of Indian music. In other words, the 'woman' conjured by Lata Mangeshkar's singing voice is the product of certain developments that are peculiar to the processes of Indian modernity.

One music critic has noted that Lata's style has become 'the ultimate measure of sweetness in a woman's voice. [And that] Its chief characteristic was the skilled use of a particular kind of falsetto which did not exist in quite the same way before her coming.'[14] Another suggests that singers from musical genres with their own distinct style began to mimic Lata's voice and that it soon 'became difficult to imagine a female voice that is not Lata Mangeshkar's'.[15] There is, it could be said, almost no precedence for Lata's voice, and the kind of femininity it conjures, in the wider sphere of female singing styles in India, especially one marked by an extraordinary diversity of expressive traditions. Given this diversity (as I show later), it is important to think about how Lata Mangeshkar's shrill adolescent-girl falsetto came to be established as the 'ideal' in 'Indian popular music and film culture in general'.[16]

My illustrations of expressive heteroglossia cannot, of course, do justice to that vast storehouse of emotions, cautionary and moral tales, laments, sensual incantations to divinities, and the constant play of historic inventiveness that is grouped under the rubric of Indian music; and hence, the random sample presented here should only be regarded as a niche in the complex iconography of Indian music. The melange of female singing styles found in the subcontinent ranges from group singing at family ritual occasions (a wedding being the most common), to organized public performances. In some instances, many earlier ritual-linked performances have become part of the commercial performance milieu.

However, no matter what the context, women's singing styles in India, at least those not connected with the film industry, have been marked by a striking heterogeneity of tonal and other styles. Thus, if the Dholi Gayikayen of Jodhpur[17] sing of a wife demanding jewellery from her husband in 'heavy' and nasal tones, then the Hindustani classical music singer Gangubai Hangal's delivery ranges between the low alto and the upper tenor ranges and frequently confuses unacquainted listeners as to the artiste's gender. Also, although the artiste's gender is not really difficult to determine in the case of an early (1911) recording by the Hindustani classical music virtuoso Zohra Bai,[18] her voice is nevertheless imbued with a quality best described as playful aggressiveness.[19] The ghazal singing of Pakistan's Farida Khanum[20] provides another example of the heterogeneity of which I speak. Khanum's voice, alternately sensuous, pleading, and cajoling, manages to reproduce the complexities of a subject position that is a combination of 'a desperate lover intoxicated with passion, a rapt visionary absorbed in mystic illumination, [and] an iconoclastic drunkard celebrating the omnipotence of wine'.[21] These examples could be multiplied manifold, with many regional and other styles vying for a place.

One perspective that seeks to account for the dominance and the subsequent stylistic homogeneity ushered in by Lata's style speaks of the 'creation of film music as a common-denominator mass-music style, produced in corporate, urban studios and superimposed on a heterogeneous audience; this audience has no active role in the creation of this music, and can exercise only indirect influence by choosing among the songs and styles proffered by the industry.²² This is, no doubt, an important aspect to consider. However, this standpoint can be usefully supplemented through an analysis of the wider *cultural* and *historical* dynamic that contributes towards constituting the field of the aesthetic, and in turn influences the representation of identities, including those linked to gender and sexuality. Consideration of aspects of the discourse of early Indian nationalism provides a good starting point towards this objective.

As feminist scholarship has pointed out, 'woman' functioned as an important sign in the masculinist constructions of the idea of the nation-to-be which comes to be represented through the notion of the 'mother-who-is-the-nation'.²³ In some versions this was achieved by representing India as a Hindu goddess. However, this formulation engendered a specific problem as far as the nationalists were concerned, in that 'the image Woman [could] be perceived to contain a charge of sexuality which always threatens to run free'.²⁴ How, then, do we deal with this dilemma? In part, it has been suggested that the resolution of the 'woman question' was achieved by identifying women not just as the carriers of 'tradition' but tradition itself: women's bodies became the site on which tradition was seen to be.²⁵ I have suggested elsewhere²⁶ that, persuasive as it may seem, this formulation of the issue should be treated with some caution as it may capture only one of several scenarios: that the *public* life of the Indian family—and 'its' women—also had a role to play in debates about engagements with modernity.²⁷ The following discussion seeks to explore this very public dimension of the 'woman question' in the career of Indian modernity through the pervasive influence of a singer who has, it would appear, crafted an entire structure of emotions in the post-colonial era.

With the coming of cinema in India, the tableau of public forms became inextricably attached to the possibilities of cinematic representation, and men and women become public figures attached to the natural and human topographies. This, it might be suggested, was a result of the particular interpretation of the term 'culture' that established itself during the modern period. This was an interpretation to which filmic techniques had an almost natural affinity. I am referring to the understanding of the culture that represented it as linked to geographical places,²⁸ and to landscape,²⁹ such that Indian culture becomes attached to specific natural and human-made sites: the Himalayas, hill-stations, the Ganges, the Taj Mahal, ruins of past 'civilizations', religious sites, and office buildings which constituted the representational iconography of the fledgling nation-state.

The relationship between geography and the nation may have received scant attention from India scholars, but its importance was explicitly recognized by nationalists of various persuasions. The pithiest example is to be encountered in the work of Sister Nivedita (Margaret Noble) and occurs in an article entitled 'Future Education of Indian Woman'. A fundamental aspect of women's education in India, Sister Nivedita was to say, must lie in making women more 'efficient'.[30] This required, among other things, the making of 'queen and housewife, saint and citizen'.[31] Such an 'efficiency drive' towards a new society, the Sister noted, required that women be imparted a geographical sensibility because knowledge constituted the fundamental building block of the consciousness of national feeling.[32] This might be achieved through resources already at 'our' disposal: 'the wandering Bhagabatas or Kathakas, with the magic lantern, may popularize geography by showing slides illustrative of various pilgrimages':

> Picture, pictures, pictures, these are the first of instruments in trying to concretize ideas, pictures and the mother-tongue. If we would impart a love of country, we must give a country to love. How shall women be enthusiastic about something they cannot imagine?[33]

It can be argued that the above derives from a 'modern' view of culture as a territorialized and fixed concept,[34] rather than as a relationship between human beings. One can contrast this with the absence of the realist convention in representing landscape in, say, certain schools of Indian art such as the Madhubani style[35] and Mughal miniatures[36] in which the landscape represents human emotional states or religious beliefs rather than standing for culture itself. A similar point has been made in relation to the absence of a realist tradition in medieval Hindi poetry that provides a contrast to developments in the modern period. Karine Schomer points out that

> nature had not been absent from [medieval] Braj poetry, but it was an idealized nature, usually relegated to the role of enhancing human emotions. ...The treatment of nature in the Dwivedi [or modern] period was quite different. Not only was it made an independent poetic subject, but it was described in realistic, concrete detail.[37]

It is precisely this modern, 'realistic', sensibility of landscape and territory that found play in early cinema.

However, even during the modern period, a sensibility of culture as a relationship between humans rather than with fixed space could also be found. A Marathi book published towards the end of the nineteenth century provides a tantalizing glimpse into this alternative world-view. The book—*Manjha Prawas*, published in Hindi as *Ankhon Dekha Gadar*—is an account of the travels of the Brahmin Vishnubhatt Godse from Pune to Mathura sometime in 1857.[38] For the modern reader, Godse's travelogue has a strangely disorienting effect. This was because the familiar, and comforting, descriptions of scenery and landscape are almost entirely absent in an account that is, instead, teeming with people, procedures, and transactions. We can only begin to comprehend this transactional sensibility if we think of it as part of a very different understanding of culture to that which we have become accustomed. It is, in fact, a different way of organizing culture.

Now, when Indian culture becomes attached to landscape and territory, the heroes and heroines of Indian films come to meet, and sing, and dance in these places which come to constitute Indian cultural and national spaces. Herein lay one of the problems for the 'woman question' in India, and where Lata Mangeshkar has been particularly helpful. This was because many of these spaces of Indian culture were public spaces, i.e. defined as 'not-home'. An important aspect of the definition of 'culture', once it becomes attached to territories and landscapes, is, indeed, its *public* nature; an aspect that is crucial in illustrating what 'Indian' culture is. Even so, how was the 'fraternal contract',[39] which was nationalism, to deal with this increasing visibility of the filmic woman 'out of place', i.e. in public spaces? Most importantly, what was at issue was not just visibility but also, given the 'musical' nature of Indian cinema, the audibility of women in public spaces. Here was a great dilemma. Indian films both contributed towards the consolidation of a national imagination on a mass scale—these sites are India, they said—but also seemed to pose a threat to one of the fundamental organizing principles of the discourses on nationalism, namely, the positioning of women within it.

It would appear that Lata's stylistic innovation offered a viable solution to the above problem of representation in the public sphere: at the same time that women's bodies became visible in public spaces via films, their presence was 'thinned' through the expressive timbre granted them. The heroines for whom Lata provided the singing voice may well have been prancing around hillsides and streets while performing a song-sequence, but this gesture which otherwise threatened male dominance of these spaces, was domesticated through the timbre, tonality, and stylistic stricture that marked that presence. The potentially powerful image of the heroine enjoying the freedom of the public space in equal measure to the male hero *and* singing in a voice that might express an ambiguous femininity was, through Lata's voice, undermined.

However, it is not enough to say that Lata provides the bridge between colonial–nationalist history and the manner in which modern cinema sought to represent women. Her 'art' is almost fundamental to another process of modernity: the recasting of the relationship between the performer and the audience. Writing at the turn of the twentieth century, Ananda Coomaraswamy, that interesting, and problematic, scholar of Indian (or, rather, Hindu) aesthetics made what is a particularly profound observation in this context. He suggested that in Indian music the relationship between the performer and the audience is one in which the audience also brings an artistry to listening: 'the listener [responds] with an art of his own'.[40] Further, that 'the musician in India finds a model audience—technically critical, but somewhat indifferent to voice production'.[41] The artistry of the performer, in other words, is not (or was not) hegemonic, as it faced the skill of the audience in receiving the performance. It is not therefore 'the voice that makes the singer, as so often happens in Europe', Coomaraswamy[42] was to note.

Lata Mangeshkar manages to break this dynamic relationship between the performer and the audience[43] and *impose* a code of interpretation through the dramatic emphasis on the singing rather than the song, through the 'sensuous perfection of the voice',[44] where now the feminine can only be articulated through a constricted timbre and style. The audience is now *instructed* on what femininity is.

One of the ways in which this dominance may have been achieved might be illustrated through reference to the relationship between orality and literariness.[45] It would appear that the wider context in which the audience exists as an active entity with *its* own artistry is the context where 'orality' continues to be a valued mode of interaction; the performative contexts of orality can be thought of as a situation where the listener may talk back, interrupt, and reinterpret. The dynamics of the oral context are those in which the artistry of the performer is not reduced to any singular characteristic, and certainly not the voice. This view finds strong support in contemporary scholarship through the *absence* of any discussion that seeks to define a norm for voice quality in Indian performative traditions. Susan Wadley's discussion of the 'performance strategies' of the artistes of the north Indian epic of Dhola is a case in point. Wadley suggests that the great popularity of the most highly regarded of these, Swarup Singh, is due to 'his magnificently expressive voice—*covering a range of performance styles*'.[46] There is no suggestion here that any *one* particular type of tonality is considered to be the mark of 'good' singing. Effective performances of Dhola, Wadley suggests, depend on two things: 'telling the story in a clear fashion and providing variety'.[47] As 'traditional' Indian music was not written music, it belonged to this milieu.[48]

Lata's music, on the other hand, derives from a 'compositional' context: because 'the elaborate arrangements [of Indian film music] reflect a precomposed and notated (i.e. written) approach to music composition and performance'.[49] The compositional or literary mode of performance can be linked to a wider sensibility about the relationship between performers and audiences, and between readers and texts: it is a sensibility that has the potential to privilege the 'expert' and disenfranchises the 'lay-person'. It is in this sense, then, that Lata's voice becomes the unquestionable authority on the feminine ideal and, inasmuch as that ideal becomes entrenched, the artistry of the audience in receiving the performance is of a far more limited kind. Here, therefore the consolidation of 'literariness' as an aspect of Indian modernity served to codify representations of femininity. This is not, of course, to suggest that 'orality' ought be treated as a fixed essence of Indian culture. Rather, the observation pertains to the broader historical and social context within which transformations in cultural forms occur.[50]

Lata's adolescent-girl voice for the adult woman comes, then, to establish the authority of the written word over the recalcitrant possibilities of orality, overriding the 'substantial amount of melodic, rhythmic, and textually expressive play'[51] that marks the latter's expressive universe. Further, through the historical association of writing with men, this also legitimized the authority of male notions of the sign 'woman'. The other aspect to this is that it simultaneously established the dominance of bourgeois notions of gender, communication, and being in the world, marginalizing other existing world-views. In this sense too, it was expressive of certain contexts of Indian nationalist discourse. Therefore Lata's voice is the simultaneous site of both gender and class.

It is interesting that when Lata did give public performances it was, as Manuel points out, just as likely that she would stand rigidly on stage and sing with her head buried in a notebook.[52] Here, at least two contexts are at play. Firstly, what matters is the voice and the way it has been defined by the 'notebook', by the authority of the writing. Secondly, Lata's own public persona (on record, cassette, and CD cover sleeves, and in magazines) is of the respectable housewife, perhaps even a mother, though a mother of the nation that has given that nation a voice; 'For the very heart of India throbs in your voice', as the lyricist Naushad Ali was to write in a ghazal in Lata's praise.[53] Lata's motherhood falls, in this context, within the realms of the 'virgin mother'. It is important that Lata has almost never been dogged by relationship-linked gossip that surrounds many other women in the entertainment industry.[54] In addition to the virgin mother thematic, there is (to resort to culturally mixed metaphors) also an aura of the cult of Meera—the medieval princess–poetess and an iconic figure in the bhakti movement—about her. Like the bhakta poets, Lata too has forsaken her sexuality and domesticity for devotion to a greater cause, namely the endowment of national pleasure through a redefinition of modern Indian feminine identity. Also, in that process, she has become the icon of virgin mother (sister?) of the nation.[55]

Therefore Lata, the mother who has breathed life into the 'national' woman (the most famous of them all, Radha, from Mehboob Khan's 1957 epic *Mother India*, comes immediately to mind) articulates a gendered intertextual space where the apparently disreputable public role of the woman as entertainer is contained by the representational strategies of motherliness and sisterliness. The most obvious contrast is with the ghazal singer Begum Akhtar who both drank and smoked, and made no effort, even in old age, to project the image of either an asexual mother figure or a generically 'respectable' grandmother.

The significance of Lata's style is also linked to the cinematic strategy in which the figure of the vamp was quite clearly differentiated from that of the heroine. The femininity that Lata, in voice and style, embodies is one in which the dangerous and uncontrollable sexuality of the vamp—expressed through dress, speech, motive, and an obsession with non-reproductive sex—is effectively eradicated. Therefore, during the period of Lata's greatest prominence, there was another female figure of public status that acted as a counterpoint to the femininity represented by the singer. I refer to the actress Helen, the most illustrious 'vamp' of the Hindi cinema. Helen, her on-screen sexuality, and her relationship to other kinds of femininities, was crucial to the meanings that came to gather around 'Lata'. It is within the space created by the split of cinematic womanhood into the productive and unproductive (and, therefore, disruptive) sexuality that Lata-ness finds a place. Of course, the cinematic manoeuvres through which women (and men) were sexualized were reflections of the broader off-screen processes where the dramas of gender and sexuality unfolded through a number of overlapping contexts. It is to the latter that I turn in the following section.

RECLAIMING THE PAST, CLEANSING THE PRESENT

The processes through which Lata's voice became established as the aesthetic epitome of Indian feminine identity can also be seen as part of the cultural politics of the making of the 'modern' Indian woman within the matrices of upper-caste Hindu milieus. In other words, Lata's singing voice was part of the broader processes of nationalist thought where the figure of the woman–citizen, inasmuch as she was the object of debate and discussion, emerged out of the skein of colonial and post-colonized caste and communal politics.

In a discussion of radio broadcasting in India, David Lelyveld has suggested that the Hindu–Muslim context is an important one for understanding the formulation of 'national programming'[56] and the attempts to inculcate a 'national' culture through All India Radio (AIR). Though Lelyveld's attention is principally directed towards exploring the strategies and manoeuvres through which Indian classical music was sought to be Hinduized in the immediate post-Independence period, I think there is an important link between his discussion and the case of Indian film music.

In what follows, I do not mean to imply that there existed at *all* levels of Indian society a fundamental hostility between Hindus and Muslims. There is sufficient historical, anthropological, and literary material to indicate otherwise. Rather, that specific historical circumstances coalesced during the second half of the nineteenth century to produce a milieu within which an anti-Muslim rhetoric was prevalent in many aspects of Indian life.

In the post-Independence period, the Hindu–Muslim angle, in the context of producing a 'national' music culture, came to the fore in several ways. Also, inasmuch as the post-colonized nation-state's cultural capital[55]—its 'ancient heritage', its various architectural landmarks, and its philosophical and cultural achievements—received as much attention as the debates around creating more economic capital, the task of producing a 'national' musical culture was taken up in a particularly conspicuous manner. Some of these debates were intrinsically linked to the supposed fate of Indian music during colonial rule. Therefore, Dr B.V. Keskar, Minister of Information and Broadcasting from 1950 to 1962, was to suggest that 'only with national independence, and indeed, primarily through radio broadcasting...,could the musical heritage of India be saved'.[58] However, Keskar did not believe that the blame for the lamentable state of Indian music could be traced exclusively to Occidental disdain for Oriental cultural forms and to 'imperial neglect' of native traditions; he was of the unequivocal opinion that the deleterious effects to which it had been subject also derived from the actions of north Indian Muslims. This community, he suggested, 'had appropriated and distorted the ancient art, turning it into the secret craft of exclusive lineages, the *gharanas*, and ignorant of Sanskrit, divorced it from the religious context of Hindu civilisation'.[59]

The wider context of Keskar's remarks is, by now, a familiar one: that the post-colonized nation-state must reinvigorate the ancient Sanskritic culture that had been neglected by the British and, more fundamentally, corrupted by the Muslims. Therefore, in another context, the 'reformist' Arya Samaj sought, through the Gurukul education movement, to revivify a 'fallen' society through the task of forming 'a sound, active and decisive character in...students'.[60] Hence, within the Gurukul schools, of 'ancient' and 'Vedic' origin, 'the students were called *Brahmacharis* on the pattern of the Ancient Gurukulas'.[61]

Keskar's thinking on Indian music was, then, heir to the history of what might be termed the 'Hindu contextualism'[62] of the late nineteenth and early twentieth century nationalist discourse in India. Also, as is well known, Keskar was not alone in his elaboration of this theme. Vishnu Narayan Bhatkhande (1860–1936) was another extremely influential figure in the movement that sought to construct a 'national' music culture by returning Indian music to its putative ancient Hindu roots.[63] These ideas formed an important subtext in debates regarding the development of a 'civil' post-colonized identity, and constituted the backdrop to the attempted Hinduization and gentrification of Indian culture. Lelyveld points out, for instance, that under Vallabhbhai Patel's reign as Minister for Information and Broadcasting (1946), the effort towards producing a purified national culture manifested in the prohibition of 'singers and musicians from the courtesan culture': anyone (as one source put it) 'whose public life was a scandal'.[64] Besides, during Keskar's tenure as minister, there came to be instituted a bureaucratic selection procedure for AIR musicians whose most explicit aim appears to have been undermining the gharana system. An important outcome of this process of linking employment prospects within AIR with 'certification from recognized music academies'[65] was the entry into the profession of many who were described as being from 'respectable' backgrounds; those, in other words, who had skirted the illicit influence of the Muslim dominated gharana and allied systems of performance.[66] All this is to say that within early twentieth-century nationalist discourse there existed a strong theme which linked the emergence of the modern Indian self to a 'pure' and 'ancient' Hindu genealogy[67] and to a 'respectable' bourgeois milieu.

An additional way of thinking about this issue is to suggest, as Lelyveld does, that 'the great enemy in this effort to construct a new music by administrative decree was the increasingly popular new style of film songs'.[68] However, it is possible to suggest that the ideology of a 'pure' and 'respectable' national culture found voice in the realms of popular (that is film) music itself, and that Lata Mangeshkar's singing style was the most obvious manifestation of this process. Therefore, I suggest that the gradual development of Lata's singing voice into what it became at the peak of her popularity—for her very early singing style carries strong resonance of the Pakistani singer Noorjehan's nasality—was part of the process of purifying—Hinduizing and gentrifying—the figure of the 'ideal' Indian woman of post-coloniality. This was to be the woman fit to carry the mantle of 'bearer of our traditions'.

From its very outset, the make-up of the Indian film industry would have caused considerable consternation to the votaries of a national 'purification' project linked to a 'great' Hindu past, for the grounds for such disquiet had been well prepared. The nineteenth-century journalist and cultural critic Bhartendu Harishchandra (1850–85) had lamented that that both Jains and Muslims had been responsible for the destruction of the Indian Sangeet Shashtra and that when 'the Muslim emperors such as Akbar and Muhammadshah did pay any attention to it, they only favoured Muslim musicians, and this led to the further decline of Hindu artistes'.[69] This theme is also salient in the life work of one of the great, and quite tragic, figures of twentieth century Indian music. In founding the first of the publicly funded Gandharva Mahavidyalayas music academies (1901), Vishnu Digambar Paluskar (1872–1931) sought not just to introduce an emerging middle-class to musical training but also to situate such training, and hence the identity of this class, within a specific moral landscape. Thus, one writer has noted that 'while there was strict discipline [at the Mahavidyalayas], there was stricter discipline in moral training. The usual odium attached to the clan of musicians was thus removed and they began to be treated with respect'.[70] Given the predominance of the gharana tradition, the point that 'the clan of musicians' acts as a metonym for 'Muslim performers' need hardly be be laboured.

The ' usual odium' that surrounded Muslims also, of course, referred to something else, namely the imagined relationship between 'Muslimness' and 'excessive' sexuality, an aspect that had a well-established colonial history. The colonial perspective of Muslim sexual rapaciousness was no doubt linked to the history of Christian–Muslim relations in Europe.[71] During the late nineteenth and early twentieth centuries, as Charu Gupta has pointed out, this perspective was adopted with great alacrity by some of the key Indian contributors to the making of a 'new Hindu national consciousness'.[72] Accordingly, 'Lecherous behaviour, a high sexual appetite, a life of luxury, and religious fanaticism'[73] came to be understood as the most salient aspects of Muslim character. This point of view got further transformed into one of 'heightened fears of sexual contact between Muslim men and Hindu women',[74] and warnings to Hindu women against contact with Muslim men.

In the opening decades of the twentieth century, then, many, no doubt, were able to read Bhartendu's comments and Paluskar's efforts as a 'correct' evaluation of the Muslim influence upon (Hindu) Indian society. Further, they may have surmised, this could now be witnessed in another sphere of Indian life, namely, in the newly established cinema industry. It is after all possible to speak of a Muslim 'cultural influence that has determined the very nature of [Indian] cinema'.[75] From its personnel, to the film-titles, to the language of the screenplays and lyrics, Hindi cinema had been deeply shaped by Muslim influences.[76] The most obvious manifestation of this was, of course, the predominance of the Urdu language in various aspects of Hindi cinema.

Saadat Hasan Manto has provided one of the most vivid accounts of the Muslim social context in the Indian film industry. Manto's pithy essays (1984) on his days as an industry worker in pre-Partition India offers us valuable social and cultural insights into an era, and an enterprise, marked by rapidly shifting contexts of transformation. One of these contexts—whose portrayal by Manto is marked both by warmth and playful wickedness—concerns the 'courtesan' background of many of the pioneers of Indian cinema. In an era when film-work of any kind was treated as disreputable and association with film-workers as equally suspect, it was natural that the industry's mainstay would be those already stigmatized by mainstream society (or, at least those who came to be increasingly stigmatized within the new moral dispensation of the national movement). Manto's essay on the actress Nargis is illustrative of this. Nargis (1929–81), he points out, was the daughter of the Muslim singer, actress, and film-maker Jaddanbai and her Hindu lover, Mohan babu. However, more importantly, there was about Jaddanbai that aura of courtesan 'disreputability' that inspired men such as Keskar and Patel to, at least implicitly, call for a purification of the national public culture. Manto describes this aspect of Jaddanbai's life in the context of her great devotion to Mohan babu:

Mohanbabu was a *raiis*, and, infatuated by the sheer magic of Jaddanbai's singing and her voice, he completely lost his heart to her. He was a handsome, educated and healthy man. But none of these attributes proved of any use to Jaddanbai [who was the main provider for the family]. Jaddanbai herself was a very prominent person of her time and there was no dearth of *khandani Nawabs* and *Rajas* willing to shower her with gold and silver at her *mujras*. However, when these showers stopped, and the skies cleared, Jaddanbai always turned to her Mohan, her true love.[77]

Such was the opprobrium attached to association with the 'morally corrupt' members of the film industry—and in particular with women of Muslim background within it, as they had doubly violated the tenets of 'proper' gender *and* occupational behaviour—that even 'respectable'

Muslims fought shy of it or, at least, attempted to keep it a secret. Manto explains that his wife and her two sisters had formed a close friendship with Nargis and would often visit her at the latter's house in Bombay. However:

> For many days my wife kept these visits a complete secret. When she did tell me, I pretended to be annoyed, and mistaking my pretence for real anger she quickly asked for forgiveness. 'Look, we made a mistake,' she said, 'but for god's sake don't ever mention this to anyone!'[78]

Jaddanbai and her milieu of 'outcast entertainers',[79] to use D.G. Phalke's self-pitying phrase, was not an exceptional aspect of the early period of Indian cinema, and it is not difficult to see how it might have provided ready-made material for a nationalist discourse organized around the theme of the 'corruption' introduced into Indian social and cultural life by Muslims. The 'low prestige of the cinema'[80] as a professional calling has been commented on by film-scholars, and my discussion here attempts to place this in the context of turn-of-the-twentieth-century nationalist discourses on gender and religious identity in 'modern' India.

In another essay on the actress Nasim Bano, Manto recalls the making of the 1942 film *Ujala*. Due to a weak story line, ordinary music, and poor direction, the film flopped and the owner of the production company, 'Ahsan sahib', had to suffer great financial loss. However:

> during the process [of completing the film] he fell in love with [the heroine] Nasim Bano. Nasim, however, was no stranger to Ahsan sahib. For, his father, Khanbahadur Muhammad Sulaiman, Chief Engineer, had been an acquaintance of Nasim's mother, Chamia. In fact, for all intents and purposes, she was his second wife. So, Ahsan sahib must have had ample opportunity of meeting Nasim on various occasions.[81]

It is this context, when 'Muslimness' and 'debauchery' became conjoined through an emerging discourse of middle-class Hindu respectability, that the project of post-colonial purification emerged; and Lata's voice was one of the several sites upon which it unfolded, though the purge, it could be suggested, was only partially successful. It is no doubt true that the classical music milieu was an explicit target for the 'reform' project discussed above, but the mass appeal of the film industry and its by-products, made it too a target of the reformers' zeal. After all, the 'good' name of the nation is most often at risk from the retrograde tendencies of its masses, and it is the always the responsibility of enlightened citizenry to shepherd the former towards the portals of citizenship and civilized action.

Through Lata's artistry, the 'disreputableness' of ambiguous tonalities and the threat of uncertain femininity—the mise en scène of Krishna Sobti's great novel *Mitro Marjani*,[82] for example—was brought into alignment with the discourses of 'pure' and controllable Hindu womanhood. The most obvious counterpoint to Lata's style was what could be referred to as the *kotha* (brothel/courtesan) style of singing, echoes of which can be discerned in, say, singer Shamshad Begum's voice. It is difficult to convey the qualities of a voice—the social and emotional contexts it may conjure for the listener—in a discussion such as this. However, it is possible to say that, through certain historical processes of which the nationalist discourse was perhaps the most important, public singing by women, unless connected to religious and ritual purposes (such as weddings), came to carry the taint of disrepute; it became the preserve of the *tawaif* (the courtesan), lower caste woman, or 'tribal' woman.[83] Also, the tonalities of such public singing, which itself remained unfettered by the definitional constraints of a 'good' voice, became associated with 'disreputable', undomesticated, conduct.

At a later point, when the 'Muslim problem', and the search for a 'proper', controllable, femininity (and hence a 'proper' masculinity) became part of the nationalist project of cultural redemption, certain kinds of voices came to be marked as an unacceptable aspect of 'proper' post-coloniality. There now emerged an inventory of 'impurities' in relation to 'proper' post-colonial femininity: included in this inventory, it is possible to say, was nasality and a 'heavy' (i.e. masculine) voice. Whilst it is true that quite a number of feminine identities came to be seen as not possessing a 'proper' voice, most commonly, however, it was the Muslim *tawaif* who became inextricably connected to *that* kind of voice. After all it was she who, in the redemptive projects of turn-of-the-century nationalism posed the greatest threat to middle-class Hindu masculinity: because she was dexterous not merely in matters of physical allure, but could also, at least as far as popular mythology would have it, match wits with her male clientele.[84]

It is therefore at this juncture, where a variety of modern processes of culture came together, that Lata's skill as a forever-adolescent voice, singing out, but through the controllable timbre of a *child-woman*, is situated. She provided another resolution of the 'woman question' in the post-colonial context: how to have women in public, but also within the firm grip of a watchful, adult, masculinity, such that the public woman became forever infantilized.

The process of 'purifying' Indian public culture took the form, then, of purging it of its Muslim associations and its connections with various realms of (non-middle-class) disreputability.[85] Lata Mangeshkar's voice, it can be argued, became the site for the unfolding of this project: a place at the crossroads of a public culture where the adolescent girl's voice–persona appeared to provide an opportunity for both expressing an *appropriately* modern femininity, and a suitably Hinduized nationality.[86] This point is nicely encapsulated in some stray comments in Harish Bhimani's hagiographic *In Search of Lata Mangeshkar* (1995). Lata sometimes cancelled her recording schedules, Bhimani says, if she felt that her voice was 'not at its best',[87] and that it may have been a lapse in her judgement (as Bhimani portrays it) that led her to record the song '*Paaon chhoo lene do…*' for Roshan's [sic] in *Tajmahal*. '[For,] it has a perceptible nasal twang to it'.[88] A few pages later, speaking of a pre-recorded introduction by Lata to 'an orchestral version of ten of her favourite tunes', Bhimani notes that 'Her voice was clear and soft. Like that of a girl on the threshold of adolescence'.[89] It is this heterosexual male fantasy of a *Hindu adolescent girl*, both controllable and ever-ready to please, that is an overwhelming aspect of the desire that congregates around Lata's voice.[90] Also, in keeping with the unbridled possibilities of fantasies, the voice that conjures the pliable adolescent girl also concurrently facilitates the invocatory gesture that imagines the 'mother'.[91]

I do not, however, mean to present Lata herself as a passive figure, merely singing to the tunes ministered by her professional mentors. There is after all no reason to assume that she herself has not been an active participant in the project of 'fine-tuning' her voice to the point of its classic recognizability. Finally, in this context, the project of purification tended, as mentioned above, to remain incomplete: therefore, whilst the 'ideal' feminine voice of Indian popular culture did, in fact, became derivative of Lata's style, the Muslim-ness of Indian filmic culture also remained an inescapable reality. Throughout the post-Independence period, film titles and song lyrics continued to borrow heavily from Persian and Urdu, and many of the most prominent lyricists and actors were also Muslim. In fact, in several films Lata was also the playback singer for Muslim on-screen characters, with the result that when she lent her voice to an on-screen *tawaif*, the *tawaif* sang with all the 'sweetness' of a girl-child![92] In these ways the project of Hinduizing Indian public culture remained unfinished and may be best viewed as a contest over the cultural terrain.[93]

THE FIVE-YEAR PLAN HERO

It is the context of twentieth-century development theory, as expressed through the formulation of the Indian planning regime, that provides the next rung of my argument. For a fuller understanding of the sign of the filmic woman who embodies Lata's voice, we have to turn to the filmic man whose identity, I suggest, is strongly linked to the nationalist economic development philosophy reified in the formulation and implementation of the Five-Year Plans. I want, then, to link the discussion thus far to the male hero of the post-Independence film era, and will refer to him as the Five-Year-Plan (FYP) hero.[94] The iconic presence of the FYP hero gained its legitimacy through both the Keynesian *and* the neo-classical models of economic thought, and he stood both for government intervention and for delayed gratification through the reinvestment of savings for the 'national' good. The FYP hero represents, in a broad sense, a particular formulation of Indian masculinity where manliness comes to attach not to bodily representations or aggressive behaviour but, rather, to being 'scientific' and 'rational'.[95]

In the Indian case, economic development policies, especially in the guise of the Soviet-inspired Five-Year Plans, traced a particular lineage to the world of science, not least through figures such as the physicist and statistician P.C. Mahalanobis (1893–1972), an active Brahmo Samaji, keen researcher of anthropometry, founder of the Indian Statistical Institute, and a leading influence upon the formulation of the second Five-Year Plan.[96] One of the ways in which the scientific nature of the FYP hero—and Mahalanobis is perhaps the most obvious real life example of this post-colonial figure—came to be represented on the screen was through the operation of very specific spatial strategies. An important aspect of this strategy was the iconic use of roads and highways in the Hindi films of the 1950s and 1960s. My gesture is to the bitumen road as a place of encounter between the hero and the heroine, as the backdrop to crucial song sequences, and as the linear space that provided the musical interlude for the display of the FYP hero's technological aptitude as he adeptly handles that epitome of modernist desire: the motor car. Indeed, roads and highways in these films seem to carry such an aura of a planned modernity—all those aspirations of 'progressing' in both literal and figurative senses—that the woman at the steering wheel and women on bicycles riding along the open highway become one of the most powerfully evocative representations of the 'modern' Indian womanhood; 'these' women come to embody a manual dexterity that marked them as visibly different.

It could also be suggested that the recurring association between the road/highway and the FYP hero really serves to emphasize another point: that of the 'natural' milieu of the FYP hero, the metropolis.[97] We get some idea of the metropolis as a structuring trope through a series of post-Independence Hindi films. Therefore:

> in films such as *Shri 420* (1955, Raj Kapoor), *New Delhi* (1956, Mohan Segal), *Sujata* (1959, Bimal Roy) and *Anuradha* (1960, Hrishikesh Mukherjee), the struggle over meaning and being in a post-colonial society takes place in a context where the metropolis is always a willful presence.[98]

Here, as in other films, the metropolis is, by turns, a site of decadence and extravagance, luring 'innocent' people into its web; a progressive influence upon 'backward' intellects, and the promise of a contractual civil society which would undermine the atavism of kin and caste affiliations, ostensibly typified by the cinematic village. However, perhaps, most importantly, the metropolis is also home to the modern, male, 'improver': the FYP hero.

Spatial strategies are particularly important representational tools in these films, in which, as I have noted in another discussion, 'the aura of the metropolis manifests itself through a new language of cinematic space, [and] where striation and secularization become important expressive principles'.[99] Therefore, the opening shots of *New Delhi* establish the sense of the post-colonial modernity that the hero hopes to find in the milieu of the city. It is a modernity that expresses itself through the measured grid of roads, traffic lights, and footpaths; and the camera, the hero, and the audience look out at these landmarks from a car being driven along major thoroughfares along which are dotted office buildings and other memorials to the nation-state. In *New Delhi*/New Delhi, economic planning and city planning come together 'at a juncture where state intervention and a geometrical sensibility of modernity produce a peculiarly post-colonial nationalist aesthetics'.[100]

In some instances, the aura of the city is figured as the capacity of the male body to infiltrate those national spaces, such as the village, that may still be under the sway of 'primitive' influences. Here, the metropolitan male body—imbued with an individualism that marks the triumph of the emphasis on personality in post-colonized contexts—fairly hurtles along national highways and train tracks, en route to the cinematic village; his object of social transformation is to be achieved through the transformation of *personalities*, and his presence as metropolitan virtues incarnate is the chief therapy. The hero is 'a projectile, clearing the way for a national space and effacing the embarrassment of backward spaces (and 'mentalities') with searing speed and unstoppable forward, always 'forward', momentum'.[101]

One way of exploring this aspect of an important filmic convention is to think of Mikhail Bakhtin's notion of the chronotope, 'the intrinsic connectedness of temporal and spatial relationships that are artistically expressed in literature'.[102] One of these, the chronotope of the road, consists in the fusing together of time and space (hence 'forming the road'). This, Bakhtin points out, 'is the source of the rich metaphorical expansion on the image of the road as a course: "the course of life", "to set out on a new course", "the course of history" and so on'.[103] Extending this discussion, we may argue that in Indian films, roads and highways become metonymic of the path to nation-hood itself: where 'people who are normally kept separate by social and spatial distance can accidentally meet; any contrast may crop up, the most various fates may collide and interweave with one another'.[104] Thus, the road and the FYP hero combine to reify the notion of progress of national life, of modernity, of the male hero as the mobile (and speedy!) agent of change, and of that 'civil' space from which all roads, and ideas of change, emanate: the metropolis. The male hero—wayfarer of Indian films has modern knowledge—scientific knowledge—as his most fundamental attitude, and this knowledge becomes the mark of post-colonized middle-class masculinity.

Indeed, the filmic hero of that era was, typically, portrayed as an engineer (building roads or dams), a doctor, a scientist, or a bureaucrat. Now, the cinematic presence of the hero was also one which could be quite easily characterized as 'camp', for the camp persona of the heterosexual hero could coexist quite comfortably with a nationalist ideology that identified post-Independence manliness as aligned to the 'new' knowledge of science and rationality which, it held, would transform the 'irrational' native into the modern citizen. We need, then, to differentiate between corporeal and *epistemological* masculinity,[105] with the latter arising out of the specific historical circumstance of post-colonized life in which nationalist discourses on gender and modernity engaged with colonial representations of the 'effeminate' native.[106] Thus, the FYP hero became the post-Independence masculinist ideal: 'homo scientificus' and 'homo economicus' rolled into one.[107] It is at this point that the relationship between Indian metropolitan and provincial culture and their different histories comes into play.[108]

It is possible to argue that the scientific career—of an engineer, or a doctor—as an avenue of social advancement was and continues to be more sought after by the provincial middle-classes rather than their metropolitan counterparts. This is linked to the specific conditions of Indian post-coloniality in which the vast majority of the provincial bourgeoisie has lacked the avenues for the acquisition of 'cultural capital'.[109] In other words, a situation where 'technical' qualifications are the prime means of social advancement for the provincial middle-classes. Therefore, in the metropolitan centres a 'Pass' degree in English literature or history from certain universities and colleges was often sufficient caché towards well-remunerated employment in, say, the corporate sector; for here 'social capital' (i.e. 'contacts') were also a part of the context. For middle- and lower-middle-class men from provincial towns and cities, however, technical qualifications provided the principal means of a reasonably secure livelihood, reflecting the differential development of metropolitan and provincial systems of education and the relationship between the English language and the 'vernaculars' in post-colonial societies. It could therefore be argued that the FYP hero is, in fact, a representation of the provincial bourgeois male and the representation of women, vis-à-vis Lata's voice, expresses the provincial male desire to keep a check on 'its' women in a time of rapid change.

Now, to make some further connections, we might also consider reading the filmic romance of the 1950s and 1960s as narratives for the 'future development' of the individual. If we bear in mind the asymmetry between Indian metropolitan and cultural spheres, then it is not difficult to speak of the provincial male (and female) as the subject of the movie romance and the complex role of the latter as the site of a narrative of the 'future development' denied by the economic process. To be 'in love' could then, in some but not all contexts, act as a metonym for 'freedom': the freedom to 'achieve', to individual choice, and, finally, to 'fulfilment'.[110] Here, my suggestion is, therefore that the Hindi film of the above era was really a compact between those who made the film and those who watched it. The (provincial male) audience found itself fully represented on the screen, and most of the song-writers and script writers were, in fact, provincial men for whom the film industry was a means of employment that did not require any formal qualifications. The 'check' which was sought to be imposed on filmic women through Lata's voice was expressed in another way which brings to the fore the provincial–metropolitan angle of my discussion. The heroine singing in a public place not only sang in an adolescent-girl voice, but also mouthed lyrics which, in addition to Urdu, also drew heavily from the various *dialects* of Hindi. In other words, from the various provincial versions of Hindi, which, in its national incarnation, has been Sanskritized in order to give it a classical genealogy.

It could be suggested, then, that Lata's voice—her artistry—was also a part of the process through which men from strong patriarchal backgrounds—the film industry people—sought to exercise control over the representation of women through both an expressive timbre and a vocabulary which resonated with more 'controllable' environment: the village and the province. The city can, potentially, be a threat to male hegemony, and the presence of the screen-woman in its public places compounded this threat. Therefore, if the heroine figure was infantilized through Lata's voice, she was also produced as familiar and speaking, or, rather, singing, in the language of 'home' and the controllable domestic space rather than a recently produced public sphere, the nation.[111]

However, it would be naive to posit a simple relationship between a 'modern' metropolitan milieu and the *lack* of patriarchal strictures; writers and thinkers such as Krishna Sobti, Fanishwarnath Renu, Rajendra Yadav also tell us something about other sites of 'progressive' thinking. It may be more fruitful, then, to suggest that if on the one hand the Lata complex emerged from the patriarchal concerns of provincial male culture, it was no less connected to the *modernization* of patriarchal forms prevalent in Indian metropolitan culture.

In addition to the 'scientific' persona of the FYP hero, it is also worth noting that his 'task' was usually positioned vis-à-vis the countryside: he acted to bring enlightenment to India's villages, a theme borrowed from, among others, Orientalist and development theory-orientated discourses about the 'irrational' peasants and their recalcitrance in accepting the logic of modernity. Now, inasmuch as the heroine sang in her adolescent girl voice and the songs were sprinkled liberally with words from village dialects, 'woman' as sign also came to represent the village (or province, e.g. *Anuradha*, 1960);[112] that which needed to be 'improved', to be made more 'rational' through the efforts of men who embodied the new knowledge which had made the West 'progressive' and India, backward. The metropolitan theme has an important history in Indian nationalist discourse,[113] and it is this which also finds play in the case of Lata and her music: men became the progressive 'metropolis' and women the backward 'countryside'. Further, the 'imbrication of sexuality, sex, gender, and nature'[114] happens in Lata's case through the voice itself: the 'natural' identity of the woman is aligned to that of the girl-child, and hence adult femaleness is naturalized by associating the adult woman as forever closer to childhood, inasmuch as in popular discourse the child is seen to be closer to nature.

Hence, either way—through 'traditional' provincial masculine politics or 'modern' metropolitan nationalist discourse—the sign of 'woman' continued to be inscribed through masculinist ideologies. The sexual politics that gathered around Lata was one that sought to rid the public sphere of the 'disreputableness' that was seen to attach to the figure of the female public performer (who was frequently non-Hindu, as well as non-upper caste), as well as conjure a figure of controllable female sexuality that would prove an appropriate companion for the sober, frugal, and rational persona of the FYP hero.

Of course, Lata's appeal did not simply disappear with the waning of the FYP hero, and she continued to have hits in the post-FYP hero period in films such as *Hum Aapke Hain Koun* (1994; directed by Sooraj Barjatya). This, I suggest, marks a situation of the resurgence of Lata-ness in the new context of late twentieth and early twenty-first century consumerist and familial modernity where the idea of Lata Mangeshkar—its model of femininity—has renewed resonance. Within this context of the 'modern' family and consumerist-as-autonomy, 'the new ideological stress on the couple is accompanied, not by a new acknowledgement of the possibility of decoupling, but by a new stress on the indissolubility of their relationship'.[115] This, as Parry suggests, is a situation in which the emphasis on the significance of the conjugal bond as a path to being modern is also one where 'wives pay a price in individual autonomy for the greater stability of their marriage'.[116] Hence, in this way, 'Lata'—once the conjunctional site of the ideologies of masculinity and patriarchy, colonialism, Indian nationalism, and the relationship between the metropolis and the province—continues to have contemporary significance.

NOTES AND REFERENCES

1. A different version of this chapter appeared earlier in *Economic and Political Weekly* 39, no. 20 (2004).
2. Another context, Lata's popularity among the recent Indian diaspora, is a project in itself, and might be explored in the context of contemporary imaginings of 'home' and 'tradition'. As Ravi S. Vasudevan points out, 'where ...[Indian cinema's] reach has extended beyond the moorings of the 'original community" and its international extensions, interesting issues arise about the nature of its attractions'. Ravi S. Vasudevan, 'Introduction', *Making Meaning in Indian Cinema*, Ravi S. Vasudevan (ed.), (Delhi: Oxford University Press, 2000), p. 8.
3. Rahul Sankrityayan's *ghummakkad* methodology, in Rahul Sankrityayan, *Ghummakkad Shashtra* (Hindi), (Delhi: Kitab Mahal, [1948] 1994), and Michel Foucault's 'genealogical' analyses, in Michel Foucault, *Discipline and Punish: The Birth of the Prison* (New York: Vintage Books, 1979) and Michel Foucault, *The History of Sexuality, vol. 1, An Introduction* (London: Penguin, 1990) have, in their different ways, helped me to think about the relationship between the discursive and non-discursive realms in a non-teleological manner.
4. I am grateful to Moinak Biswas for raising this issue.
5. K. Hansen, *Grounds for Play: The Nautanki Theatre of North India* (Berkeley: University of California Press, 1992).
6. Karine Schomer, *Mahadevi Varma and the Chhayavad Age of Modern Hindi Poetry* (Berkeley: University of California Press, 1983).
7. This discussion is based on information gathered by Mr Har Mandir Singh 'Hamraaz' of Kanpur. I am grateful to Hamraazji for his kind assistance in this and other matters.
8. 'Fan clubs' are a particularly important part of film culture in south India, though they seem to be chiefly organized around screen stars rather than film music. Perhaps the greater prominence of playback artistes in north India as

compared to the south accounts for this. S.V. Srinivas provides an interesting account of the activities of fan clubs devoted to the Telugu superstar Chiranjeevi. S.V. Srinivas, 'Devotion and Defiance in Fan Activity', in Ravi S. Vasudevan (ed.), *Making Meaning in Indian Cinema* (Delhi, Oxford University Press, 2000).

9. 'Saga of the Compiler's Odyssey': *http://hamraaz.org./sco1.htm*.
10. Ibid.
11. Ibid.
12. Peter Manuel, *Cassette Culture: Popular Music and Technology in Northern India* (Chicago: University of Chicago Press, 1993), p. 267, 10n.
13. Manuel, *Cassette Culture*, p. 52.
14. Raghava Menon quoted in Manuel, *Cassette Culture*, p. 53.
15. Chandavarkar quoted in Manuel, *Cassette Culture*, p. 53.
16. Manuel, *Cassette Culture*, p. 53.
17. The main singers of the Dholi Gayikayen ('Female singers with drum accompaniment') group whose recording I possess are Jamila Kulsum and Natha Bai. The Dholis are a caste of professional musicians from Rajasthan and commonly perform at Hindu ritual occasions. The singing is accompanied by large drums known as the *dhol*. See Varsha Joshi, 'Drum and Drummer in the Peasant Society', in R. Joshi and N.K. Singhi (eds.), *Folk, Faith and Feudalism* (Jaipur: Rawat Publications, 1994). I am grateful to Ann Grodzins Gold, Varsha Joshi, Manohar Lalals, Nancy Martin, and Shirley Trembath for responding to my request for information. The recording I have access to was made by the Social Work and Research Centre at Tilonia in Rajasthan, and is part of its archive on folk-music.
18. Cassette recording: *The Festival of India*, vol. I, The Gramophone Company of India Ltd., 1987 (?). Here, Zohra Bai sings in *raag* Bhopali.
19. As stated earlier, I am aware of the limitations of such a *description* of voice qualities, and invite the reader acquainted with Indian music to evaluate my statements in the light of personal experience. Of course, many will already be familiar with the performers and performance style I refer to, as also with the ritual singing mentioned. From my own experience, the principal criterion for inclusion in the latter is usually perceived to be kin responsibility rather than a predefined voice quality; in his autobiography, Mahatma Gandhi was to note that during Hindu marriage ceremonies 'women, whether they have a voice or no, sing themselves hoarse'. M.K. Gandhi, *An Autobiography: Or The Story of My Experiments with Truth* (Ahmedabad: Navjivan Trust, [1927] 1990), p. 7.
20. Cassette recording: *The Best of Farida Khanum. Urdu Modern Songs*, vols. 1 and 2, 1992, The Gramophone Company of India Ltd.
21. S.R. Faruqui and F.W. Pritchett, 'Lyric Poetry in Urdu: The Ghazal', in Barbara Stoler Miller (ed.), *Masterworks of Asian Literature in Contemporary Perspective: A Guide for Teaching* (New York: M.E. Sharpe, 1994), p. 94.

22. See Manuel, *Cassette Culture*, p. 53. The issue of a fortuitous fit between Lata's voice and the technology for public recordings is also sometimes offered as an explanation for its popularity; there is always some merit in arguments that tell us something about the intersection between technology and culture, but to leave matters at that is merely to defer to technological determinism.
23. S. Zutshi, 'Women, Nation and the Outsider in Contemporary Hindi Cinema', in T. Niranjana, P. Sudhir, and V. Dhareshwar (eds.), *Interrogating Modernity, Culture and Colonialism in India* (Calcutta: Seagull, 1993), p. 94.
24. Ibid., p. 102.
25. Partha Chatterjee, 'The Nationalist Resolution of the Women's Question', in K. Sangari and S. Vaid (eds.), *Recasting Women: Essays in Colonial History* (New Delhi: Kali for Women, 1993a); and, in the same volume, Lata Mani, 'Contentious Traditions: The Debate over *Sati* in Colonial India'.
26. S. Srivastava, *Constructing Post-Colonial India: National Character and the Doon School* (London: Routledge, 1998), ch. 4.
27. See also Susan Bayly, 'Vietnamese Intellectuals and Postcolonial Times', *Critique of Anthropology* 24 (3): 320–44, (2004) and Tanika Sarkar, *Hindu Wife, Hindu Nation: Community, Religion, and Cultural Nationalism* (Bloomington: University of Indiana Press, 2001).
28. James Clifford, *The Predicament of Culture: Twentieth-Century Ethnography, Literature and Art* (Cambridge, Mass.: Harvard University Press, 1988); A. Gupta and J. Ferguson, 'Beyond "Culture": Space, Identity and the Politics of Difference', *Cultural Anthropology* 7(1): 6-23, (1992).
29. R. Gibson, 'Camera Natura: Landscape in Australian Feature Films', in J. Frow and M. Morris (eds.), *Australian Cultural Studies: A Reader* (Sydney: Allen & Unwin, 1993).
30. Sister Nivedita, *Hints on National Education in India* (Calcutta: Ubodhan, 1923), p. 59.
31. Sister Nivedita, *Hints on National Education in India*, p. 57.
32. Ibid., p. 59.
33. Ibid., p. 61.
34. My most immediate reference is to recent work in anthropology that has sought to problematize this spatial consciousness within anthropological theory. A representative sample of discussions can be found in Gupta and Ferguson, 'Beyond "Culture"'.
35. U. Thakur, *Madhubani Painting* (New Delhi: Abhinav Publications, 1982).
36. M.C. Beach, *Mughal and Rajput Painitng* (Cambridge: Cambridge University Press, 1992).
37. Karine Schomer, *Mahadevi Varma and the Chhayavad Age of Modern Hindi Poetry* (Berkeley: University of California Press, 1983), p. 11.
38. Vishnubhatt Godse, *Ankhon Dekha Gadar* (Eyewitness to the Mutiny), translated with an Introduction by Amritlal Nagar (Delhi: Rajpal and Sons, 1986).

39. C. Pateman, *The Disorder of Women: Democracy, Feminism and Political Discourse* (Cambridge: Polity Press, 1989).
40. A.K. Coomaraswamy, *The Dance of Shiva: Fourteen Indian Essays* (New Delhi: Munshiram Manoharlal, 1974), p. 103.
41. Ibid., p. 103.
42. Ibid., p. 104.
43. The milieu to which I am referring at could be better described as constituted through the 'patron–performer–audience nexus'. See K. Hansen, *Grounds for Play: The Nautanki Theatre of North India* (Berkeley: University of California Press), p. 251.
44. Coomaraswamy, *The Dance of Shiva*, p. 103.
45. I could be accused here of falling into the kind of romanticism—based on the speech-writing binary—that Derrida critiques in Levi-Strauss's work. However, one can argue that cultural contexts where orality continues to be a major aspect of social interaction, whilst not intrinsically morally 'superior' to 'writing' contexts (indeed, this would be a banal point), may have *different* modes of sociality. This may or may not have any implications for the presence or lack of hierarchies; rather, the question is one of investigating the variations of sociality, rather than asking: 'Do we really know what writing is?'. Jacques Derrida, *Of Grammatology* (Baltimore: John Hopkins Press, 1976). Also Christopher Johnson, *Derrida: The Scene of Writing* (London: Phoenix, 1997). The issue, specifically, is about the *different* forms of power (not their lack!) that characterize different interactional contexts. Oral contexts, no matter how contingent, *can* have their own social and cultural dynamic, and this does not in itself, suggests the reduction of 'textuality' to a 'second order ideological expression'. H.K. Bhabha, *The Location of Culture* (London: Routledge, 1994), p. 23.
46. S.S. Wadley, 'Choosing a Path: Performance Strategies in a North Indian Epic', in S.H. Blackburn, P.J. Claus, J.B. Flueckiger, and S.W. Wadley (eds.), *Oral Epics in India* (Berkeley: University of California Press, 1989), p. 81. (Emphasis added).
47. Ibid., p. 97. See also Hansen, *Grounds for Play*, on north Indian Nautanki theatre.
48. Lest this be regarded as a variety of romanticism on behalf of 'tradition', we should remember that even in the relatively structured milieu of an Indian classical music concert in urban India, the audience has considerable scope for (vocal) interaction with the performer (see also Hansen, *Grounds for Play*, pp. 243–51); and this in a post-colonial context with a long history of instruction on the 'proper' relationship between audiences and performers. However, I am also mindful of Kathryn Hansen's comment (personal communication) that not *all* 'traditional' performance genres were necessarily strictly oral, and hence my view on orality may be open to dispute.
49. Manuel, *Cassette Culture*, p. 50.

50. The general point Ravi S. Vasudevan makes is also applicable here: 'Traditional form', he says, 'far from being fixed or fixing of cinematic convention, has been selective and open to revision'. 'Introduction',Vasudevan (ed.), *Making Meaning in Indian Cinema*, p. 11.
51. Hansen, *Grounds for Play*, p. 243
52. Manuel, *Cassette Culture*.
53. Quoted in H. Bhimani, *In Search of Lata Mangeshkar* (New Delhi: Indus, 1995), p. 16.
54. There have only been vague discussions about one relationship.
55. For more on *bhakta* poets, see the special issue on 'Women Bhakta Poets', *Manushi*, nos. 50–2 (Jan.–June, 1989).
56. David Lelyveld, 'Upon the Subdominant: Administering Music on All India Radio', in Carol A. Breckenridge (ed.), *Consuming Modernity: Public Culture in a South Asian World* (Minneapolis: University of Minnesota Press, 1995), p. 55.
57. P. Bourdieu, 'The Forms of Capital', in J.G. Richardson (ed.), *Handbook of Theory and Research in the Sociology of Education* (New York: Greenwood Press, 1986).
58. Lelyveld, 'Upon the Subdominant', p. 55.
59. Ibid.
60. S.S. Pandit, *A Critical Study of the Contribution of the Arya Samaj to Indian Education* (New Delhi: Sarvadeshik Arya Pratinidhi Sabha, 1974), p. 211.
61. Ibid., p. 156.
62. S. Srivastava, *Constructing Post-Colonial India: National Character and the Doon School* (London: Routledge, 1998).
63. Lelyveld, 'Upon the Subdominant'.
64. Ibid., p. 57.
65. Ibid., p. 58.
66. I am aware that at this time AIR had several Muslim musicians on its staff and recognize that *everyday* relationships between Hindu and Muslim musicians may, in fact, have been quite cordial. However, meta-discourses, such as those of Hindu nationalism, are not, usually, about complexities of practices.
67. R. Sunder Rajan, *Real and Imagined Women* (London: Routledge, 1993); Partha Chatterjee, *The Nation and its Fragments: Colonial and Postcolonial Histories* (Princeton: Princeton University Press, 1993).
68. Lelyveld, 'Upon the Subdominant', p. 59. See also S. Chakravarty, *National Identity in Indian Popular Cinema, 1947–1987* (Austin: University of Texas Press, 1993) and E. Barnouw and S. Krishnaswamy, *Indian Film* (New York: Columbia University Press, 1963), pp. 200-205.
69. Bhartendu Harishchandra, *Pratinidhi Sankalan* (essays in Hindi edited by Kamala Prasad), (New Delhi: National Book Trust, 1995), p. 117.
70. B. Chaitanya Deva, *An Introduction to Indian Music* (New Delhi: Publications Division, Government of India, 1992), p. 106.

71. See, for example, B. Kapferer, *Legends of the People, Myths of State: Violence, Intolerance, and Political Culture in Sri Lanka and Australia* (Washington: Smithsonian Institution Press, 1988), esp. pp. 127–32.
72. Charu Gupta, *Sexuality, Obscenity, Community: Women, Muslims, and the Hindu Public in Colonial India* (New York: Palgrave, 2001), p. 243.
73. Ibid., p. 243.
74. Ibid., p. 298.
75. Mukul Kesavan, 'Urdu, Awadh and the Tawaif: The Islamicate Roots of Indian Cinema', in Zoya Hasan (ed.), *Forging Identities: Gender, Communities and the State in India* (Boulder, Colorado: Westview Press, 1994), p. 245.
76. Also, although, as Kesavan points out, 'Muslim influence' may not itself be a simple term to define, it is nevertheless one we can meaningfully employ. Further, this is not to suggest that other non-Hindu groups such as Parsis and Christians did not have a presence in the film industry; rather, that at the time Muslims formed a considerable proportion of film-industry workers, and that the idea of 'Muslim influence' had considerable public currency. I owe this point to a discussion with Kathryn Hansen, though do not claim to represent her point of view.
77. *Raiis*: literally, a wealthy man; also a man of leisure, given to 'pleasures'. (All translations from Hindustani texts by the author). S.H. Manto, *Meenabazar* (Delhi: Rajkamal Paperbacks [1962] 1984), p. 14.
78. Manto, *Meenabazar*, p. 17.
79. S. Chakravarty, *National Identity in Indian Popular Cinema, 1947–1987* (Austin: University of Texas Press, 1993), p. 37.
80. Ibid., p. 39.
81. Manto, *Meenabazar*, pp. 19–20.
82. Krishna Sobti, *Mitro Marjani* (New Delhi: Rajkamal Paperbacks, [1967] 1994).
83. Hence, the 'professional' singer of Hindi films—as opposed to the 'spontaneously' melodic heroine, who was liable to break out into song at any time in order to express her 'inner' self—was usually the *tawaif* figure; the (Hindu) heroine who aspired to be a professional singer was usually a representative of the 'modern' woman, and carried within her an *unsettling* aspect. Illustrative examples of this may be found in films such as *Anuradha* (1960) and *Abhimaan* (1973), both directed by Hrishikesh Mukherjee.
84. See, for example, Premchand, *Sewasadan* (Delhi: Rajkamal Paperbacks [1921], 1994). This aspect of courtesan characterization was perhaps most successfully propagated through the medium of Hindi films. Therefore, in films such as *Kala Pani* (1958; Raj Khosla), *Sahib Bibi Aur Ghulam* (1962; Abrar Alvi), and *Chitralekha* (1964; Kidar Sharma) the courtesan is a figure of mysterious sophistication.
85. There is another interesting aspect to the aura of middle-class respectability that subsequently gathered around Lata. Her own family background was, in

the context of early twentieth century culture, an ambiguous one, for her father, Master Dinanath, had been a very well-known singer and actor on the Marathi stage and, hence, may have been somewhat at the margins of 'respectable' Maharashtrian society; to reiterate his strong opposition to a life on the stage for his daughter, Dinanath is reported to have said that 'this work might offer money and fame, but not social standing'. Bhimani, *In Search of Lata Mangeshkar*, p. 83. The degree to which Lata's own career also constitutes a drive towards attaining 'respectability' must remain a point of conjecture. I am grateful to Kathryn Hansen for raising this issue.

86. In more recent times, Lata has openly associated with activities linked to the 'Hindu fundamentalist' Rashtriya Swayamsevak Sangh (RSS) and other similar organizations. These have included involvement in public events, such as fund-raisers, sponsored by organizations such as the Shiv Sena, and, singing songs for a documentary on RSS's founder Dr Hegdewar (*Organiser*, 7 Nov. 2004). I have chosen not to devote much space to this aspect as such activities in themselves may not say much: the actor Dilip Kumar, a Muslim, has also appeared at Shiv Sena organized rallies. Lata's current association with, say, the RSS, only makes sense in light of the longer social history of which she is a part.

87. Bhimani, *In Search of Lata Mangeshkar*, p. 21.

88. Ibid.

89. Ibid., p. 34.

90. This of course begs the question of the grounds of women's attraction to Lata's voice, a research project in itself. However, given what Raheja and Gold have to say about the abundant 'sexual play' in the songs of rural women in Uttar Pradesh and Rajasthan, the admiration for Lata's 'pre-sexual' style merits careful scrutiny. See G.G. Raheja and A.G. Gold, *Listen to the Heron's Words: Reimagining Gender and Kinship in North India* (Berkeley: University of California Press, 1994).

91. From the 1990s, Hindi films have witnessed the incursion of other kinds of female voices, such as those of Ila Arun in Subhash Ghai's 1993 film *Khalnayak*, and Sapna Awasthi in the 1998 film *Dil Se*, directed by Mani Ratnam. These 'other' tonalities provide Indian public culture with a resonance that is markedly different from that of Lata's style, as well as pointing to a ferment over the meaning of desirable femininity, or at least to an opening up of the question of feminine identity.

92. Interestingly, Lata's sister Asha Bhonsle, who specialized in providing playback voices for 'non-domesticated' female characters, also occasionally sang in an adolescent-girl voice (e.g. in *Sahib Bibi Aur Ghulam*—the '*Bhanwara bara nadan hai*' number picturized on Waheeda Rehman). However, these songs were usually regarded as oddities in Asha's repertoire.

93. Of particular interest is Lata's playback role in films which were predominantly about Muslim contexts, such as *Mere Mehboob* (1963; H.S. Rawal).

94. Masculinity has had a varied career in Hindi films; for some other examples see Chakravarty, *National Identity in Indian Popular Cinema*, especially ch. 6; Sudhir Kakar, *Intimate Relations: Exploring Indian Sexuality* (Chicago: University of Chicago Press, 1990); and Madhava Prasad, *Ideology of the Hindi Film: An Historical Construction* (Delhi: Oxford University Press, 1998). It should also be added that the singing voices that most typified the FYP hero were those provided by Mohammad Rafi and the 'earlier' Kishore Kumar. The dominance of Lata's voice was part of the same process that established the styles popularized by Rafi and Kishore Kumar as the norms for male singers. I have been led to be explicit about this at the suggestion of Madhava Prasad (personal communication).
95. S. Srivastava, 'The Garden of Rational Delights: The Nation as Experiment, Science as Masculinity', *Social Analysis*, no. 39, pp. 119–48, (1996).
96. In a 1922 edition of the *Records of the Indian Museum*, Mahalanobis published a statistical paper entitled 'Anthropological Observations on Anglo-Indians of Calcutta, Part I: Male Stature'; his interest in anthropometry led him to also do some work in England in 1927 on the so-called Pearson's Coefficient of Racial Likeness. Information compiled from Ashok Rudra, *Prasanta Chandra Mahalanobis: A Biography* (New Delhi: Oxford University Press, 1996) and from Indian Statistical Institute (n.d.) '"Professor", the Founder' (obtained via the Indian Statistical Institute website). See also Partha Chatterjee, *The Nation and its Fragments: Colonial and Postcolonial Histories* (Princeton: Princeton University Press, 1993b), ch. 10.
97. The following discussion has been adapted from S. Srivastava, *Constructing Post-Colonial India: National Character and the Doon School* (London: Routledge, 1998), pp. 165–7.
98. Ibid., p. 165.
99. Ibid.
100. Ibid., p. 166.
101. Ibid.
102. M.M. Bakhtin, 'Forms of Time and of the Chronotope in the Novel. Notes Towards a Historical Poetics', in M. Holquist (ed.), *The Dialogical Imagination: Four Essays by M.M. Bakhtin* (Austin: University of Texas Press, 1990), p. 84.
103. Ibid., p. 244.
104. Ibid., p. 243.
105. Srivastava, *Constructing Post-Colonial India*.
106. Mrinalini Sinha, *Colonial Masculinity: The 'Manly Englishman' and the Effeminate Bengali in the Nineteenth Century* (Manchester: Manchester University Press, 1995).
107. During the 1970s and 1980s, the epistemological masculinity framework of Hindi films was most conspicuously undermined by superstar Amitabh Bachchan's film persona. See, for example, Prasad, *Ideology of the Hindi Film*.

108. For a discussion of aspects of the relationship between Indian 'metropolitan' and 'provincial' cultures, see Nita Kumar, 'Provincialism in Modern India: The Multiple Narratives of Education and their Pain', unpublished paper, 2003.
109. P. Bourdieu, 'The Forms of Capital', in J.G. Richardson (ed.), *Handbook of Theory and Research in the Sociology of Education* (New York: Greenwood Press, 1986).
110. Film songs play a considerable role in the promotional activities of 'sex-clinic' operators in Delhi and Mumbai. Inasmuch as sexuality has become an important area for the expression of contemporary individuality and autonomy, it further highlights the popular association between filmic romance and the possibilities of achieving one's 'full' potential. See S. Srivastava, 'Non-Gandhian Sexuality, Commodity Cultures and a "Happy Married Life": Masculine and Sexual Cultures in the Metropolis', in Sanjay Srivastava (ed.), *Sexual Sites, Seminal Attitudes* (New Delhi: Sage, 2004).
111. During the past two decades, Hindi song lyrics appear to have moved away from the earlier reliance on both the dialects as well as Urdu. This may be due, among other factors, to the urban background of contemporary lyricists, Hindutva politics, NRI audiences, and recognition of the non-middle-class audiences for films.
112. Interestingly, Kaali presents a different perspective in his analysis of the 'Old Nativity' film from Tamil Nadu, within which the 'urbane woman' comes to represent both the city and modernity. Sundar Kaali, 'Narrating Seduction: Vicissitudes of the Sexed Subject in Tamil Nativity Film', in Vasudevan (ed.), *Making Meaning in Indian Cinema,* p. 107. As Kaali also points out, in this context, 'The taming of the educated, urbane woman is the means by which male lack is liquidated, or rather, projected onto the female'. Ibid., 107. This was also, of course, true of Hindi cinema, though more frequently its 'city girl'—barring roles portrayed by actresses such as Nargis and Saira Bano—was not the film's heroine.
113. Srivastava, *Constructing Post-Colonial India.*
114. C.A. Holmlund, 'Visible Difference and Flex Appeal: The Body, Sex, Sexuality, and Race in the *Pumping Iron* Films', in S. Birrell and C. Cole (eds.), *Women, Sport, and Culture* (Champaign, IL.: Human Kinetics, 1994), p. 305.
115. Jonathan Parry, 'Ankalu's Errant Wife: Sex, Marriage and Industy in Contemporary Chhattisgarh', *Modern Asian Studies* 35, no. 4 (2001), p. 817.
116. Ibid.

The Mapping of Guru Dutt's Comedic Vision

DARIUS COOPER

Not much (if any at all) critical attention has been focused on Guru Dutt's earlier filmic efforts in mapping out 'comedy's utopian dimensions',[1] especially in his full-length comedies *Aar Paar* (Heads or Tails, 1954), and *Mr & Mrs 55* (1955), or his carefully orchestrated comedic moments focused around the conspicuous presence of comedian Johnny Walker in *Pyaasa* (The Thirsty One, 1957) and *Kaagaz Ke Phool* (Paper Flowers, 1959). Taking my cue from his sad protagonist's musical utterance in *Pyaasa*:

> *Gham se ab ghabrana kaisa*
> *Gham sau baar mila...*
> (Why should I be afraid of sorrow
> Having encountered it a hundred times...)

what I wish to undertake in this essay is to evaluate the 'other' side of Guru Dutt's talents which lay in his 'emotional detachment from the fate of his individual characters',[2] primarily in his two comedies *Aar Paar* and *Mr & Mrs 55* in directorial contrast to his narcissistic involvement with the tragic characters of *Pyaasa* and *Kaagaz Ke Phool*. The buffoon/architect of *Sahib Bibi Aur Ghulam* (Master, Mistress and Slave, 1962), however, achieves happiness *in spite* of his tragic odyssey because of his small town naiveté and yokel culpabilities. Dutt's working out of the romantic comedy format in *Aar Paar* and *Mr & Mrs 55* follows very closely 'the remarkable tenacious pattern of New Comedy as defined by Northrop Frye (in which): What usually happens is that a young man wants a young woman, that his desire is resisted by some opposition, usually paternal, and that near the end...some twist in the plot enables the hero to have his will'. (Frye, 163.)[3]

In addition to these two films, I also wish to examine the important role played by the celebrated Hindi film comedian of the times, Johnny Walker, not only in *Aar Paar* and *Mr & Mrs 55* but also in the two tragically centred films *Pyaasa* and *Kaagaz Ke Phool*. His 'semiotic significance' and how Dutt manages to successfully 'contain his given roles within the individual narratives'[4] of both the comedies and the tragedies in which he features opens up fascinating areas for critical exploration. Finally, I would like to add one more layer to this essay and show how Dutt's comic vision was constructed through the creative mediums of the song and dance musical elements he inserted into these chosen film narratives. He obeyed very accurately, it seems to me, the advice given by Gene Kelly's character to his dancing and singing troupe in the 1950 musical *Summer Stock*, 'We're trying to tell a story with music and song and dance and not just with words. For instance, if the boy tells a girl he loves her, he doesn't just say it, he sings it.'[5] I will try to show, through a careful selection of Dutt's alphabet of comedic songs and dances from *Aar Paar, Mr & Mrs 55, Pyaasa,* and *Kaagaz Ke Phool*, how *through* a song and how *as* a dance, the comedic 'language (and moment of these films) is in a sense transfigured, and lifted up into a higher, more expressive realm'.[6]

Born on 9 July 1925 in a Saraswat family of Mangalore, this eldest son of the Padukone family clan was always taken for a Bengali. Gurudutt Padukone simply *became* Guru Dutt. Educated in the liberal climate of Calcutta and dissatisfied with conventional mores of education, he joined Uday Shanker's dance school in Almora for two years. In keeping with his restless nature, he made the leap from choreography to film-making by joining the famous Prabhat Studios in Pune where he patiently and assiduously learnt every aspect of film-making.

In 1954, with *Aar Paar*, Guru Dutt started his own production company and never looked back till *Sahib Bibi Aur Ghulam*, his last film in 1962. On 9 October 1964, he committed suicide but the cinematic work he has left behind makes him a giant on par with film-makers like Satyajit Ray and Ritwik Ghatak, who for me, form the first great formidable troika of Indian cinema.

Dutt's comedic utopian vision is directed at commenting on a certain kind of Indian community that was being formed in the independent Indian nation between 1954, when he makes *Aar Paar*, and 1955 when he followed up with *Mr & Mrs 55*. The utopian possibilities of being, for the first time, an Indian nation, released from over two hundred years of British rule, but also struggling with the difficulties of creating its own intrinsic social and cultural order, are translated very accurately in the determination of the romantic couples of both films to live 'happily ever after' in the nouveau post-Independence Bharat of the 1950s.

Guru Dutt's comedies were made during the euphoric period that lasted in India between 1951 to 1957. The nation's utopian tilt was visible in the many changes that were being implemented to make many dreams, realities. Pavan K. Varma catalogues these changes very accurately in *The Great Indian Middle Class*:

> Newspapers write about them. Films romanticized them...
> All in all, there was a diffused sense of buoyancy and promise.[7]

The 'most seductive goal...was', as Varma notes, 'the pursuit of modernity...[as] interpreted in the Nehruvian sense of shedding the shackles of the past and adopting a rationalist and scientific outlook'.[8] The image of the new Indian was of one who had to break with the past, or in Nehru's celebrated words from *The Discovery of India*, to progressively throw out all 'the dead wood of the past; all that was dead and had served its purpose had to go'.[9] This new Indian, in the words of another thinker, D.K. Rangrekar, 'must be able and willing to tear himself away from his family ties; flout customs and traditions...think of the future rather than the past; concentrate on material gains rather than dwell on kismat'.[10] Guru Dutt's comedies very clearly reflect this ideology, not only in the formulations of its plots and the thoughts and actions of its characters (as this essay will strive to show) but also in the very conscious adoption of the Hollywood 'modernist' mode of telling his comic stories. (The Hollywood model would *remain* even when he switched from the comic vein to the tragic!)

The overwhelming influence of the Hollywood model on Indian film-makers was historically present even *before* Indian Independence. As Guru Dutt received his formal and foundational training in making films at the famous Prabhat Studios in Pune, let us look at some of the seminal works, especially comedies, made there by many of his mentors under the powerful influence of Hollywood. In Master Vinayak's *Lagna Pahave Karun* (Let's Get Married, 1940) and *Sarkari Pahune* (Guests of the Government, 1942), historian Ashish Rajadhyaksha informs us that 'the Gundyabhau–Chumanrao duo' of these films are planned along lines very strongly 'reminiscent of Laurel and Hardy'.[11] Master Vinayak's 1939 satire, *Brandichi Batli* (Bottle of Brandy) addresses the problem of Western prohibition and Gandhian morality in a series of carefully structured gags learnt and transcribed from Hollywood's great comedians. The timid clerk in a municipal office who, under the influence of brandy, 'gets embroiled in a series of adventures, including a famous scene in a bar',[12] clearly bears affinity with the antics of the Chaplin, Keaton, and the Mack Senett school of comedy. Dhirendranath Ganguly's (a non-Prabhat satirist, but nonetheless a Bengali) *Bilet Pherat* (The England Returned, 1921) 'startled everybody', in Rajadhyaksha's words, 'with his quixotic notions of love and morality, [especially] Ganguly's acting [which] incorporated a lot of Hollywood slapstick...'[13]

In Dutt's filmic oeuvre (both comic and tragic), I detect a very stubborn and curious reluctance to deal with an Indian culture on its own intrinsic and inherently native terms. Very rarely did he adapt for any of his films a celebrated or popular Indian novel or Indian short story. (The only exceptions are *Sahib Bibi Aur Ghulam* (Master, Mistress, and Slave, 1962) based on the Bengali novel by Bimal Mitra, and *Chaudhvin Ka Chand* (Fourteenth Day of the Moon, 1960) that is set entirely in a Muslim Lakhnavi culture and is based on an Urdu story 'Jhalak' written by Saghir Usmani. Reluctant to plunge into the predominantly decadent ethos of the Bengali feudal order in pre-Independence India, he ghost-directed *Sahib Bibi Aur Ghulam* and had Abrar Alvi's name signed on as director. For the Muslim saturated *Chaudhvin Ka Chand*, M. Sadiq, a Muslim director, was chosen. This time he did not ghost-direct, and the results are obvious: though it was his most successful commercial film, on artistic and aesthetic grounds, it is his worst offering. In his 1959 *Kaagaz Ke Phool* (Paper Flowers), the film-maker protagonist of Dutt's film is supposedly making a film version of *Devdas* (Saratchandra's famous Bengali novel) but we never *see* any scenes of *Devdas* shot by him either projected in a theatre *or* even in the editing room. We never even see him directing his actress Shanti as the film's main heroine in the studio. All that one remembers of *Devdas* is a bullock cart that acts as a prop during the '*waqt ne kiya*' song sequence and a pair of street musicians singing and dancing on a studio street.

Dutt's reliance on Hollywood as his primary teacher is seen in the way in which he orchestrated the fluid movements of his camera; the way in which he arranged his *mise en scène*; the way in which his song and dance moments were created *out* of his narrative stream; and the way in which he edited his images. One astonishing discovery I made when I was teaching Preston Sturges's great comedy, the 1948 *Sullivan's Travels*, was to find how cleverly Guru Dutt had borrowed the train suicide scenes from Sturges's film and transcribed them in his 1957 film, *Pyaasa* (The Thirsty One). Several plot elements, such as that of the tramp borrowing the hero's coat; having his foot caught in the rails; and raising his hands in a crucified position in the glaring lights of the approaching steam-locomotive, were all duplicated along with the series of scenes in the railway yard bearing the same kind of lighting techniques and editing rhythms. The elaborate tracking and crane shots in the interiors of the studio in *Kaagaz* are so reminiscent of Orson Welles in *Citizen Kane*, especially the depiction of the enclosed world of Xanadu. Dutt's singular efforts at reviving the screwball traditions of Hollywood comedy and the Hollywood musical (song and dance) routines (that are particularly focused on in this essay) clearly show that notwithstanding his trained Shantiniketan Uday Shankerian roots in theatre and dance, it was Hollywood that was his consummate teacher and inspiration.

Even the tension in his characters is clearly enunciated between their nativist/Indian roots and their need to impose on them Westernized personas. In *Aar Paar*, the Iranian Rustom trying to play Hollywood's cynical Western noir figure finds his essence more under the Irani prayer topi rather than the imported silk shirt. However, in *Sahib Bibi Aur Ghulam*, *choti bahu's* '*bibi*' essence is destroyed by the Indian feudal zamindari system whereas Jaba's liberated femininity thrives under her Westernized Brahmo-Samaj upbringing. While *choti bahu* sings Hindustani songs of putting her husband's 'dust' into her *sindhur*, Jaba composes naughty libidinal songs about her '*bhola*' lover on the 'piano'. In the same film, Bhootnath's progress from country bumpkin to respectable architect is achieved at the cost of abandoning the dead Indian wood of his past. This is first indicated by the squeaky polished shoes and argyle socks he takes to wearing under his village dhoti–kurta. Then, when he eventually becomes an architect, the dhoti–kurta is abandoned for the English sahib's khaki overseer's uniform.

With the exception of *Sahib Bibi Aur Ghulam* and *Chaudhvin Ka Chand*, all his films are situated in the Westernized centres of Bombay and Calcutta. His metropolitan characters think, dress, act, and emote like Westernized Indians along the Rangnekar model previously cited. They eat and drink in Westernized hotels and live in homes that bear very few Indian signifiers. Their language is an interesting mixture of Hindi and English. Most important, their musical preferences in song and dance are Western, even when the songs are sung in Hindi. What one finds, rather (as I show), is a very strong influence of the great Hollywood musicals whose strategies and inventiveness he successfully anglicizes in his Indianized musical moments.

As Guru Dutt's filmic career commenced with the category of 'comedy', why did he make only two comedies and abandon that category to embrace the opposing one of 'tragedy'? In trying to show the links between these two phases, I want to trace this transition in relation to the emerging Indian nation-state as it is the most significant backdrop in both his comedies and tragedies.

In 'The Frames of Comic "Freedom"', Umberto Eco points out that while 'he sees the tragic as dealing with "eternal" problems [life and death, love and hate]...comedy seems more closely linked to specific social habits'.[14] In his two comedies, Dutt makes a concentrated effort to begin his examination of the emerging Indian nation-state by showing us how the newly liberated nation was interested in asserting its independence by deliberately parodying many rules and rituals in order to find its new *avaaz*. What was conspicuously noticeable in the newly-awakened aura of India was the mischievous conduct of subversion. As new kinds of rules were being insisted upon by the personal institution of family in the domestic space and by professional dictats in the work place, and as the home and the office, the street and the café, the private car and the public taxi, the public park bench and the private club seat were being imposed upon by all kinds of 'the majesty of the forbidden norms'[15] of what was acceptable in the metropolis and what was not, comedy, in the carnivalesque sense of deliberate transgression, became the most appropriate strategy to point to the absurdity of such a calculated national resolve.

When Dutt's comic protagonists throw their pies on the puffed up faces of the so-called nouveau guardians of morals in the newly emerged Indian nation-state, we enjoy such forbidden behaviour and applaud the direction those pies are taking. Why Dutt's comedies are carnivalesque is because Dutt was aware that the carnival itself had a limited lifespan, especially as the serious task of nation building continued. As new hierarchies and institutions loomed in the future, and as new norms were gradually developed and introduced in accordance with different kinds of pressures and demands constantly being made on the people, both individually and collectively, he realized he would have to abandon comedy and find a serious way of coming to terms with these changes.

Between 1951–7, the carnivalesque spirit allowed for 'the abandoning of social roles in favour of a more fluid conception of identity'[16] in India. Illiterate taxi-drivers and unemployed cartoonists could become temporary husbands on hire and getaway drivers for criminals before crowning their efforts as garage owners and newspaper editors, as Dutt's heroes in *Aar Paar* and *Mr & Mrs 55* clearly show. During this period, life in India was subject to carnivalesque laws that insisted on shattering the concerns of hierarchy in the pursuit of freedom. A respectable daughter could abandon her duty to her hardworking father and elope with an honest lover who had spent a few months in jail for speeding. A wealthy niece could break down all the locked doors of her stern aunt's mansion and elope with an unemployed cartoonist who slept most days on a park bench. The regenerative carnival spirit made corpulent landladies more feared, on the day rents were due, than their timid landlord spouses. Dutt's comedies accurately depict how, within this short period, the Indian people had 'extended the carnival into the realm of their everyday lives [and were trying] to make its resistance a permanent rather than a temporary state'.[17]

The buoyant mood in India started changing, however, after 1956. Nehru's 'living proof of the validity of a certain past and also the guarantor of a future [in which the educated (metropolitan) class's] pre-eminent participation would be ensured'[18] was now being seriously questioned because of the failure of many of his plans; the prevalent atmosphere of rampant corruption, and the disastrous defeat at the hands of China in 1961, created a nationalized hypocrisy, especially amongst the affluent and average Indian middle class. The nation was being abandoned and national interest was being replaced by personal interest. The rules that were being violated in this climate could not be examined under the carnivalesque rubric. Eternal problems related to life, death, love, and how one's very existence could dictate one's essence had to be investigated if this *new* nation was to be saved. Its enemies were many and they were all within India. As comedy did not have the equipment to deal with this alarming national predicament, Dutt chose tragedy as his new instrument through which he decided to dissect the nation's rot. The ones violating the rules had to be exposed; what was wrong with the rules had to be stated and restated and the awful truth revealed to the audience. They had to be made aware of where they were going. '*Jinhé naaz hain Hind par/voh kahaan hai?*' (Those who are so proud of India, where are they?) became the thesis, not only for his first tragic film, *Pyaasa*, in 1957, but for all the subsequent tragic films that followed. Comedy was not however completely abandoned in his tragic canvas. It was there, but now it had a marginalized presence, and with the help of his superb comedian, Johnny Walker, Dutt, again using the Hollywood format, found interesting ways (as I will show) in integrating comedy's marginal significance into the more ambitious designs of his tragic vision.

According to Frye, 'the heroes in New Comedy are innocents [who are] socially attractive. The humour often centres around misunderstandings involving the protagonist. The hero is usually of the low mimetic mode. He is like one of us, and we respond to a sense of his common humanity'.[19] We don't get an immediate evaluative pulse on Kalu Birju's essential character in *Aar Paar* when we first meet him in prison at the beginning of the film. He is a taxi driver sentenced for speeding. He wears the same prison uniform, and like the rest of the convicts he is eager to get out. He does two months before his term expires for good behaviour. However, once he steps out, a certain kind of comic individuality is established by all the indexical signs Kalu displays in asserting a certain kind of masculinity as the proud but struggling man of the metropolitan Bombay street. Dutt presents him initially as a marginalized character having no 'home' to go to. (He does go to his sister's place, but his brother-in-law evicts him for his temporary status as ex-jailbird). His appearance, as Nasreen Munni Kabir rightly notes, bears 'a hint of the Chaplinesque',[20] and in that mould he appears as the proverbial footloose figure of the bum roaming the city streets by day and sleeping at nights at the doorways of closed shops with another ragamuffin character, the young boy Elaichi, who ekes out a living selling 'grams, old papers and Hindi film-song books' on the streets. With his Muslim topi arrogantly tilted at the conventional world of respectable bourgeois values (*from* whom he hopes to secure some kind of employment) and his trousers manfully upturned at the cuffs to show his instant readiness for any kind of trouble, there is one thing that Kalu is very proud of which is 'to walk with my head always lifted'. Not crushed by his imminent *bekari*, Kalu is repeatedly shown trying to improve his impoverished existence. For example, after finding a temporary job at a private garage, we see Kalu spending his 'off' evening hours trying to learn English to move up in the tough (un)educated urban world of Bombay. When he is corrected on his desi pronunciation of the English word 'g(e)irl' by the garage owner's daughter Nikki, Kalu's response is offered in a funny augmented English sentence, 'thank you very much kindly', a phrase he has picked out from one of those numerous but sloppily written rapid English primers promising him mastery over Shakespeare's language in seven easy steps!

Preetam, the comic hero of *Mr & Mrs 55*, shares a lot of Kalu's Chaplinesque attributes. He too is introduced to us as a peripheral character. We first see him asleep on one of the benches under a row of wooden stands at a tennis court. In reality, he is a *bekaar* (or unemployed) cartoonist constantly under the care of his photographer friend, Johnny who pays his rent, feeds him, and even gives him, on formal occasions, his own suit to wear. Unlike Kalu, Preetam 'is educated' but like Kalu he is prepared to do anything in order to survive (and improve) his precarious day-to-day existence.

It is interesting to mention here that Guru Dutt plays both these characters as a comedian, and the comedy 'stems from mistakes and mishaps arising from their efforts to conform to social roles'.[21] As their representative comedic performer, Dutt inevitably propels his characters of Kalu and Preetam into the flow of mainstream Indian society where they *are* finally accepted. As their filmic creator, he doesn't really descend into their troubled psyches as he was wont to do when he played the roles of the tormented poet in *Pyaasa* and the disturbed film-maker in *Kaagaz Ke Phool*. In those films, even when given the opportunity for communal acceptance, these characters choose to deliberately 'wander away from the crowd at the end [unlike] the community which embraces Kalu and Preetam in its celebration'.[22] Dutt plays the roles of Kalu and Preetam in a very transparent way. They are presented as being very confident about who they are and what they want. Even when circumstances force them to adopt an 'expressive anarchy' of personality 'marking their imperfect integration into the social order', their cynicism never wearies them nor deters them from 'working towards the resolution of their respective anarchies'.[23]

'A typical feature of New Comedy', in Frye's words, 'is the struggle [that takes place] between the hero and a *senex* figure, an older, usually paternal figure'.[24] In *Aar Paar*, the *senex* figure is the garage owner Lalaji who functions as Kalu's rival in two ways: proud of his blue-collar working-class status, Lalaji treats all his mechanics (including the recently hired Kalu) as inferiors. In the professional space of his garage, there is only one Master mechanic: himself! Kalu's mechanical skills may be as good, or as one suspects, even superior to Lalaji's, but as his paid worker, he is never praised for them. As far as Lalaji is concerned, Kalu is just one more hired grease monkey, though he grudgingly allows him to sleep in his garage. However, when Lalaji blunders into Kalu romancing his only daughter Nikki inside the garage and is further mortified to learn of Kalu's previous prison sojourn, he has no hesitation in throwing Kalu out. Lalaji believes in upholding conventional respectability on *both* fronts: the professional and the domestic. Neither a mechanic nor an ex-jailbird will do for his garage, or for his daughter! To win Lalaji's professional and domestic approval, therefore, becomes a formidable challenge for Kalu who has now been exiled from both spaces by this fearful *senex* figure.

In *Mr & Mrs 55*, the *senex* figure for Preetam assumes the form of Sita Devi, the old battleaxe aunt who, in Nasreen Munni Kabir's definition, is 'a crusader of women's rights who means to protect Anita from men. Anita's late father had wished to see her married, so he stipulates in his will that Anita will only inherit his fortune if she is married within a month of her twenty-first birthday. Sita Devi plans to contrive a marriage which will be immediately followed by a divorce, thereby fulfilling the terms of the will while also preserving Anita's independence.'[25] What is interesting about both these *senex* figures is the comic roles Dutt makes them play as substitute mothers. The absent mother in *Aar Paar* is periodically visible in the maternal instincts of Lalaji, and she refigures in *Mr & Mrs 55* as the matriarchal aunt who mothers not only Nikki but also loves to play the role of the symbolic matriarch for her feminist followers. This gives Dutt the opportunity to, in Kathleen Rowe's words, 'direct corrective laughter onto the matriarch [and other *senex* figures like Lalaji representing her]'.[26] They represent 'a dreaded domesticity and propriety, a fearful symbol of a community'[27] which in Sita Devi's case would only *include* women and in Lalaji's case would *exclude* skilled mechanics and ex-jailbirds.

Consequently, both become 'targets for the hatred of repression mobilized by comedy',[28] especially from the perspective of our two heroes. Preetam's caricature of Sita Devi (in one of his cartoons) attired in Roman toga, standing on a Roman chariot with a whip in one hand while Anita and Preetam are drawn on all fours pulling her chariot, applies also to Lalaji, the dreaded patriarch with the spanner in a man-in-black mechanic's overalls.

If Sita Devi and Lalaji occupy strong centres within their respective social orders, Preetam and Kalu embrace the status of picaresque characters, who within the tradition of Dutt's New Comedy, are presented as 'searching for a place within a social order, which is itself undergoing dramatic social change'.[29] In *Aar Paar*, Lalaji's narrow social and domestic order is cut off from the real world that begins outside his garage door. His inclusive universe revolves only around his garage with its predictable theatrics of mechanics, machines, grease, and tyres providing him his daily bread and butter. Behind this working area lies his domestic space where we see Nikki performing her daily rituals as the dharmic daughter: cooking his meals and pressing his feet. The only other person who is allowed entrance into this exclusive father/daughter space is an old Muslim crony with whom Lalaji plays his daily game of chess. Both areas are threatened when Kalu, the homeless, rootless, unattached *outsider* dares to intrude, challenging not only Lalaji's professionalism in relation to the automobiles he repairs but also his consummate position as patriarch when threatening to spirit away his only daughter.

In *Mr & Mrs 55*, when Sita Devi hires Preetam into a marriage of convenience with Anita, she wants to prove to her female followers that *this* is all that males are fit for as they can be driven to do anything for 'a price'. She is however unaware that her social order of female emancipation which she practises is really a fraud. In one scene, we see her female followers secretly discussing 'beauty tips' when the old battleaxe is busy hauling the whole of MANkind over the coals. In her own home where she holds these rabid male-bashing meetings, her primary critic is her commonsensical native Maharashtrian maidservant who sees through her repressive tendencies. Having never found love in her own youth, Sita Diva is determined not to see her own niece succeed. The maidservant, happily married, is constantly shown reiterating this criticism to Anita whose sole confidant she has become.

She warns Anita that her aunt's feminism is bound to fail because it is predominantly 'Westernized'. Preetam's intrusion, in fact, causes a significant breach in the aunt's deliberate Westernized upbringing of Anita, especially in relation to the conflicting issues of love and marriage. Preetam finds a way to not only prick the aunt's feminist balloon but also to confirm the maidservant's nativist critique. After he forces Anita to elope, he takes her to his brother's home in a nearby village. Here, Anita is exposed to the concern and kindness of Preetam's traditional Hindu sister-in-law who registers her happy connubial state with every act and gesture, even when on occasion (as she shyly confesses to Anita) her husband slaps her!

As picaresque heroes, both Kalu and Preetam, in Richard Bjornson's catagorization, are 'initially shown as lacking the strength and absolute integrity to impose their wills upon a hostile world'.[30] Initially, when they try, they are rudely rejected. In *Aar Paar*, Kalu prides himself in knowing everything about cars: from driving them to fixing and taking care of them. In *Mr & Mrs 55*, Preetam is a talented cartoonist who prides himself in caricaturing the follies and double standards of the urban metropolitan Indian. Even so, when they try to express their skills in the correct way, Lalaji refuses to have his cars (and his daughter) even touched by an ex-convict, and Sita Devi not only heaps scorn on the masquerade of the hired husband but also suspects very strongly that in his cartooning skills he is 'a communist'. Thus, in Bjornson's terms, 'they have to adapt themselves to diverse situations by serving different masters, inventing clever ruses, or wearing a variety of masks during a peripatetic life of alternating good and evil fortune'.[31] Rejected by Lalaji professionally and by Nikki personally (when she refuses to elope with him), Kalu has no choice but to descend into the coils of the underworld where he is willing to serve as the driver of the getaway car for the captain and his gang planning a daring daylight heist. When Preetam's skills as a cartoonist fail to interest any of the city's newspaper editors, he is compelled to participate in a fake marriage of convenience arranged by Sita Devi, and by doing so himself becomes a cartoon. However, both men are shown embracing their respective masquerades in a true Darwinian sense of adaptability. They wear these temporary masks of the 'other' authentically, and when the time comes to radically remove them, they save the women they love, punish the bad guys, and proudly enter their social orders of respectability to be welcomed most resoundingly by the same *senex* figures who had cast them out of their briefly glimpsed edens. Both films, in the proverbial comedic tradition, 'depict their successful integration into the world once they have learned their lessons through their adventures'.[32]

Both *Aar Paar* and *Mr & Mrs 55* 'also illustrate a paradigm structure of the screwball comedy' of the romantic type where 'the focus is on sexual confrontation and courtship':[33] Kalu's with Nikki in the former and Preetam's with Anita in the latter. However, Dutt's narrativizing of their romance in a prominent screwball comic vein assumes the predominant characteristic of 'the reaffirmation comedies [which] concentrate on the reestablishment of the couple after circumstances ...have succeeded in separating them'.[34] This idea of the screwball comedy emerges from the cultural myth of the Indian Dream which Dutt is at great pains to establish notwithstanding the anarchic way the lovers in both films reaffirm their coming together. 'The viability of the (Indian) hard work ethic and the (Hindu) conservative notions of marriage and family'[35] are very evident in both films. 'While Dutt's romantic characters are initially presented as having temporarily fallen short of these ideals,'[36] the emphasis of his comic narrative 'steer the couples back towards the goals and commitments they have abandoned'[37] or have not yet been able to achieve. This clearly implies that in Dutt's comic vision, his abiding faith in Indian society is never really abandoned or doubted. His couples *will* come together and embrace the notions of conventional marriage *and* hard work, which will, as a result, enable them to function effectively and productively *within* the respectable bourgeois/middle-class Hindu/Indian norms they had briefly contested. Dutt does not allow his couples, especially in their screwball romantic entanglements, to confront, either Prufrock's 'overwhelming question' of loveless sterility or Hamlet's forbidding 'there is something rotten in the state of Denmark' fatalism. These concepts Dutt was to embrace with his tragic couple of the poet and the whore in *Pyaasa*, who can only come together in a utopian off-screen space far away from the city and *Kaagaz Ke Phool*'s doomed pair of the film-maker and his protege actress: the former as a corpse on a directorial chair and the other, doomed like Penelope, to weave and unweave stitches of her repressed passions in sweaters designed only for a corpse.

In *Aar Paar*, Kalu is loved by two women. Nikki, Lalaji's daughter, is screwball comedy's 'good' woman: virginal and devoted to the two men in her life—her father and Kalu. In the scene when her love for

Kalu is tested and found wanting—she refuses to cut the umbilical cord which ties her to her father and elope with Kalu—the first major separation occurs. Kalu's demand that they elope is not unreasonable. He goes to great efforts to prove to Nikki that his jail stint was not the result of a criminal act but for rash driving. He even has this confirmed to her in person by taking her to his jail warden, who actually provides him with a written certificate clearing him of all convict metonymies. However, when in spite of all this, Nikki fails to choose him over her father, Kalu resolves to permanently sever their relations.

Now enters the second woman, the cabaret dancer Rita, comedy's 'bad' woman who has been nursing her love for Kalu in the wings for a long long time. In the presentation of this second romantic liaison, it is she who is shown chasing Kalu in a bold and aggressive way. Kalu on the rebound, humiliated by his rejection, enjoys being the object of Rita's powerful sexual attentions and utterances. He enjoys flirting with her in a salaciously screwball comedic fashion. Psychologically, it helps him lick his recently received Cupid wounds and also keeps his wounded masculinity intact.

In Kalu's romantic scenes with Nikki, the screwball comic element is essayed, but always at a chaste level. She takes the lead by correcting all the hilarious nativisms that enter his speech as he struggles to achieve mastery over the English language. She admires his persistence, especially in his cockeyed way of viewing and renewing the world. She is overtly delighted by all the efforts he makes to woo her with the style and swagger of a Westernized male film hero, openly defiant of all conventional Indian norms and practices. In his company, she suddenly feels alive. Life seems to offer her so much more than the daily routine of preparing her father's medicine, wiping his grease-stained hands, and quietening his constant nagging complaints. Kalu opens up a whole new world for her which she has never seen: a world of colour and excitement, far beyond the narrow horizons she was compelled to glimpse through her father's garage doors. There is also a mounting physical awareness, but proximity has not yet attained sexual complicity. Nikki has never known a man *that* way and Kalu is shrewd enough to postpone all sexual enthusiasm after first legitimizing this bond in marriage.

Rita's romantic scenes with Kalu, on the other hand, reverberate overtly only at the libidinal level. Her interest in Kalu is instantaneous. Her gaze traps him from the first steps Kalu takes at the Captain's Sakli

Street nightclub where she dances. She admires his confident handling of the Captain's loudmouthed thugs. In a song, '*Babuji dheere chalna*' (Dear Sir, walk cautiously), she even tries to warn him against stepping on too many toes there. However, when he continues to show her that he can take care of himself, despite being (in her own song's term as) '*vo akela to lakhho hai dushman*' (or one pitted against many enemies), she is hooked. After the song ends, she continues to flirt with him, and is thrilled when Kalu responds with equal abandon. In keeping with the sexual innuendo tradition of screwball comedy, Dutt invests the Rita/ Kalu conversation scenes with very suggestive 'comic lines of dialogue and short, often abrupt sight gags...seizing [particularly] on those individual lines of dialogue'[38] that emphasize a distinctive cut and thrust approach to sexuality. As the flirting between the two gathers comedic momentum, Kalu tells her brazenly although he is just a motor mechanic, he considers his face 'a model', not only for women like her, but for *all* attractive women! Later, when she conspires to bring her 'troubled' car into his garage and only wants him to 'repair' it, the verbal 'car' imagery that Kalu flings at her relating to his 'face' is wonderfully exchanged (in the dialogue that follows) in which not only 'the face' but the entire 'body' (both his and hers) are sexually indexed:

'*Kya dekhoon*', [what should I see?], Kalu slyly asks her as he starts poking under the hood of her car. '*Sub kutch*', [everything] she offers, arrogantly thrusting her entire body at him.

However, when she realizes that Kalu will not surrender to her sexually, as he still belongs to Nikki, she decides to make Nikki pay for this indiscretion and has her kidnapped by the Captain. This move, however, provides Kalu with an excellent opportunity of saving Nikki, thereby enabling him to stake his claim very firmly, not only as Lalaji's benefactor, but also as his soon to be son-in-law. In the end, Lalaji has no hesitation in embracing Kalu, not only as a family member but also as the heir and new owner of his daughter and garage.

In *Mr & Mrs 55*, the screwball romance between Preetam and Anita 'depends on unpredictability which often takes the form of incongruity'.[39] Their first meeting sets the tone for all their subsequent incongruous get-togethers. Anita, literally falls into his lap as she dozes during the tennis match. So stunned is he by her overwhelming intrusion, that he is completely dumbstruck, as she collects herself hastily, and runs away from one of her aunt's spies keeping tabs on her. Their next meeting in the park is once again worked out in incongruous terms by Dutt. Strolling in the park, Anita encounters a very sleepy and a very hungry Preetam on a park bench. When Preetam insists he was trying to sleep in order to ward off hunger, Anita, who is a complete stranger to the very idea of hunger, offers him the same advice and in doing so, becomes an intertexual twin of that silly French queen (who was subsequently *beheaded* for this remark) who suggested that if bread was found wanting, he (like the French peasants) should eat a cake or biscuits, instead!

In both these scenes, the humour arises out of one's partner's inability to resolve the incongruity arising out of the comic situation. Preetam cannot fathom how a very rich and pretty woman unexpectedly fell into his lap (and life). For her part, Anita, cannot understand how a shabbily dressed man on a park bench can substitute hunger by sleep and, furthermore, make so much fuss about absent bread when cakes and biscuits are so freely available in the city's bakeries. It is, however, the second incongruity that enables Dutt to set up the reaffirmation comedy plot angle. As Anita is the upper-class partner in this romantic liaison, madly in love with a tennis player who shows not the slightest inclination to return or even acknowledge her love, she is the one who has not only to be humbled but also taught to commit herself to the man who truly loves her.

Following the dictates of the screwball romantic comedy tradition, 'the upper-class partner must also give up something. Because she has focused her energy on the relationship, she must be willing to give up her life of wealth to secure the relationship.'[40] Dutt arrives at this schema by first eliminating the 'blocking character' of the tennis player through the comic ploy of a letter situation in which the tennis player's intentions are conveyed to Anita. Johnny, who is expected to hand deliver this letter to Anita suddenly develops cold feet. He therefore entrusts this uncomfortable mission to Preetam who is unaware that Anita is the chosen recipient. To make the incongruity work even more effectively, Dutt chooses a darkened film auditorium where Preetam is given a film-ticket and told to hand the 'letter' to the girl who will be seated next to him. In the dark, when Preetam hands over the letter to a woman seated to his right, she proves out to be a respectably married woman who complains loudly to her spouse about Preetam's insistent and neighbourly indiscretions. Anita's late arrival, as the woman occupying the *other* empty seat to his left, relieves Preetam's initial embarrassment, but when on reading the letter Anita bursts loudly into tears, Preetam's credentials as the proverbial pervert in the dark are now firmly confirmed, and he has to flee the cinema hall before the outraged male patrons rise en masse to beat him up.

Another 'shock' is in store for Preetam when he subsequently turns up at the Marriage Registrar's Office and is finally revealed as Anita's mock husband on hire. Separation is insisted upon not only by the aunt *senex* figure, but also by Anita who is doubly appalled at Preetam's recent (mis)conduct. However, as they *are* legally married, Preetam forcibly abducts her and they bicker all the way to his sister-in-law's pastoral retreat. There, amidst simple and rural surroundings, a poor but happily married woman reawakens in our rich and spoilt heroine a genuine love for Preetam and clears away all circumstantial misunderstandings. However, another separation is immediately imposed with the forcible arrival of the aunt who drags Anita away and locks her up in her own mansion's master bedroom.

The final incongruity that enables Anita to prevent Preetam from leaving Bombay, 'the city of merchants', for Delhi, 'the city of kings', is instigated by a linguistic device rendered, in Geeta Dutt's sensuous voice, of an old monumental K.L. Saigal 'love song' which commences with the address to one's '*preetam*', which in Hindi means 'beloved'. As this song plays loudly on the radio in the room where our Preetam is packing his suitcases to leave for the airport, Dutt dissolves into another radio in Anita's locked bedroom where the same song is playing. It is the song, and especially the singer's soulful reiteration of the word 'preetam' that compels the momentarily exhausted Anita to overthrow all of her aunt's restrictive ploys, break down all the doors, open all the windows, and rush to the airport to reunite with *her* Preetam.

In Guru Dutt's comic universe, Johnny Walker's character functions 'as a [strategic] invader of [Dutt's] diegetic world'.[41] In the earlier comedies, Johnny initially 'operated as a figure who was peripheral to the narrative'.[42] He functioned as someone who was 'not fully bound by [the film's] plot, and had no deep personal stake in it'.[43] However, as his presence in every succeeding Dutt film began receiving very appreciative approvals from the Indian audience, Dutt was able to make Johnny's character 'circulate [more closely] around his romance plots [but] still without overwhelming them.'[44]

As Rustom, the Irani-barman/*guallawalla* (or one who sits at the *gulla* or till dispensing money) in *Aar Paar*, Johnny's role is peripheral for most of the film till the end when he makes the successful leap from being a lackey in the Captain's criminal gang to helping Kalu cleverly rescue Nikki and also capture the gang. But in *Mr & Mrs 55*, Dutt has Johnny playing a more concerned avuncular role as Preetam's benefactor, especially at the end of every month, when the tough *senex*-landlady comes banging on their door for rent. The gap between Johnny, as comedic sidekick, and Dutt's heroes perceptibly narrows when we come to the two tragic films.

As Abdul Sattar, the nomadic barber and oil massage man in *Pyaasa*, Johnny figures as the important third part in the insulted trinity whose other two members are the hero, Vijay and the heroine, Gulabo. As a *hajjam*, Abdul is excluded and looked down upon by Indian society in the same condescending manner as the disgraced unemployed poet, Vijay and the commodified/shameful whore, Gulabo. Abdul is not 'fully bound by the film's plot'[45] but plays a very loyal and committed role, often functioning as Aristotle's intervening agent, a humorous *deus ex machina* figure. He helps Vijay escape from the lunatic asylum where he has been incarcerated by his cruel brothers. He also protects Vijay and Gulabo during the stampede in the hall after Vijay is forcibly thrown out.

In *Kaagaz Ke Phool*, Johnny is finally given a well deserved family inclusion. As Rocky, hero Suresh's brother-in-law, he shares with the estranged Suresh all the marginalizations imposed upon him as well by his wealthy Jewish parents and sister who, like Suresh, consider him a family disgrace. However, notwithstanding Rocky's Bertie Wooster philandering lifestyle, he is the one who tries very hard to bring the estranged actress Shanti from her self-imposed exile in the village to the studios, in the hope, that she will end Suresh's solipsistic immersion into poverty and gradually lure him back under the studio's arc lamps. But unlike Abdul's textual interventions in *Pyaasa*, Rocky in *Kaagaz Ke Phool* is given his own subtext where a lot of screen time is devoted to showing how he can independently forge his own romantic pursuance of Miss Juliet Singh, his award-winning horses' vet. This enables Dutt to let Johnny loose on many improvised critiques and observations levelled humorously on Indian modes of self-enforced bachelorhood which he has tried to maintain before succumbing to Cupid's arrows and domesticity with his prize-winning stallions on the race track and his Juliet sing(h)ing at home!

Johnny Walker's comedic odyssey in Guru Dutt's films follows an interestingly worked out trajectory, calculatedly progressing from being a liminal figure existing on the edges of civilization and contesting its dictats...[to] celebrating social transgression, fluid identity and bodily pleasure.'[46] Dutt exercises Johnny's clowning by making him play two conspicuous roles: a ritual one and a civic one. In his ritual role, he makes Johnny's character 'explore the comic interplay of order and disorder' and in his civic role, he makes him 'amuse and question' centres of power and authority.[47]

As Rustom, in *Aar Paar*, Dutt makes Johnny emerge (in our first glimpse of him from behind a bar in the Sankli Street nightclub) as a wonderful presence of cultural indecisiveness: suggested first by his fancy and imported silk shirt, under whose tactile feel, he plays the wisecracking noir tough guy role and his native Irani prayer topi under which he struggles to overcome his timid and essential Zoroastrian self. This condition is comically supported by the Bombay 'footpath' argot utterances that Rustom has mastered and which he flings out expertly as impromptu orchestrated comments every time he participates in some kind of comic violation. Every violation, for Rustom, is however humorously measured in the *gullawalla*'s calculated ideology of the cash nexus—which he wittily defines for us as '*a baara aneeka phatka hota*' or a twelve-anna hit. This schizophrenic personality split of tough henchman/timid Irani is further enhanced by the distinctive feminizations Dutt makes Rustom often give to the many objects with which he comes into contact in the tough masculine world he inhabits. '*Eeesko park karoni pehle*' (why don't you park *her* (i.e. the car first), he will declare in a thin feminine voice to his driver buddy before responding, gravely, in a thick masculine tone to whatever question he is asked by his boss sitting in the back seat.

Another humorous refrain which Johnny adds to most of his funny dialogue exchanges is the repeated English question, 'what is your idea?' which no one seems to hear and everyone seems to ignore except the audience who are repeatedly tickled by its reappearance. When a fight erupts in the bar and one of the gang members is knocked down and feels a sudden loss of manhood, Rustom intervenes, props him up, and offers the comforting palliative. 'No *faida*! *Kaunsa* punch *maara*! Now, what is your idea?' This combination of churned Angrezi and Hindustani syllables accurately point to Rustom's split existence, and when Kalu finally gives him the opportunity to liberate himself from the clutches of the captain's criminal gang, Rustom willingly grabs it. He cheerfully hangs up his gang's sterilized silk shirts for the wisecracking Iranitopiwalla restaurant patron that, in his heart of hearts, he really is and to which he finally reverts at the end of the film.

In *Mr & Mrs 55*, Johnny is not only a freelance journalistic photographer, but also a close friend and roommate of the often jobless and idle Preetam. Being more worldly-wise, he is also a shrewd Machiavellian protector, especially at the end of every month when the roof of their rented apartment threatens to explode with the impending arrival of their feared corpulent Goan landlady. Then we see Johnny going into full comic gear. For 'fifteen days', as he informs Preetam, he has been 'working on Mama', (i.e. the landlady), appealing to her maternal instincts from the perspective of two talented but unfortunately 'orphaned' tenants, wheedling not only many free meals for both of them but also extracting timely postponements for recent and long overdue rents. The 'other fifteen days', however, he works 'on Papa' (i.e. the landlady's timid husband), flattering, cajoling, inflating, and boosting his severely henpecked libido till it intercedes on their jointly circulated male behalf on this last day of the month. Capitalizing also on the couple's 'childless' familial state, Johnny aces his comic routine by forcing Preetam, on the last day of every month, to improvise in different degrees, a very convincing and cartoonish suicidal ritual for the sake of their adopted 'mama and papa', and with his own fervent and hysterically funny pleas of 'help *karo*, help *karo*', he sees to it that their room's roof stays, at least for another month, temporarily over their heads.

In the scenes where Preetam is absent, Dutt makes Johnny play the role of the prowling Casanova who has not yet succeeded in coaxing a woman to his bed. Notwithstanding his assumed rakish presences, he has not gone beyond offering every new conquest 'a lollipop'. In one very bold scene, Dutt shows Johnny whispering to his tennis player friend to get him some 'dirty pictures' from Paris; but besides this one schoolboyish indiscretion, Johnny remains the eternal aspirant of love till he is eventually smitten by the pretty stenotypist recently appointed in the magazine office. It will take Johnny a couple of songs before he can finally win her over, and I shall discuss one of these musical numbers later on in this essay where Johnny is shown making his romantic intentions very clearly (and very cleverly) to his intended.

Johnny's skills as a barber and oil masseur in *Pyaasa* are given a different comedic and social impetus by Dutt. As Abdul Sattar, we see Johnny ply his trade with a great deal of social enthusiasm as well as personal expertise. In a wonderful song, written especially for him by Vijay:

> *Sar jo tera chakraaye*
> *Ya dil duba jaaye*
> *Aaja pyaare paas hamaare*
> *Kahe ghabraaye, kahe ghabraaye...*
>
> (When your head hurts
> And when you're feeling blue
> Come to me instantly
> There is no need to be afraid)

Dutt defines Abdul's 'pleasure-driven mentality against a succession of exhausted killjoys and dupes of the Indian social order' whom he revives single-handedly by practising his professional skills literally and socially on their aching heads and bodies.[48] We see him massaging away, in one instance, the business '*ragda*' that a financer/banker has recently suffered; and removing (in another instance) with those same skilful fingers, the slinging rebukes of an angry girlfriend from the troubled scalp of an aspiring young man in '*pyar*'. 'Masters and servants; leaders and members of the public,' he cheerfully tells us in his song, all have to surrender 'their heads' under his hands in order to find relief. As a result of this song, business has tripled for this struggling but always cheerful barber as he optimistically wends his way through the park where clients from all walks of life await him.

In *Kaagaz Ke Phool* Dutt finally gives Johnny *family* recognition. As the hero's brother-in-law, Johnny's character embraces the same exclusion the hero suffers at the hands of his ex-wife's thoroughly anglicized Jewish family sired by Sir B.B. Varma. Named Raakesh by his parents (an interesting pun, as the Hindu name cleverly enunciates all his *rakish* tendencies), he chooses to go by the nickname Rocky amongst his affluent high society friends. Rich, idle, and eccentric Rocky has one hobby: breeding prize-winning stallions who collect prestigious turf awards all over India. A firm believer in permanent bachelordom, Dutt gives Rocky an entire song where he personifies for a south Indian brahmachari, one Mr Iyer, all the troubles that marriage and any other kind of serious commitment to 'a female' can bring to those who are committed fiercely to the Dionysian spirit, both in and out of their cups. It is indeed in precisely carefully calculated *whisky pegs* that Rocky, in another comic scene, appropriately sums up his wayward relationship to his *proper* parents and *properly* brought up sister. This comic advice is given to the hero by Rocky when the former is unceremoniously thrown out of Rocky's house. Considering that to be a *peg* in the right direction, Rocky philosophizes:

Before meeting the old man, you must remember first to have a full peg of whisky. Before meeting the old dame, however, you must have two pegs of whisky. And before meeting your ex-wife and my sister? My dear chap, have the whole flask!

While witnessing Johnny Walker's characters in Guru Dutt's films, one is reminded of the claim made by Steve Seidman that 'the comedian's awareness of the spectator's presence and the assertion of his own presence are factors which work towards described enunciation.'[49] Even though Johnny, as a comedian, 'is dropped into the centre of a ready-made fictional world, the fictional identity he assumes is torn between the demands of conforming [as a character] and the need to deviate [as a performer]'.[50] Why Johnny Walker's comedic contributions work so well in Guru Dutt's films is because Dutt understood that 'no performer in a film can ever really function as an enunciator—the comedian [should be] allowed, at specific and regulated moments, to masquerade also as an enunciator.'[51] As Dutt's principal comic character, Johnny is given tremendous license to rearticulate and improvise over his scripted lines and directed jests. Johnny Walker, himself confirms this in Nasreen Kabir's book on Guru Dutt when he says:

He used to tell me...here is your scene, your dialogue, this is the shot. If you can do better, go ahead. That's what he would say, then off I'd go. In each rehearsal, I'd say some lines extempore. In every rehearsal I would come up with something new. Guru Dutt used to love that. He used to look at everyone on the set and see if the lightboys, the cameraman, the assistants, were laughing at my dialogues... That's how we worked. The reason why I did so well in all of Guru Dutt's films was that I had found the man who knew how to draw out my talent; otherwise, it would have stayed within me.[52]

Dutt allows Johnny to spontaneously create many of the proverbial film-comedians' 'fictional ruptures; [especially] through his looks at the camera or by his direct address'[53] to the spectator witnessing that particular comedic enunciation. In *Mr & Mrs 55*, every time Johnny is asked by Preetam to pay on his behalf, Johnny reaches for his wallet and issues to Preetam *and* to us as the audience, the comical command of '*moo udhar*' (turn your face elsewhere). Or if another character within his diegetic space fails to grasp the subtleties of any of his improvised jokes that he has unleashed on him, Johnny will once again address him *and* us by directly looking at the camera and imploring: 'Why don't you *samjoo* (or understand)?'

Such 'idiosyncratic ways of speaking and moving, (and) eccentric facial and bodily gestures'[54] are fully exploited and incorporated by Dutt into Johnny's comedic characters. Hence, Johnny's funny scenes became critical 'performance sequences (and acquire) a semi-autonomous status within the film narrative functioning as set pieces pleasurable in their own right.'[55] Thus it is from a resplendent high angle that Dutt makes *Pyaasa*'s Abdul Sattar enter the park where he plies his *tel-malish* (oil massage) trade singing his signature song. Such an entrance not only befits Johnny's status as the film's most important comic performer, but it also situates Johnny's character within the park which now becomes Abdul Sattar's privatized theatrical space into which Johnny Walker, the comedian, can inject his celebrated comedic talent.

Similarly, in *Kaagaz Ke Phool*, before Rocky can musically enter his anti-marriage song, Dutt makes him shrewdly arrange the diegetic area over which he will unfurl his mockery of Cupid. He marshalls all the men to one side of the room and instructs the band to begin. Targeting all the women on the other side of the room and placing old Mr Iyer deliberately at the centre, he proceeds to unload in song, one by one, all his anti-connubial diatribes. Rocky works the room like a master, expertly launching his witty utterances at the women while at the same time weaving them into an octopus formation around poor Mr Iyer; and just when he feels he has succeeded in tying poor Mr Iyer into all manner of alarming feminine knots, he is mortified to learn that all his efforts have been in vain as Mr Iyer reveals himself to be stone deaf! What makes both these scenes so comically innovative is the way Dutt shoots them. Both of them are filmed by Dutt in long takes, and his stationary camera maintains a deliberate distance to enable Johnny 'to preserve his comic performance's integrity'.[56] Johnny's highly 'styled movements [sic] is calling to attention *how* his act is [being] performed more than *what* is being done.'[57] (Italics are mine.)

Michael Wood, while describing Gene Kelly's and Donald O'Connor's spirited dance 'Moses Supposes' from *Singin' in the Rain*, draws our attention to:

> A whole bunch of domestic objects [which one] rounded up and danced with. These are precisely the connections that great musicals make; these are just the continuities they insist on; our speech can be nudged into music, our way of walking can be edged into a dance; and the things in our house are all possible props for an improvised ballet.[58]

In many of Guru Dutt's musical song and dance numbers, Dutt creates the musical moments out of the precise environment in which he locates his characters. What Jane Feur categorizes as 'environment choreography' abounds in Guru Dutt's musical numbers. In fact, an 'environmental conception for choreograph (becomes for Dutt, especially in his comedies) his favorite "hobby horse".'[59]

The first quality of environmental choreography that one observes in Dutt's comedic musical numbers is the way in which he makes his performers 'make use of props at hand, things perhaps intended for other ends, to create the imaginary world of the musical number'.[60] He makes his characters very creatively rebuild the musical number around their own intimate environment.'[61]

The song/dance number from *Aar Paar*:

Sun sun sun sun zaalima
Humko tumse pyaar ho gaya...
(Listen, listen you flirt.
I have fallen in love with you.)

erupts spontaneously between Kalu and Nikki in Lalaji's garage. The verbal duet and the dance movements of the couple are choreographed in unison *around* the conspicuous object of a *car*. When each one sings a verse, Dutt isolates the singer and frames him/her separately through the car window. After they tease each other in song, passing from window to window, Dutt brings them musically together in the song's finale where they confess their attraction for each other seated side by side on top of the car's roof.

Their second romantic duet also takes place *inside* Kalu's *cab* after he has successfully established before her that he is not a criminal with the attestation of his ex-warden. As he drives her home in his cab, Nikki apologizes to him in the song:

> Ye lo mein haari piya
> Hui teeri jeet re
> Kaahe ka jhagda baalam
> Nayi nayi preet re...
> (I admit I have lost
> And you have won.
> So why continue this quarrel
> In this new awareness of our love...)

As *she* is the principal singer and *he* is the recipient of her song, she is shown as being literally pushed by the song from her *chaste* side, in the front seat of the cab, to his more *tactile* side. Nikki's song succeeds not only in dissolving Kalu's anger but also having him respond by placing one arm around her shoulder while the other one deftly manoeuvres the cab through regular traffic.

In *Mr & Mrs 55*, we see Johnny declaring his love to the pretty stenotypist by carving out a song and a dance out of the very office space where she works. He enters her work-area during the lunch-break when the other workers have conveniently abdicated their customary presence at their desks to go to the canteen, and pretends to be searching for 'something'. The following verbal transaction sets up very cleverly the suggestive preamble to the song that is to follow:

> Girl: What are you searching for?
> Johnny: That which I have lost.
> Girl: What have you lost?
> Johnny: That which I am searching for.

The crucial 'that' in this prosaic exchange becomes in the song his '*jigar*' or 'heart' which he has 'lost'. Attracted by his wit, the girl joins him in the duet, in an effort to find it. What is so accurately developed as the song proceeds is Dutt's choreography which shows both characters expressing surprise and delight at discovering each 'object' belonging to the girl: her purse; the drawers of her desk; the space under her office chair and desk; her typewriter; her blotting pad; all the objects where he has *left* his heart for her to *find* under the spell of love. The tracking and circular shots continuously employed in the search enables the couple to physically come together finally under her desk, but just as they are about to embrace for the very first time, the other workers return, and the song ends. However, what they had been looking for they have finally found, thanks to the propelling enactment of the dance and the bold pronouncements in the song.

The mesmeric effect that Nikki has on Preetam (when she suddenly falls into his lap) in *Mr & Mrs 55* is first verbally suggested in the song's words which begin:

> *Aji dil pe hua aisa jaadu*
> *Tabiyaat machal machal gayi*
> *Nazren jo milin kya kisi se*
> *Ke halat badal badal gayi.*
>
> (My heart was struck by such magic
> My state of mind's disturbed,
> The moment my eyes met another's
> I felt myself transformed.)[62]

Dutt heightens this effect by having Preetam sing this song through a series of *changing* environments which are unable to distract Preetam's in-love hypnotized state. Preetam bursts into the song's first verse during the regular tea drinking ritual with Johnny in the Irani restaurant. The second verse is next imposed on poor Johnny as both of them wait for their bus at their accustomed bus stop. Preetam climbs into his third verse along with Johnny and all the other passengers as they enter the bus and is flung spontaneously out into his fourth verse when he and Johnny get thrown out of the bus for not having money to pay their fare. Undaunted, Preetam continues to serenade Johnny all the way home, and finally wraps up the song by actually wrapping his arms around a street lamp and embracing it as his absent loved object Nikki.

Jane Feur's observation that:

> In prop numbers and elsewhere, Hollywood musicals employ choreography which could only by a great stretch of the imagination be called 'dancing'. Such 'non-choreography' implies that choreography is cancelled out... By cancelling choreography as a calculated dance strategy, non-choreography implies that dancing is utterly natural and that dancing is easy...the continuity between walking and dancing is always stressed,[63]

is fully endorsed by Dutt not only in Johnny's office space number and Preetam's environmental one, but also in the following song from *Mr & Mrs 55*:

Udhar tum hasein ho Idhar Dil jawan hai.
(There you stand, so youthful in happiness
Here I stand, palpitating with youth as well...)

Here, the continuity between Preetam's (who sings this song) *walking* on the ground and Nikki's identical stance on the balcony above him is choreographed with the camera *dancing* around the lovers. The vertical crane shots, orchestrated to chime with the horizontal tracking shots, synchronize the *shrinkage* of space between the lovers so that when they meet at the song's finale, it is at a harmonious point to which he has ascended and she has descended!

Another musical convention that Dutt borrows from the Hollywood musical is his marvellous way of 'putting audiences into the film for the purpose of shaping the response of the movie audience to the song and dance moment in the film.[64] In a song like:

Kabhi aar, kabhi paar, laaga teer-e-nazar
(When our looks meet with arrow-like precision)

from *Aar Paar*, Dutt creates a certain kind of natural audience that spontaneously gathers around this impromptu song sung by a construction worker on a building site.[65] She acts as a chorus to indicate to Kalu and Nikki their powerful attraction for each other when they first meet. The song circulates around Nikki's stalled car that Kalu is trying to start. The song comments not only on a stalled car, but is aimed more precisely on an exciting relationship that could also be jump-started. Once the construction worker–singer starts her song, her other working companions join in and cordon the embarrassed pair below. Also as Kalu needs his friend Elachai and his gang of street urchins to push Nikki's stalled car, they too join the song as a secondary chorus. Further, as both these filmic audiences sing and dance in unison, urging all primary signs of love to finally emerge between these two, we too are induced by Dutt to sing and dance along with these two groups, thereby enlarging their prospects of coming together by shedding all their inhibitions.

Guru Dutt's cinema, whether comedic or tragic, implicated us all as well and what this essay tried to show is how he could do it, wearing very successively, though for a short time, the face of the laughing and the naughty muse.

A lengthier version of this essay appears in *In Black and White: Hollywood and the Melodrama of Guru Dutt* (Seagull Books, 2005) and portions are also drawn from a chapter on 'Dutt's Aesthetics of the Hindi Film Song'.

NOTES AND REFERENCES

1. This is Northrop Frye's definition as indicated by Kathleen Rowe in her essay, 'Comedy, Melodrama and Gender: Theorizing the Genres of Laughter', in Kristine Brunovska Karnick and Henry Jenkins (eds.), *Classical Hollywood Comedy* (New York: Routledge, 1995), p. 47.
2. Ibid., p. 48.
3. Ibid., p. 47.
4. This is Richard Dyer's notation as cited by Kristine Karnick and Henry Jenkins in their essay 'Introduction: Acting Funny' from their book *Classical Hollywood Comedy*, p. 151.
5. Jane Feur's *The Hollywood Musical* (Bloomington and Indianapolis: Indiana University Press, 1993), p. 49.
6. Ibid., p. 52.
7. Pavan K. Varma, *The Great Indian Middle Class* (New York: Penguin Books, 1999), p. 65.
8. Ibid., pp. 41–2.
9. As cited by Varma, in his chapter 'The Age of Hope', from *The Great Indian Middle Class*, p. 42.
10. Cited in ibid., p. 42.
11. Ashish Rajadhyaksha and Paul Willemen, *Encyclopaedia of Indian Cinema* (London: Oxford University Press/British Film Institute Publication, 1999), p. 235.
12. Ibid., p. 278.
13. Ibid., p. 244.
14. See Karnick and Jenkins in 'Comedy and the Social World' from their book *Classical Hollywood Comedy*, p. 272.
15. Ibid., p. 272.
16. Ibid., p. 271.
17. Ibid., p. 276.
18. Varma, *The Great Indian Middle Class*, p. 69.
19. See Karnick and Jenkins in their 'Introduction: Funny Stories' from *Classical Hollywood Comedy*, p. 73.
20. Nasreen Munni Kabir, *Guru Dutt: A Life in Cinema* (Delhi: Oxford University Press, 1996), p. 52.
21. See Karnick and Jenkins, 'Acting Funny', p. 156.

22. Ibid., p. 167.
23. Ibid.
24. Karnick and Jenkins, 'Funny Stories', p. 73.
25. Kabir, *Guru Dutt*, p. 60.
26. See Kathleen Rowe's essay 'Comedy, Melodrama and Genre' in *Classical Hollywood Comedy*, p. 46.
27. Ibid., p. 46.
28. Ibid.
29. Karnick and Jenkins, 'Funny Stories', p. 77.
30. Ibid., p. 77.
31. Ibid., p. 78.
32. Ibid.
33. Lee Kristine Karnick, 'Commitment and Reaffirmation in Hollywood Romantic Comedy', in *Classical Hollywood Comedy*, p. 131.
34. Ibid., p. 131.
35. Ibid.
36. Ibid.
37. Ibid., p. 132.
38. Ibid., p. 144.
39. Ibid., p. 129.
40. Ibid., p. 133.
41. Karnick and Jenkins, 'Funny Stories', p. 20.
42. Ibid., p. 21.
43. Ibid.
44. Ibid.
45. Ibid.
46. Karnick and Jenkins, 'Acting Funny', p. 156.
47. Ibid.
48. See Karnick and Jenkins, 'Funny Stories', p. 76.
49. See Frank Krutnick, 'Genre, Narrative and the Hollywood Comedian', in Kristine Karnick and Henry Jenkins (eds.), *Classical Hollywood Comedy*, p. 24.
50. Ibid.
51. Ibid.
52. Nasreen Kabir, *Guru Dutt*, p. 64.
53. Krutnick, 'Genre, Narrative and the Hollywood Comedian', p. 24.
54. See Karnick and Jenkins, 'Acting Funny' in *Classical Hollywood Comedy*, p. 152.
55. Ibid., p. 153.
56. Ibid.
57. Ibid.
58. As cited by Jane Feur in *The Hollywood Musical* (Bloomington and Indianapolis: Indiana University Press, 1993), p. 3.
59. Ibid., p. 5.

60. Ibid., p. 4.
61. Ibid., p. 6.
62. Kabir, *Guru Dutt*, p. 67.
63. Fleur, *The Hollywood Musical*, p. 9.
64. Ibid., p. 26.
65. I have borrowed Fleur's words from her essay, 'The Narrative Audience', in *The Hollywood Musical*, p. 31.

Index

Aa Ab Laut Chalen xviii
Aaj Ki Awaz 55
Aakrosh 56, 70
Aar Paar 156, 157, 160, 162, 163, 165–9, 173, 174
   approach to sexuality in 170
   romance in 169
   senex figure in 165
   song/ dance numbers in 178–80, 182
Abbas, Khwaja Ahmad 58
Abhiman 56
Abhinavagupta, *rasa* theory of xvi
Achchut Kanya 67
actor-god, and comedy in Kannada cinema 103–6
   phenomenon in south Indian cinema 104
'ahistoricity', of Indian popular film 35
Ajanta frescos, 'continuous narrative' of 35
Akhtar, Javed 67, 74, 76, 77
Alam Ara 55, 66
Ali, Naushad 132
Ali, Salim 74
All India Radio 133
   Muslim musicians in 151n
   selections of musicians for 135
Allen, Woody 78, 79
Amar Akbar Anthony 72
Amrit 71
Amrohi, Kamal 65
An Evening in Paris 56
Anand 56

Anand, Dev 63
Anand, Siriyavan xix, xxi
Andaz 56
Andhi 56
Ankhon Dekha Gadar (*Manjha Prawas*) 129
Ankur 56, 70
antakshari, game on TV channel 61–2
anti-war films xvii
Anubhav 56
Anuradha 146
Aradhana 56, 100
Ardh Satya 70
'art', in India and the West 35
   forms 97
   and modernity 130
'art' / parallel films xi, 70
   theory-oriented 9
Arun, Ila 153n
Arya Samaj, Gurukul education movement of 134–5
Ashirwad 56
Astika, Indian philosophy of 7
attention bubbles 8–9
Avadhi 68
Awara 55
Awasthi, Sapna 153n
Ayodhya Ka Raja 56
Azmi, Kaifi 58

Bachchan, Amitabh 68, 74, 75, 105, 154n
   use of Bambaiya Hindi in films 72–3
Baiju Bawra 69

INDEX

Bakhtin, Mikhail 143
balance of opposites, in popular cinema 98
Balachander 112, 113
Bambaiya Hindi 72–4
Barjatya, Suraj 42, 45, 46, 146
Barsat 77
Barthes, Roland 36
Bawarchi 55
Bazi 55
Begum Akhtar 132
Being and Nothingness 8
Benegal, Dev 81
Benegal, Shyam 70
Beta 56
Betab, Pandit Narayan Prasad 58
Beyond the Pleasure Principle 101
Bhabhai Ki Churiyan 70
Bharat Milap 71
Bhartrichar's *Sphota* theory 12
Bhatkande, Vishnu Narayan 134
Bhavantarana 70
Bhave, Vinoba xxiii
Bhimani, Harish 140
Bhojpuri 68, 69
  films in 69
Bhonsle, Asha 125, 153n
Bhumika 56, 70
Bhuvan Shome 56
Bicycle Thief 37
Bilet Pherat 159
Bjornson, Richard 167
Bobby 99
Bollywood Cinema 56
Bombay 116–17
  communal riots in xvii
  narration of 117–18
  strength of 117
Bombay films xvii–xviii
Border, storyline on India-Pakistan war xvi–xviii
Braj 68
  poetry 128

Brandichi Batli 159
Carnivalesque spirit 161, 162
caste, and commercial politics 133
causality 123
'Chakle' (poem) 54
Chakravarty, Sumita S. 56
Chandavalliya Thota (Kannada film) 101, 102
Chandni Bar 73
characters, larger-than life, in films xiii
Chitegu Chinte (Kannada film), spoofing in 106
Chitralekha (novel) 60
Chaudhvin Ka Chand 159
Chopra, Anupama 75, 76
Chugtai, Ismat 58
cinema, as academic study 51
  'mainstream' xi, 26
  as modernizer 96
  quality of 78
  see also popular cinema
Cinema Bhasha aur Hindi Samvadon ka Vishleshan 59
Cinematic language, and style xv
civil society, state and 115
civilization, Indian xxi
class character, in Raj Kapoor's films 99
classical Hollywood cinema, as the norm 32–4
classical music, Indian, Hinduization of 133, 135
  milieu 138
'co-authorship', concept of 24
cognitive activity, role of 7
colonial-nationalist history, Lata Mangeshkar and 130
colonialism 147
Coomaraswamy, Ananda 130
comedian, and awareness of spectator's presence 177
comedies 87
  in Kannada and south Indian films 103

screwball 168, 171
comic, collapse, of authority 87–120
    narrative 168
        dissolution, films in the mode of 118
commercial cinema, in Bombay xxiv, xvii, 91
    differences and limitations of xxvi
communal harmony, in films 115, 119
    in the mode of noble melancholy 116–19
communal violence 117–18
communication, bourgeois notion of 131
consensus, notion of 114
'consumer co-author' 24, 25
continuous linear time, notion of 35, 41
Cooper, Darius 156
Cosmopolitan, concept of xiii
Coward, Harold G. 12
'creator co-author' 24, 25
cricket, in Hindi films xviii.xx
Crystal, David xiii
culture, definition of 129
    of India 127–8
    of Indian politics, and popular cinema xi–xxvi
    and landscape 127–9
    and relationship between humans 128, 129
    studies, in cinema xiv, 51

Damini 56
Dasgupta, Probal 1
Dastak 56
Deewana 55
Deewar 56
Deleuze, Giles 52
Derrida 11
    critiques 150n
Detectives 9
Devdas 68, 90, 159
Devi Devayani 66
Dharmendra 74, 75

Dharti Ke Lal 56
Dhola, performance strategies of artists of 131
Dholi Gayikayen, of Jodhpur 126, 148n
Dhool Ka Phool 56
Dhyanabhanga 10
dialect, emergence of, in Hindi cinema 69
    Hindi 67–9
dialogue, 'director' 64
    in Hindi films of 'golden period' 63
    songs and 61–5
    stilted xiii
    writing, for films 76
Dil Ek Mandir 56
Dil Se, songs from 64
Dilip Kumar 60, 63, 64, 65
Dilwale Dulhaniya Le Jayenge xviii
Dinanath, Master 153n
Discovery of India 158
Do Bigha Zamin 67
Don 68
Dravidian languages 71
Drishti 70
Dushman 55
Dutt, Guru 54
    comedic vision of 156–83
    metropolitan characters of 161
    musical convention borrowed from Hollywood by 181–2
    musical songs and dance in films of 179 161
    reliance on Hollywood 160
    tragedy in 163
Dutt, Sunil 69
Dutta, J.P. xvii
Dwarakesh 104

Eco, Umberto 161
economy/economic, India's xiii
    policies 141
Electoral politics xxiv
Elizabeth, Hollywood film by Shekhar Kapur 81

Emergency, imposition of, in 1975 xxii
  opposition to xxii–xxiii
Emmerich, Roland 38
Encyclopaedia of Indian Cinema 51, 57
English, educated middle class xii
  global, and NRI Hinglish 79–81
  importance of, in socio-economic and cultural life xii
  status of xiii
English August 81
'escapism', in Indian popular cinema 26

family, dramas, in Hindi films 37
  and parental figures, in films 37
  values in cinema xiv
fantasy, and fairy tales 25–6
  agential character of 12
  and discourse 7–10
  and popular cinema 1–22
Farz 55
Fellini, Frederico xiv
female, 'disreputableness' attached to public performance 146
  identity 125
  stereotypes 73
feminine voice, 'ideal', of Indian popular culture 140
femininity 130
  'proper' post-colonial 139
  and space of the nation 122–33
feminist scholarship 127
festivals, of Indian films xi–xii
Feur, Jane 181
Film Comment, on Bollywood xii
Film Language: A Semiotics of the Cinema 52
film(s), critics xvi
  feature, as master narrative 3, 4
  writing xv
  see also cinema
Filmindia 123
folk songs, in dialect 68
Five-Year-Plans 141
  hero 141–7

'scientific' persona of 144, 145, 146
folk taboos, of naming an evil 101
foreign locales, for songs in films 61
form and structure, of popular cinema 26, 95–7
Foucault 11
Freud 101
Frye, Northrop 156, 157, 163, 165

Gandharva Mahavidyalaya music academies 136
Gandhi, Indira xxiii
  populism of xxiv
Gandhi, Mahatma 7, 59, 71, 148n
  and Hindustani 54
  Marxist and Ambedkaraite critique of xxi
  rediscovery of xxiii
Gandhi, Rajiv, decline in popularity of xxv
Ganeshan, Shivaji 102
Ganga Jumna 68
gangster films, of the West 41
Ganguly, Dhirendranath 159
Gauriganesha (Kannada) 107–12, 113
  comic reversal in 111
  and *School Master* 107, 111
  structure of 110
gender 1, 127
  bourgeois notion of 131
  identity 122
  and sexuality 133
  speculation on 122–47
Ghai, Subhash 24, 57, 153n
gharana tradition 134, 135, 136
Ghatak, Ritwik 157
ghazals 68
  singing 126
global film theory xiii
global mass culture xxv
Godard, Jean-Luc xiv
'golden period', dialogues from Hindi films of 63
Godse, Vishnubhatt 129

The Good, the Bad and the Ugly 38
'great disintegration' 105, 111
The Great Indian Middle Class 158
Gubbar Singh episode, from *Sholay* 74
Gulzar 64
Gupta, Charu 136
Gupta empire, erotic art of 6

'Hamraaz', Har Mandir Singh 123–4
Hangal, Gangubai 126
Harishchandra, Bharatendu 136
Hasan, Kamal 112
Helen, on-screen sexuality of 133
Hema Malini, in *Sholay* 74
heroes, in Hindi cinema 105
   of Indian films 143–4
   picaresque 167
   of post-Independence era 141
   see also Five-Year-Plan heroes
heterosexual hero 144
'high cinemas' xii
Hindi,
   -film script, in search of 76–8
   language, in Hindi cinema 51–81
   poetry, medieval 128
   song lyrics 155n
   writers 60
   and Urdu writers 57–61
Hindi Film Geet Kosh 123, 124
Hindu,
   -Muslim conflict 115
   national consciousness 136
   womanhood, 'pure' and controllable 139
'Hindu' rate of growth xii
Hindustani
   language 71
   of Hindi cinema 53
   and Urdu 54
   meaning of 54
   titles of films in 56
Hindutva xxi
'Hinglish' 79
   in *Bandit Queen* 81
   in *Bollywood Calling* 81
   in Hindi cinema 79, 81
   in *Hyderabad Blues* 81
   NRI 79–81
   in *Rockford* 81
historicity, time and 35–8
history 5
   nature of 99
Hollywood cinema 32
   classical 32–4
   family dramas in 37
   influence of 158–9
   musicals 181, 182
Hollywood Ending 78
horror films, of the West 41
Hum Aapke Hai Koun, Lata Mangeshkar's hit songs from 146
   and the absent of 'first cause' 42–5
   celebrations in 42, 46
   narratives in 43–4
   'pre-history' in 44
   reference to Ramayana in 45

iconic codes 117
Ideology of the Hindi Film 56
images, production of 11
India, cinema in, and classical Hollywood cinema 33
   and illusion 10–14
   logical farce of 6–7
   melodrama in 25–6
India–Pakistan, war of xvi–xvii
Indian Filmography 124
Indian People's Theatre Association (IPTA) 58
individualism, emergence of 89
The Intimate Enemy 6
Ishq Ishq Ishq 35

Jaddanbai, (singer/mother of Nargis) 137, 138
Jafri, Sardar 58

Jain, Madhu 80
Jalti Nishani 56
James Bond 36
Jataka 87
Jeans xviii
Johnny Walker 156, 157, 163
　family recognition in films 176–7
　funny dialogues of 174–5
　in Guru Dutt's films 172–8
　songs picturized on 176
　status of, in films 178
joint family, as theme 101
Jwar-Bhata 60

Kaagaz Ke Phool 156, 157, 159, 160, 164, 168, 173, 176
Kabir, Nasreen Munni 165, 177
Kakar, Sudhir 24
Kal Ho Na Ho xviii
Kamaleshwar 60
Kannada cinema, birth of actor-God and new comedy in 103–6
　heroes' clothing in 89
　history of 88–9
　on joint family and filial loyalty in 101
　narratives of 102
　romantic love in 88
Kannada literature, Navya literary movement in 89
Kannada popular cinema, founders of 102
Kannada-speaking public 88
Kapoor, Prithviraj 65
Kapoor, Raj xiv, 63, 90, 96, 98, 99, 110
　audience for films of xv
　and B.R. Panthul 90–5
　films of 91
　lovers in films of 97
Kapoor, Shekhar 81
Kashmiri, Agha Hashr 58, 59
Kathavachak, Pandit Radheshyam 58
Kaul, Mani 52
Kaviraj, Sudipta 62

Kazmi, Kikham xvii
Kelly, Gene 157, 179
Kesavan, Mukul 54, 55, 67
Keskar, B.V. 134, 135
Khamoshi 55
Khan, Ajmal 74
Khan, Amir 69
Khan, Bade Ghulam Ali 69
Khan, Mehboob 132
Khan, Yusuf *see* Kumar, Dilip
Khanna, Rajesh 100
Khanum, Farida 126
Khari boli, rural character speaking in 67
Khaya Gatha 70
Khilafat 71
Khosla, Raj 54
King, Christopher 54
Kishore Kumar 154n
Kismat 26
Kukunoor, Nagesh 81
Kulavadhu (Kannada film) 101
Kulsum, Jamila 148n
Kurosawa, Akira xiv

Lagaan 68
　admirers of xx
　and historicism xix–xxi
　and the nation-state xix–xx
　criticism of xix
　mythic material in xxi
　reading of xx–xxi
　success with audience xviii
Lagna Pahave Karun 158
Lagna Patrika, comedy in 104
Lal, Lakshminarayan 59
Lal, Vinay xi
landscape, and culture 127–9
language, aspect of 8
　classical Indian theory of 12
　of French films 52
　of Hindi films 52, 57
　of Hollywood cinema 52

and meta languages, problem of 10
spoken by women characters 73
Language and Cinema 52
Lath, Mukund 14
Laurel and Hardy 159
Lawrence, Friar 29
Leone, Sergio 38, 39
Lelyveld, David 133, 135
Listeners' Bulletin 123
locations, for picturization of songs for films 96
love story, in Indian popular films 31, 37
lowbrow literature xiv
Lucknow Pact 70
Ludhianvi, Sahir 54, 58, 70
'lyrics' writers 58
Lysistrata (play) 119

Madhubani style, of art 128
Madhuri *123*
The Magnificent Seven 38
Mahabharata 29
Mahabharat (play) 58
Mahalanobis, P.C. 141
Mahatma Vidur 71
Mainstram film theory, political discourse of 5
see also cinema
Mandukya Upanishad 11
Mangeshkar, Lata 122
  adolescent girl's voice of 139, 140, 146
  authority on feminine ideal 131
  as epitome of feminine identity 133
  femininity and space of the nation 122–33
  mimicking the voice of 125
  playback singing for Muslim characters 141
  public persona of 132
  recordings of songs of 125
  'voice' of 122
  voice as representing modern femininity and Hinduized nationality 140
Mani Ratnam 79, 116, 117, 153n
Manmatha Leelai 112
  meta-language in 113
Manthan 70
Manto, Saadat Hasan 58, 64, 137, 138
marriage, in cinema 112–13
Marx, Karl xx
masculinity, cultural politics of Indian 122
  in Hindi films 147, 154n, 163
  Indian 141
Masoom 55
Mathur, Malati 73
Matila, Bimal Krishna 6
Maya Darpan 70
Maya Machhindra 56
Mazumdar, Rajni 72
McGregor, R.S. 55
media, culture 25
  role of xxii
Meenakshi 71
Meera, cult of 132
melodrama, Indian 25–6, 94, 100, 119
  mono-dimensional 102
  multidimensional 101
Mera Naam Joker 110
Meta-narratives, of history 36
metaphor, use of, in cinema 12
metropolis, in Hindi films 142
metropolitan, male body 143
  and provincial culture 144–5
  theme 146
Metz, Christian 52
middle class, culture xxv
  India's xxiv
  respectability 152n
'middle' films xi
Milan 69
mimicry 106
Mishra, Vijay 56

INDEX

Miss 1993 56
Mitra, Bimal 159
Mitro Marjani (novel) 139
modern, formal pampering of, and balancing of opposites 97–8
modernity 3–4, 96, 97, 122, 127, 130, 131, 158
   women's role in 127
Mohammed, Mahathir xiii
Monteiro, Anjali xv
Morris, Desmond 2
Mother India 67, 132
Mr & Mrs 55, comedy in 156, 157, 158, 162, 164, 170–2, 175, 178, 180–2
   romance in 170
   senex figure in 165
Mughal miniatures 128
Mughale-e-Azam 55, 65–7
   singing in 69
   Muslim subject-matter in 66
   Urdu dialogues in 65, 66
Mulvey, Laura 1
Mumford, Lewis 8
music, compositional/literary mode, of performance in 131
   of popular cinema xi, 123, 129
   'playback' singing 123
   and relationship between performer and audience 130
   'rights' 61
   sale of commercial 123
Muslim cultural influence, on Indian society 136–7
'Muslim socials' (films) 55
Muslims, musicians during Muslim rule 136
   social and cultural life of artists among 137–8
'Muslimness', and 'debauchery' 138
myth, and pre-history in Hindi cinema 6, 36, 37
mythology, elements of 28
   in Western films 36

Nag, Ananth 107
Nagar, Amritlal, writing for films 60
Nagaraj 87
Nair, Mira 81
The Naked Ape 2
nakedness, and clothing 3
Namak Haram 55
Nandy, Ashis xi, 6, 80
Nargis 137, 138
narratives, in popular cinema 26, 33, 37, 52
   causality as backbone of 33
   models 3–4
narrative style, of cinema xv
Nartaki 71
Nasim Bano 138
Natha, Bai 148n
national culture, Hinduization and gentrification of 135
   of music 134
   'pure' and respectable 135
National Identity in Indian Popular Cinema 56
nationalism, Indian 127, 129, 147
   discourse on 123, 129
   histories of xix
   oppressive xix
naturalism, in films 5–6
Natyashastra, of Bharata 10
Nautanki artists 123
Neeraj 60
Nehru, Jawaharlal, and defeat in Indo-China war 162
   on new Indian 158
New Comedy 156, 163, 165, 166
New Delhi 142
new wave directors 71
Nietzsche 11
Nihalani, Govind 70
Nishant 70
Nivedita, Sister 128
Non-Cooperation 71
Noorjehan, nasality of 135

novels, Indian, in English xiii
  as master narrative 3
  role of 3
nudity, categories of 2
  see also nakedness
Nutan 69
Nyaya school 7
O'Conor, Donald 179
Once Upon a Time in the West 38
One Language, Two Scripts 54
'orality' 131
  and literariness 130–1
  performative contents of 130

painting medium 34
Paluskar, D.V. 69, 136
'pan-Indian' audience 26
Pandian, M.S.S. 104
Panthulu, B.R. 90, 98, 99
  and Raj Kapoor 90–5
Paranjape, Makarand xx
Pardes xviii, 80
Parekh, Jabri Mall 78
Parsi theatre 58
  study of 59
Patel, Vallabhbhai 135
The Patriot 38
performers, and audience 130, 131
personalized vocabulary 64
Phalke, Dadasaheb 59
Plato, dreams and night in 11
Polydor, records of dialogues of *Sholay* by 76
popular cinema, as centre of Indian politics xi–xxvi
  features of 3
  as fiction 25
  form of 89, 95–7
  India and fantasy 1–22
  narrative structure and forms in 24–46
  romantic love in 95
  study of xi–xvi

transgression in 95–6
popular culture, new interest in xxiii
  speculation on 122–47
  see also culture
popular music, in the West 62
populism, attraction of xxii
portraits, in films 31
Prabhat Studios, Guru Dutt joining 157, 158
Prasad, M. Madhava 56, 57, 63
Premchand 71
  and Hindutva 54
  writing for films by 60
Progressive Writers Association (PWA) 58
  Convention 60
provincial bourgeois male hero, of Indian films 144
public culture, 'purifying' Indian 140
Public singing, by women, as disrepute 139
public spectator 87
  use of concept of 88
Pyaasa 54, 70, 156, 160, 164, 173, 178
  tragic couple in 168

Qawwali 68
Qayamat Se Qayamat Tak 55

Rafi, Mohammad 154n
Rag Darbari (novel) 62
Raghvendra, M.K. 24
Rahman, A.R. 77
Raj Kumar, dialogue delivery of 64
Raj Kumar (Kannada actor) 104
  as super-ethical hero 105
Raj Nartaki 71
Raja Harishchandra (play) 59
Rajadhyaksha, Ashish 51, 57, 159
Ramachandra, Phani 107, 108, 113
Ramachandran, M.G. (MGR) 104, 105
Ramana Maharshi, use of metaphor 12
Ramayana, reference to, in films 45, 46

Index

Ramrajya 45–6, 71
Rangeela 72
Rangoonwala, Firoz xvii
Rangnekar, D.K. 158
Rao, N.T. Rama (NTR) 104, 105
rape scenes, in cinema xiv
rasa, notion of 33
Ray, Satyajit xiv, xv, xvii, 157
   Oscar Award to 79
Raza, Rahi Masoom 58, 66, 76
   dialogue writing by 76–7
realism, in cinema 37
'regional' cinema xi, 26
Renu, Fanishwarnath 145
Rig-Veda 70
Rijn, Rembrandt Van 34
Roads, and highways, in Indian films 143
Roja, on politics in Kashmir 102, 116–19
   terrorism in xvii
romance/ romantic love 97, 144–5
   and cinematic form 88–90
   narrative of 168
   in popular cinema 95
   screwball 170–1
Romeo and Juliet 29
Rowe, Kathleen 165
Roy, Bimal 79
rural films 67–8
Rushdie, Salman 62, 81
Rustom va Sohrab (play) 59

Saath Saath 62
Sadgati 79
Safar 55
Sagar, Ramanand 77
Sahib Bibi Aur Ghulam 55, 159, 160
Saigal, K.L. 68
Samsara process 7
Sangam 26, 40
Sangeet Karyalaya, of Hathras 123
Sangeet Shastra, destruction of 136
Sanskrit 6, 7
Sanskritic culture, neglect of 134
Sanskritic Hindi 53, 69–71
   in Parsi plays 59
Sanskrit titles, of Hindi films 56, 57, 70
Sarkari Pahune 158
The Satanic Verses (novel) 62
Sathyu, M.S. 106
satires 103, 104
Satre, Jean-Paul 8
Satya 73
Saudagar 26, 27–34, 39
   Characters of 29
   'episodic' character of 31
   narrative of 24, 27–8, 32, 33
   songs in 30
Saxena, H.S. 64
Schomer, Karine 128
School Master (Kannada film) 90–1, 95, 100
   importance of guru and value system in 94
   popularity of 91
   strength of film 102
   sub-plots in 92–3
Science 5
   fiction films 9
In Search of Lata Mangeshkar 140
The Secret Politics of Our Desires xxv, xxvi
The Secret of Santa Vittoria 38
secularism, death of 119
Seidman, Steve 177
Sen, Sushmita xii
senex figure, in films 165, 168
'serious' films, 112
Seth, Vikram 62
Seton, Marie xvi
Sevasadan (novel) 60
sexuality, in films 1, 100, 127, 170
singers, public place of 123
Shahani, Kumar 70
Shailendra, Pradip 60
Shakuntala 71

196 INDEX

Shamshad Begum 139
Shankar Parvati 71
Shantaram, V. 79
Sharma, K.D. 124
Sharma, Pandit Mukhram 77
Sharma, Pandit Narendra 60, 70
Sharma, Ram Bilas 70
Shatranj Ke Khilari
Sholay 26, 55
  characterization in 40
  episodic quality of 40
  Hindi use in 74–6
  narratives in 38–42
  as 'realistic' 39
Shree 420 80
  songs from 62
Shukla, Srilal 62
Shyamalan, M. 'Night' 81
Silsila 68
Singh, Swarup, singer of epic Dhola 131
Singh, V.P., decline in popularity xxv
Sippy, Ramesh 38
Sirk, Douglas 26
The Sixth Sense, Hollywood film 81
Sobti, Krishna 139, 145
social films, comic scenes in 103
society, changing nature of 89, 99
  disintegration of values in 91
songs, in Hindi films 30
  in cassettes and CDs 61
  -dance routine xi, 95
  and dialogue 61–5
  production and circulation of 61
  role of 14
space(s), bridging of 30
  speculation on 122–47
spectator, great disintegration and ambivalance 113–16
sphota theory 12
spoof, and comedy 106
Srinivas, M.N. 89
Srivastava, Sanjay 122
Stam, Robert 52

state, and civil society, discourses of 115
  role of, and culture 115
sthayi 114
subalternity, concept of xix
A Suitable Boy 62
Sullivan's Travels 160
Sultanpuri, Majrooh 58

Tagore, Sharmila 100
Tajmahal, Lata Mangeshkar's songs in 140
'talkies', beginning of 51, 61
Talks with Sri Ramana Maharshi 12
tapori language 72, 73
Tarang 70
tawaif 139
Teesri Kasam 68
television audience xv–xvi
Thackeray, Bal 117
time, and historicity 35–8
  in Indian art 34–5
Todorov, Tzvetan 25
tradition, as theme 90
tragedies, in Guru Dutt's films 157
translation, strategy of internal 98–102
'transnational globalism' xx
Trivedi, Harish 51
twilight, enchantment of 11

Ujala 138
Urdu, entitlement of 53–7
  in Hindi cinema 53–5, 57, 137
  and Hindustani vocabulary 63
  titles of films 56, 57
  writers and Hindi writers 57–61
Usmani, Sahir 159
Uttara-Mimamsa 7

Vaisesika school 7
'Vakya Geetanjali', programme in Radio Ceylon 124–5
vamp, sexuality of 132–3
Vanity Fair 81
Varma, Pavan K. 158
Vasantasena 71

Index

Vasvani, Kishore 59
Verma, Bhagwati Charan 60, 70
vernacular forces xiii
Vinayak, Master 158
violence, in cinema xiv
   political nature of 116
voice quality, in Indian performance tradition 131
vulgarity, commercialism and, in films 60

Wadley, Susan 131
Waqt 55
Western cinema, historical anchoring of narrative in 36

Western pop music 123
Willemen, Paul 51, 57
Willis, Bruce 81
women, degradation of portrayal of 1
   education of 128
   as entertainer 132
   and gender and occupational behaviour 137
   singing style of 126
   as tradition 127
Wood, Michael 179

Yadav, Rajendra 145

Zohra Bai 126